# PCs made easy

## A PRACTICAL COURSE

## STAGE 3

# PCs made easy

## A PRACTICAL COURSE

## STAGE 3

**Reader's Digest**

THE READER'S DIGEST ASSOCIATION, INC.
PLEASANTVILLE, NEW YORK / MONTREAL

PCS MADE EASY
A PRACTICAL COURSE – STAGE 3

Published by the Reader's Digest Association, Inc., 2002,
by arrangement with De Agostini UK Ltd

Reader's Digest and the Pegasus logo are registered trademarks
of The Reader's Digest Association, Inc.

READER'S DIGEST PROJECT STAFF
Senior Editor: Don Earnest
Designer: Jennifer R. Tokarski
Production Technology Manager: Douglas A. Croll
Contributing Copyeditor: Nancy Humes

READER'S DIGEST HOME DIVISION
Editorial Director: Christopher Cavanaugh
Senior Design Director: Elizabeth Tunnicliffe
Marketing Director: Dawn Nelson
Vice President and General Manager: Kiera Kuhs

THE READER'S DIGEST ASSOCIATION, INC
Editor-in-Chief: Eric W. Schrier
President, North America Books and Home Entertainment: Thomas D. Gardner

*PCs made easy* was created and produced for
The Reader's Digest Association, Inc. by De Agostini UK Ltd,
from material originally published by De Agostini UK Ltd,
in the UK in periodical form as *Computer Success Plus*.

Copyright © 2000, 2002 De Agostini UK Ltd

Front cover center photograph: Rob Lewine/Corbis Stockmark

Library of Congress Cataloging in Publication Data

PCs made easy : a practical course.
    p. cm.
    Contents: [3] Stage three
    ISBN 0-7621-0380-9 (v.3)
        1. Microcomputers. 2. Computer software.

QA76.5 .P3675 2001
004.16—dc21
                                                        00-045880

Address any comments about *PCs made easy* to:
Editorial Director, Reader's Digest Home Division,
Reader's Digest Road, Pleasantville, NY 10570-7000

To order additional copies of *PCs made easy*, call 1-800-846-2100.

You can also visit us on the World Wide Web at **rd.com**

Printed in the United States of America

# CONTENTS

# Windows

# Keep a healthy hard drive

**With Windows' disk tools, you can make sure that your computer is always achieving its optimum performance by preventing problems and correcting them if they occur.**

A computer is a complicated, fragile piece of equipment, and every now and then things can and do go wrong. It can get accidentally knocked, for example, just like other electrical equipment in your home. When a PC is switched on, even what might seem like a small knock could affect the computer's hard drive, where all your programs and documents are stored. Such knocks can interfere with the data that is stored on the drive and this could make a single file – or even whole areas of the hard drive – impossible to use. As a result, any data stored there could be lost.

### ● Don't just turn your PC off

Similar problems often arise when the PC is turned off before open documents are closed. Make sure that everyone using your computer – especially any children who share it – knows that the only safe way to turn a computer off is to select the Shut Down option from the Start menu. If you do this, Windows will check to make sure that any open documents have been properly saved before shutting down.

Less frequently, hard drive problems can also occur as a result of faulty software, quite outside your control.

Even when it is working properly, your computer's hard drive can become clogged up. As a result of this, you might find that it seems to slow down, and opening and saving takes longer than it did when the PC was new.

All these problems are easily cured with Windows' programs called System Tools. There's a tool to deal with each problem.

### ● Instant cures

When a stored document has been damaged, it is said to be corrupt. Sometimes the file won't be accessible at all: you might, for example, see an error message appear when

you try to open a corrupt letter in Word. Even if the document isn't that important, you should always repair the damage to the disk so that it cannot affect other documents in the future. The ScanDisk tool can check your hard drive for errors and will automatically repair any it finds.

If your computer seems to be running slower than it used to, you can tune it up and get it back up to speed by using the Disk Defragmenter. This reorganizes the data on your hard drive so that programs can start, and your documents can be opened or saved, as quickly as possible. It doesn't change the way you have arranged the documents and folders on your disk, so you'll still find everything where you left it.

We'll also look at Disk Cleanup, another of Windows' System Tools. This program can automatically delete unused and unwanted files that are taking up disk space.

# Checking your hard drive for errors

**If you suspect that files on your hard drive have become damaged or corrupted, a simple-to-use Windows program called ScanDisk might solve the problem.**

ANY OF the files and data stored on your hard drive can become corrupted. In most cases you can repair this damage, although it is likely that the files can be recycled only as free space rather than reclaimed. ScanDisk is the tool to use for such tasks.

**1** To start ScanDisk, press the Start button and select Accessories from the Programs menu. Select System Tools from the Accessories menu and single click on the ScanDisk icon.

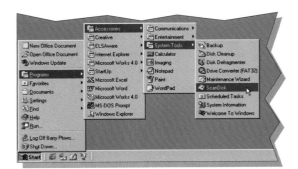

**2** The ScanDisk dialog box lets you select which drive to check. Select the C: drive by clicking on the relevant item in the list of drives.

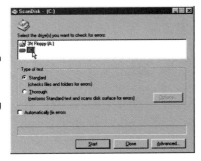

**3** You have the choice of a Standard or Thorough disk scan. The Standard option checks only the files and folders stored on the hard drive, whereas the Thorough option checks the physical surface of the hard drive. Most of the time you should choose a Standard scan, the quickest of the two options. You will need to select a Thorough scan only if you want to make absolutely sure there are no errors, or if you have already detected errors through a Standard scan.

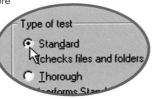

**4** After selecting a Standard scan, make sure that the final box, labeled Automatically fix errors, is checked. Press the Start button. ScanDisk works through the disk without asking you to confirm any disk repairs it needs to do.

**5** ScanDisk will now begin to scan the hard drive. You will see several stages indicated by the progress bar that appears at the bottom of the dialog box.

**6** When ScanDisk has finished checking your hard drive, you will see a panel of information. Most of this is only of interest to computer experts, but the first line will tell you about any errors ScanDisk found.

If ScanDisk finds damaged areas of the disk, it will try to read the information stored there and save it to a safe place on your hard drive. These 'rescued' files are usable only by computer experts, however, so you will have to rely on back-up copies of affected documents.

Note: if you selected a Thorough scan, the ScanDisk process will take a much longer time to complete – anything from 30 minutes to a few hours, depending on the size of your computer's hard drive and the amount of material stored on it.

## CHECKPOINT ✓

### GIVE YOUR COMPUTER A PHYSICAL

☑ If you're running Windows 98, you can use its Maintenance Wizard to keep your PC in good working condition. You can also schedule regular checkups using the ScanDisk and Disk Defragmenter System Tools.

☑ If you're using Windows 95, you need to schedule and perform these checks yourself. Use ScanDisk (see the example on this page) whenever you suspect there is a hard-drive problem with your computer. ScanDisk runs quickly and the Standard scan will alert you to any major problems that might exist. You need only do a longer Thorough scan every six months or so. Most people need only run the standard Disk Defragmenter every four months. But if you install lots of programs or games, consider doing it every two months.

# Defragmenting your hard drive

**Your hard drive can slow down as more programs and files are stored on it, but a simple operation will soon have it running as quickly as possible.**

YOUR HARD drive can slow down as it tries to keep up with all the files stored on it. This problem – fragmentation – is not too serious but can be avoided if you use Windows' Disk Defragmenter tool to reorganize your hard drive. It does this by moving files around on the hard drive. Don't worry about finding them: the files appear in exactly the same place, but your hard drive can now find them more quickly.

**1** To start Disk Defragmenter, click on Start and select Accessories from the Programs menu. Select System Tools from the Accessories menu and click on the third option of the drop-down menu: Disk Defragmenter.

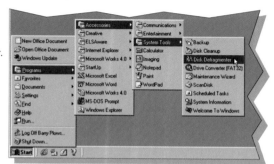

**2** You will be asked to select the drive you want to defragment. First, though, click the settings button.

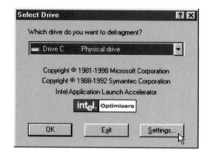

**3** In the dialog box that appears, make sure that the first option is checked. This lets Windows optimize the performance of your PC. Click the OK button and then click OK again to proceed.

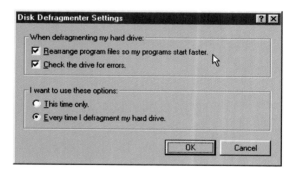

**4** The defragmentation process will start and you can see it happening by watching the progress bar in the center of the dialog box. You can run other programs at the same time, but you'll find your system will operate more slowly while defragmentation is going on. To see how the hard drive is being rearranged, click the Show Details button.

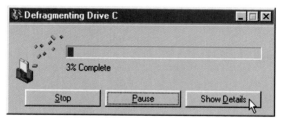

**5** Now you can get a visual idea of what the Disk Defragmenter tool is doing. The small squares represent one cluster of data on the hard drive. Press the Legend button (inset) and you'll see a pop-up panel that describes what each of the different colors refers to.

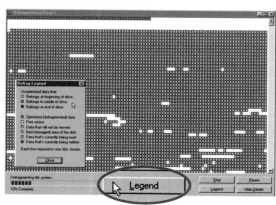

**6** When the process is finished (the larger your hard drive and the more information that's stored on it, the longer it will take), a dialog box will appear, asking if you now want to quit Disk Defragmenter. Press the OK button. You should now notice a marked improvement in the performance of your computer.

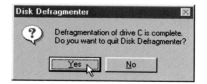

# Cleaning up your hard drive

**As you use your computer, many files are created that you will never need again. Here we see how to get rid of them to free up valuable disk space.**

WINDOWS COMES with Disk Cleanup, a special program that automatically roots out useless old files in just a few minutes, saving you many megabytes of hard drive space in the process. When you run Disk Cleanup, it lets you choose which types of files to look for and delete. You can, for example, select temporary files created when you access the Internet.

**1** To run Disk Cleanup, click on the Start button and select Accessories from the Programs menu. Select System Tools from the Accessories menu and click on Disk Cleanup.

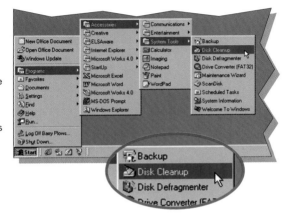

**2** In the Select Drive dialog box that appears, make sure that drive C: (if this is your hard drive) is selected, not the floppy disk. Then press the OK button.

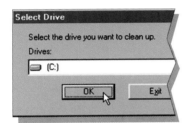

**3** Disk Cleanup shows you the types of files it can clean up. Initially, only two options are checked. Temporary Internet Files and Downloaded Program Files cover the different types of files – Web pages, graphics and so on – that are stored on your PC from your travels on the Internet. It's easy to collect several thousand in just a week's browsing.

**4** Check the Temporary files option if you want to delete the various files that programs such as Word create behind the scenes. Correctly running programs delete such files automatically, but crashes can cause the programs to forget this task.

**5** If you upgraded from Windows 95 to Windows 98, the setup program probably stored your old Windows 95 setup – just in case Windows 98 didn't work properly and you needed to uninstall it. Once your PC has been running Windows 98 without problems, it's safe to delete the old files. Check the Delete Windows 98 uninstall information option to do this.

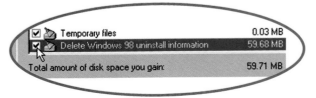

**6** Press the OK button and confirm your choice when Windows asks you. It then deletes the various files you have identified as being superfluous. It takes only a few minutes to recover the disk space.

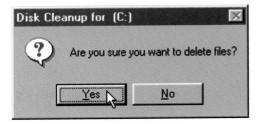

# Installing new software

**Whenever you buy a new piece of software, you have to load it from the CD-ROM or floppy disk onto your PC's hard drive. Here we show you how easy it is to install new programs.**

Loading or 'installing' new software is much the same as putting any new data onto your PC from a CD-ROM or floppy disk. But instead of copying the files yourself, your PC will run a setup program to install the new program on your PC's hard drive for you.

When you insert the new program disk and go through the installation process, all you are doing is transferring these instructions, bit by bit from the floppy or CD-ROM, onto your PC's hard drive. Once they are on the PC, they provide it with a new range of instructions that you can use directly, just as you use any of the programs already on your PC when you bought it.

### ● Hard drive space
With a small piece of software, you might be transferring only a few files. With a major software package, you might be transferring most of a CD-ROM's contents. It depends on how the program will be used. Reference programs that provide you with data, images and sounds, such as Microsoft's Encarta, require only a little hard drive space because the program reads the data directly from the CD-ROM (the CD-ROM needs to be in the CD-ROM drive for the program to access the information on it). But major programs, such as Word or CorelDRAW, can take up over 100MB of space on your hard drive when they are fully installed on your PC.

### ● Installation time
The time it takes to load software varies from program to program. Clearly the larger the program, the longer it takes to load. But some major programs take much longer to install

than others because they ask a lot of questions before they even begin to install the files. This is because these types of programs are also used in offices where it is important to know who is using the software and whether it has been properly licensed. Even with the largest programs, the installation process rarely takes more than half an hour – and usually much less.

**Successful Installation**

World Reference Atlas has been successfully installed on your computer.

To run World Reference Atlas, simply double click on its icon in the DK Multimedia group in Program Manager.

Be sure to send in the registration information for your new software.

[ OK ]

*You'll be able to install most software successfully simply by inserting the supplied CD-ROM and following the instructions given by Windows.*

### ● Installation options
Most programs let you choose how much of the software you wish to install, but most home users usually install the entire program. With the CorelDRAW program, for example, the default option for installation is called Typical and, as the name suggests, it will install all the files that most people typically use. Other options are Compact, which installs only the essential files

*Installing a new program can often seem daunting, but usually it involves nothing more than answering a few on-screen questions put to you by Windows. Any changes to your PC setup are made automatically.*

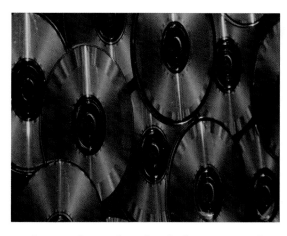

*Installing new software will seem less of a daunting prospect when you understand what happens during the installation process.*

## Checking available space

Before you install a new program, you must make sure that there is enough space for it on your hard drive. The box in which the software comes will tell you how much space it will take up. You can check how much is available for it on your hard drive by double-clicking on the My Computer icon, then clicking on the C: icon with the right mouse button. Select Properties from the list of Options that appears and you'll see your hard drive displayed as a pie chart (left), showing the way your hard drive space is being used. The lighter area shows how much space is free, while the darker area shows the amount of space currently occupied by other files.

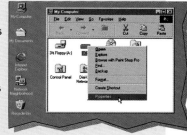

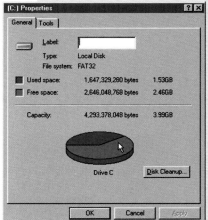

to save disk space, and Custom, which allows you to choose exactly which files to install. The Custom option is really intended for advanced users. Unless you have very little space on your hard drive, it's best to use the Typical option. This also applies when installing other Windows programs.

### ● Installing other software

Most large programs have a number of extra applications as well as the main program functions. These include items such as fonts and clip art. While you should install all the main program functions, check how much space these extra files take up before you install them. If they take up a lot of memory, they might not leave you with much room to install anything else on your hard drive. If you think they are going to clog up your hard drive, you can leave all these items on the CD-ROM. If you are in any doubt, *always* leave them on the CD-ROM – you can install them when and if you need them at a later date.

All you have to do to start most of the software you are likely to buy is to insert the CD-ROM. This starts the

*The icon for the CD-ROM drive features an image of a CD disc, with the letter that signifies the drive underneath it.*

program responsible for managing the installation process. If you have any older software programs that you also want to install, they might not include the special autostart software that is a necessary requirement. If this is the case, there is no other option but to install the software manually, which is a more time-consuming process. The same techniques are also used to install programs from floppy disks.

Some programs will ask you to restart your computer once a program has been installed. This is because they have installed special files that work closely with Windows. For technical reasons, Windows needs to close down and restart before they can work. Only then will you be able to run your new software properly.

**HARDWARE REQUIREMENTS**
Whenever you buy new software, make sure you check its hardware requirements first to make sure your PC is able to run it. Here's a summary of CorelDRAW's requirements:
☑ Windows 98, Me, 2000, NT or XP
☑ 133MHz Pentium processor
☑ 32MB RAM (64 recommended)
☑ At least 200MB of hard drive space (300MB recommended).
☑ CD-ROM drive
☑ Super VGA display

# How to Install CorelDRAW from CD-ROM

**In Stage 2, pages 68–89, we introduced you to the graphics program CorelDRAW. Here we show you how to install the program from a CD-ROM, a process that involves steps common to other installation programs.**

**1** To start the installation, you need to insert the CorelDRAW CD-ROM labeled 1 into your CD-ROM drive. The CD-ROM will autostart and a window will appear, giving you several options. Click the Install option.

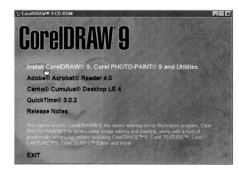

**2** The Install program will then analyze your system (to see how much memory you have, how fast your processor is and so on). When it's finished, another window will appear, asking if you are sure you want to continue. To do so, press the Next button.

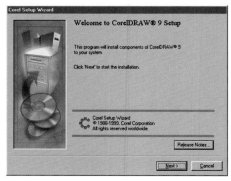

**3** The next window displays the License Agreement, which asks you to agree not to copy or lend the software illegally. The following window asks you to type in your name and the name of your company (if relevant). This information is not really essential and merely helps to register the product. Press the Next button and a window will give you a chance to check your entry; press Next if everything is correct.

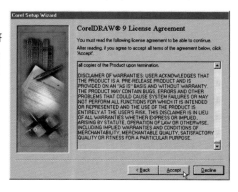

**4** The next screen asks you to enter the product serial code for your copy of CorelDRAW; this code is different for each copy of the software and it is important that you don't lose it (the code is printed on a registration card that you'll find in the CorelDRAW box). It is a good idea to copy it down somewhere else in case you lose the original. When you've typed in the code, press the Next button to go on.

**5** You will now be presented with the installation options. There are three options from which to choose. The Typical installation will be selected for you by CorelDRAW by default, so press Next to proceed.

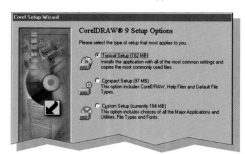

**6** The installation program checks to see what spelling dictionary you want to use. Make sure the right one is selected before proceeding.

**7** A new window asks you exactly where you want to install the software. CorelDRAW suggests the best location, so simply click Next to move to the next step. Click the Yes button when asked to confirm this step.

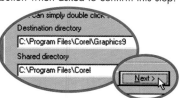

**8** Click the Next button when the program asks you which Start menu Folder to use for the CorelDRAW programs. Then click the Install button on the next screen.

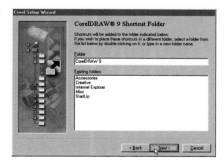

**9** The following windows are the final parts of the setup process. There is a progress window showing how the transfer of instructions is going (right above). When this is finished, you will be asked by the program if you want to register the software online, but you can do this at a later date. When a window tells you that your installation is complete, click OK. The final step is to restart Windows (see Why Restart Your PC? box, previous page).

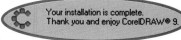

# Installing software manually

**Sometimes your PC won't automatically know you are trying to install a new program. All this means is that you have to make a few extra choices and input it yourself.**

SOME SOFTWARE doesn't start automatically – this means you will have to find the setup or install file on the CD-ROM (the software manual will tell you the exact name of the file to look for). Here we show you how easy it is to load new programs onto your PC manually.

**1** For software that doesn't autostart, you need to locate the setup or install file on the CD-ROM. To do this, go to the My Computer icon on your Desktop (right) and double-click on it.

**2** When the My Computer window opens, you will be able to see the CD-ROM drive. It has a small picture of a disc and the letter that the drive has been designated is underneath (in this case, D:). Double-click on the icon to open the CD-ROM drive window.

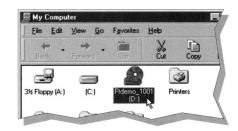

**3** The contents of the CD-ROM will then be displayed. Often, the file you need to double-click on to start the setup process will be called Setup and you'll spot it right away. Sometimes, this file is called Install and you might have to look through many files and folders to find it.

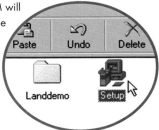

**4** When you double-click on the Setup (or Install) file, the installation process begins. As the installation proceeds, you might have to answer some simple questions about your computer's setup, or confirm that the software is making acceptable choices about where and how it will work on your computer.

## PC TIPS

### Finding the right file

Sometimes when you click on the (D:) icon to view the contents of a CD-ROM, you can find yourself presented with a whole page of files (right). You can organize these to make it easier to find the file you need by going to the View menu, selecting Arrange Icons and then clicking on by Name (right). All the files on the CD-ROM will then appear in alphabetical order, making it easier for you to find the Setup file.

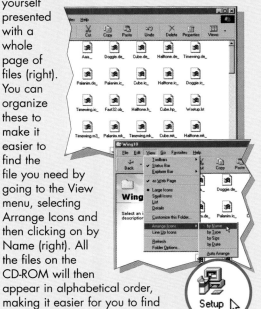

## Another method to start manual installation

**1** If a program you have just bought doesn't install automatically and you don't like the manual method explained above, here's another way to do it. Click on the Start button and choose Run from the menu that appears.

**2** Now Windows needs to know the location of the file, so click on the Browse button.

**3** You will then see a dialog box that allows you to look at the contents of your hard drive and the other disk drives on your computer. Choose your CD-ROM drive from the pull-down menu at the top of the screen.

**4** It is now just a matter of locating the file that starts the setup process. Remember that in most cases this involves running a computer program that monitors the installation process for you, so it will be called either Install.exe or Setup.exe. Double-click on this file to begin the installation process.

# Installing new typefaces

**You don't have to stick to the typefaces that come with Windows. By adding new fonts to your computer – either those that come with new programs or others that you buy separately – you can give your work a new look.**

Among the first fun things you can try with a word processor are the different typefaces (called fonts) installed on your computer. Experimenting with curious sounding Arial, Algerian or the more traditional Times New Roman is great fun.

Windows comes with several fonts, but when you install some new programs you might have the option of adding more. Some printers even include new fonts. However, sometimes you might find that you need to use a particular font that isn't on your system. For example, you might need a solid, chunky font for headlines in your club newsletter, or an elegant, scriptlike typeface to create imposing looking certificates for the school sports awards.

*Windows comes with a number of typefaces that you can use in almost any program. You can also add your own.*

You will find that changing fonts can radically alter the look and tone of your text. Some fonts are simple and clear, others more ornate or eye-catching, and ideal for posters. You should beware of using too many strikingly different fonts in any one document. More than two or three typefaces in a letter or document is likely to make it look a mess.

### ● Adding new typefaces
Some software adds new fonts for you, but you can also install them using the Windows Control Panel. The fonts will be copied from the CD-ROM or floppy disk to your hard drive. Once you've added your new fonts, you'll find that they are available in almost all your Windows programs – not just the programs they came with.

*It's easy to install new typefaces (called fonts), and there are even some on your original Windows CD-ROM that you can install right now.*

## WHY ARE THERE SO MANY TYPEFACES?

Some typefaces have many subtle variations. Arial, for instance, is made up of several slightly different typefaces, all created from the same basic shape: Arial, Arial bold, Arial italic and Arial bold italic. If you create a letter using the Arial typeface and then use Word's bold button, Word uses the Arial bold variation to form the letters on your screen and on the printed page. These closely related variations make up a font 'family'. Programs such as Word 'hide' these simple variations from you: you need only choose the basic typeface and then decide whether you want bold, italic or both.

# Adding new fonts

**New fonts are supplied on program disks or as special font disks. To see what's involved in installing them, we'll add two fonts from the Windows CD-ROM.**

**1** Open up the Control Panel and double-click on the Fonts icon. This icon doesn't start a program; instead it's a shortcut to a special Fonts folder on your hard drive.

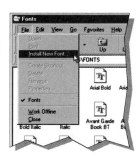

**2** The Fonts folder appears and you'll see the fonts installed on your computer. They might be displayed in list form or as small icons. This is how the folder appears in large icon form (an option in the View menu).

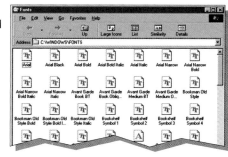

**3** To install a new font, click on the File menu and then select the Install New Font command from the drop-down list of options.

**4** You'll see the Add Fonts dialog box. Initially, the listed Fonts box says 'No fonts found'. This is because it always starts by looking on your C: drive. We'll add some fonts from the Windows CD-ROM. Insert it into your CD-ROM drive and then select your CD-ROM drive from the Drives list (right).

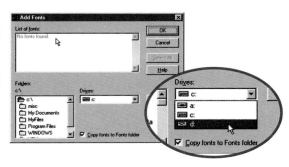

**5** Use the Folders list and double-click on the tools folder, then click on reskit, the desktop and the minitel folder. Windows will find two fonts and list them at the top of the dialog box. Note: there are several slightly different versions of the Windows CD-ROM; it is possible that yours will not have these files or it might have different files.

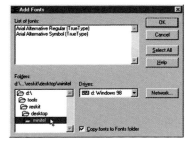

**6** Pick the fonts you want to add. To select a single font, you need only click on it to highlight it. However, in this exercise we want to add both fonts. The simplest way to do this is to press the Select All button and then press the OK button. As soon as you do so, Windows will copy the fonts into your Fonts folder.

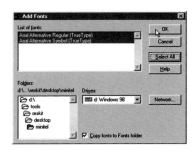

**7** To use one of your new fonts, start Word. From the Font list, choose Arial Alternative (or the name of any of the fonts you have found and added). Now, whatever text you type will be in the new font.

## SYMBOL TYPEFACES

The Arial Alternative Symbol font added above is used for special symbols (shown below) rather than text. You can select it from the Font list (Step 7) or you can use it via the Symbol command from Word's Insert menu.

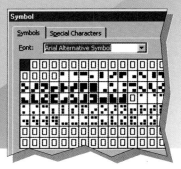

# Installing Windows' extra programs

**Windows is not just one program: it's made up of many different programs. Most will have been copied to your computer's hard drive when it was built, but some very useful programs are contained on the Windows CD-ROM for you to add if you need them.**

If you have used several computers, you might find that Windows varies slightly from one to the next. Although the basic operations are the same, you will probably have noticed that some of the minor functions are different. For example, it is possible that the Backup program (which allows you to copy your work files from the computer to external Zip or floppy disks) is present on one PC, but missing from another.

This happens for two reasons. First, PC manufacturers might choose slightly different installation options when copying the Windows files to the computer's hard drive. Differences also show up because Microsoft has released several updated versions and major revisions of Windows since Windows 95 was launched in August 1995.

● **Typical installations**

Most of the time, PC makers add Windows to the computer through a 'typical' installation. This copies only the most commonly used programs to the computer's hard drive, ready for you to use. There are many other components, however, which are not copied in the typical installation. Most of the time, you won't even notice they are missing, but it is useful to know how components help Windows work, what types of extra components are available on your Windows CD-ROM and how to load them into your computer when you need them.

● **Loading extra components**

A component is a specific part of Windows that can be added or removed from your computer without affecting how the rest of Windows works. The most important components are installed as standard, but some of the less essential ones are not.

These uninstalled components are not necessarily any less useful than the others, but might be specific to a particular type of computer. For example, you do not need the components that control sound if you don't

**WHAT IT MEANS**

COMPONENTS
*Windows is not a single program. Instead, it consists of the central operating system software, with a collection of separate pieces of software (such as Backup and Calculator) arranged around it. These peripheral programs are known as components. Most can be installed or uninstalled on your computer as you choose, without affecting the overall functioning of Windows.*

have a multimedia computer. Some components are left uninstalled because they are of interest only to more experienced computer users. For example, business users with networks can load components that check how their computers are being shared between different users.

Several uninstalled components are left out merely because they are a little frivolous – and leaving them out saves hard-drive space. For example, Windows has some sounds and pictures that are fun to add but are not really essential for the efficient operating of the computer, unless you have space to spare.

### ● Important components
However, there are also times when adding certain components can be very useful. For example, it is well worth having the Character Map program to help you to add special characters and symbols to your documents.

Although the Character Map component comes on the Windows CD-ROM, it's not normally installed at the same time as Windows. Here, we'll show how to add this mini-program to your computer as an example of how to add any extra component.

You need to install the extra Windows components by using a different method from the way you install other new software (see pages 12–15). Instead, you use a special part of the Add/Remove Programs tool that is located in the Control Panel. The Add/Remove Programs tool keeps track of all the Windows components that have already been installed on your computer. It can also quickly show you what other options are available on the Windows CD-ROM.

# The Add/Remove Programs tool

**It is worth learning how to use this important tool properly, because it can be used for a variety of housekeeping tasks that will help to keep Windows running smoothly.**

*To start the Add/Remove Programs tool, first open the Control Panel (above) and then double-click on the Add/Remove Programs icon (below).*

THE ADD/REMOVE Programs tool handles many Windows housekeeping tasks. With it you can install or uninstall programs and add or remove Windows components. You can also use it to create a special floppy disk, which can help if your computer has problems starting Windows or to solve emergencies.

You start the tool through the Control Panel (left). You will then see a dialog box with three tabs at the top: Install/Uninstall; Windows Setup and Startup Disk (right).

With the first tab, you can remove unwanted programs from your computer's hard drive. You might want to do this to recover some hard-drive space from programs you no longer need or to remove a program that isn't working correctly (see page 11). You should always use this option to remove programs, instead of just deleting them by dragging them into the Recycle Bin.

On the page opposite we've shown how to use the second tab – Windows Setup – to add components from the Windows CD-ROM.

The third tab has just one button, Create Disk. You use this to make a special floppy disk called a Startup Disk. This stores important system files that Windows can use to restart the PC properly if a problem occurs with your hard drive.

*The Install/Uninstall tab lets you remove unwanted programs from your computer and add new programs. It provides a list of programs that are already installed on your computer. To remove one, select it and press the Add/Remove button.*

*The Windows Setup tab provides a way to load the many components that are supplied with the Windows CD-ROM.*

*You need only use the last option once: it will create a special floppy disk for use in emergencies. Keep this Startup Disk somewhere safe. Should Windows not start up correctly, you can use this disk to get going again.*

# Installing the Character Map program

**The Character Map program is one of the more useful extra components in Windows. It is easy to install and takes up only a small amount of hard-drive space.**

THE CHARACTER MAP program is a useful tool that you can use to see the full range of letters, numbers and symbols in your fonts. Once installed, you can call it up to view the contents of any font on your PC. You can copy and paste characters from Character Map into your documents – even if the program doesn't have an Insert Symbol command.

**1** Open the Add/ Remove Programs dialog box, as shown on the previous page, and click on the Windows Setup tab. This displays a list of Components. Items that are checked are already installed on your computer; those without have not yet been installed.

**2** We want to install the Character Map tool, which Windows classifies as a System Tool. Click on this item and then press the Details button (inset) to see further information on this option.

**3** The System Tools window appears and lists all the individual components available. In this case, there are several tools, some of which are already installed.

**4** Click on the box next to Character Map to add a check. Press the OK button to return to the previous dialog box.

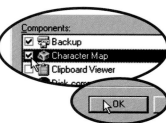

**5** Windows returns you to the Add/Remove Programs dialog box. Click the OK button.

**6** After a moment, you will be asked to insert the Windows CD-ROM into your computer's CD-ROM drive. Press the OK button and you will see a progress window to confirm the copying process.

**7** Once the copying has finished, the Add/Remove Programs tool will close automatically. Use the Start button to look in the Accessories folder. Click on the System Tools and you will see that the Character Map component has been added to the menu of programs.

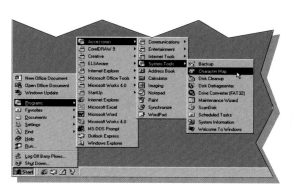

# Windows' extra components

**Windows comes with a number of extra components that are not part of a typical installation. Here is a selection of some that might prove useful.**

ALL OF THESE fun and functional options are included on your original Windows CD-ROM. These programs can be installed on your hard drive by following the procedure used to install the Character Map.

### ● Multimedia Sound Schemes

We have already shown how an external microphone can be attached to your computer for recording new sounds (see Stage 1, page 89). However, if you don't have a microphone, or don't want to be bothered recording new sounds, then you can use the collections of alternative sound effects offered by Windows. Each collection of sounds follows certain themes, such as wild animals, robots and so on. If you install and select them, they will replace the sounds that you hear.

### ● Direct cable connection

This useful program lets you connect two PCs using a cable. You can then transfer files from one to the other. It's a lot faster than swapping floppy disks between two PCs and you can transfer any size file (floppies can accommodate files up to 1.4MB in size).

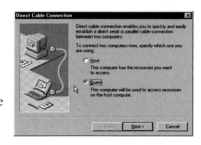

### ● Quick View

Quick View is a useful program that allows you to preview a document without having to open it in the program that created it. The advantage of this is that Quick View is very fast, so it's easy to use if you are searching for a particular file where you know the contents but not the name. Quick View works not only with many types of text files, but also with picture files, such as those created by the Microsoft Paint program.

*Quick View can show you the contents of files much more quickly than the program that created them can open them for editing.*

*If you can't find Windows' built-in games, check in the Games section of Accessories.*

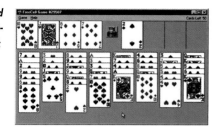

### ● Games

Windows is supplied with a number of games. These are entertaining enough, but comprise simple card games and beat-the-clock routines, rather than action games.

### ● Clipboard Viewer

Some of these smaller programs are left out of the typical installation because they 'clog up' the Start menu and can be confusing to first-time users. The Clipboard Viewer is one of the items left out. It's a tiny program that allows you to view any information that you have copied to the Clipboard. This can occasionally be useful if you need to check what is in the Clipboard before pasting it into a new position.

# Windows timekeeping

*Your computer's clock keeps going even when you switch off your PC. It knows when you load programs and when you save files. Here's your guide to how Windows keeps track of time and, therefore, your work.*

K eeping track of the time and date, even when the computer is switched off, is an important function that your computer performs almost invisibly. The small clock in the bottom-right corner of the Windows screen might be the only thing you have noticed that indicates your computer's timekeeping.

The ability to tell the time comes from your computer's internal clock. This clock has its own battery that keeps the clock ticking, even if you don't use your PC for several months. The time stored in this clock is displayed on the toolbar in Windows to give you a convenient on-screen clock to refer to while you're working.

### ● Clocking on

Windows also uses the clock for its own purposes to time-stamp and date-stamp files and folders every time you create, modify or save them. You can see how this works at its simplest by double-clicking on the My Computer icon to open the My Computer window. From this window, open your computer's hard-drive (C: drive) folder by double-clicking on it. Inside, you'll see a number of folders. Move your mouse pointer to the

*If you go to the View menu on a Windows window and select Details, you'll see the last date and time you modified the files in that window.*

*You don't have to alter the year on your PC – it happens automatically. Your computer has calendars programmed with all the dates up to 2099.*

View menu and select Details. You can then see the last time and date you modified the folder or its contents. Because Windows uses the time and date on your PC's clock to update this information, it is important to make sure that both these details are set accurately, otherwise the modified date will be completely useless to you. Windows gives you the power to do this using the Date/Time dialog box (see How to set the time and date, opposite).

### ● Putting the clock back

The Windows Date/Time dialog box also includes an option that allows it to adjust automatically for daylight saving time. As long as you leave this option switched on, Windows will automatically put your PC's clock backward or forward an hour on the right date.

The first time you switch on your computer after there has been a time change, Windows will warn you about the adjustment it's about to make and give you the chance to check that it's correct. It is important, therefore, to make sure that not only the time and date are correct, but also that your PC knows exactly where it is in the world.

*Once the correct time has been entered into your computer, all the changes you make to your documents will be time-stamped by the PC's internal clock.*

## WHAT IT MEANS

**TIME-STAMP AND DATE-STAMP**
*Every file and folder stored on your PC includes information about the time and date when it was last modified. Whenever you modify a file or folder, Windows updates this time and date information. Updating the time is called time-stamping, while updating the date is called date-stamping.*

# How to set the time and date

Here we show you how easy it is to set the date and time on your PC. We also show you how to set up or alter different time zones.

**1** Like many other Windows settings, time and date can be managed from the Control Panel. Click on the Start button, choose Settings, and then Control Panel. Double-click over the Date/Time icon to open the Date/Time Properties dialog box.

**2** This is the dialog box for both the time and date. We want to change the month to September, so move the mouse pointer to the arrow to the right of the window with the month displayed (in this case, October). Click on the arrow, scroll down the menu and click on September.

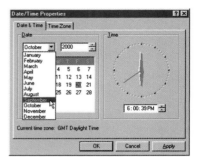

**3** To change the year, click on the up arrow by the year window to add one year at a time, or the down arrow to subtract a year. To change the day, click on the number of the day you wish to use in the main window.

**4** Changing the time can be done by highlighting the hour and clicking the up/down arrows to the required hour, then moving along to the minutes and seconds and changing them as required. Alternatively double-click on the figures and type in the new number.

This feature has hidden powers. For example, if you can't find a file on your hard disk, do a time search with the Find option in the Start menu (see Stage 2, pages 8-9).

0

**5** One thing to pay close attention to is the Current time zone, which is at the bottom of the window. In our example, it says GMT Daylight Time, which is fine if you live in London, but most people don't. Click on the Time Zone tab to change this.

**6** This is the Time Zone screen. Click on the arrow to the right of the current time zone and a long list of all the world's possible zones will appear (far right). Choose the one that suits your location by scrolling down the list. We've selected Eastern Time (US & Canada).

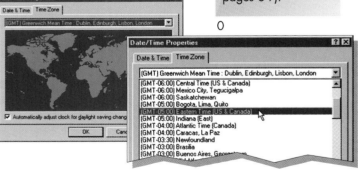

**7** When all your time and date settings are correct, click OK to put them to work. As usual, there is an Apply option that allows you to see how the changes you made will affect the screen. Check that everything is correct and then press OK.

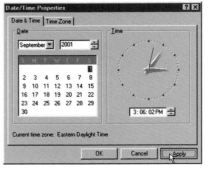

## PC TIPS

### Double-quick time

There are two quicker ways of reaching the Time/Date Properties dialog box than through the Control Panel. The first is to move your mouse pointer to the clock in the bottom-right corner of the screen and double-click on it. Alternatively, you can move the mouse pointer to the clock, click with the right mouse button, and then select Adjust Time/Date from the pop-up menu.

# Software

## CorelDRAW™

# Printing on envelopes

*Now that you are using your word processor to create perfectly presented letters, why not complete the picture and give a great first impression by printing professional looking envelopes as well?*

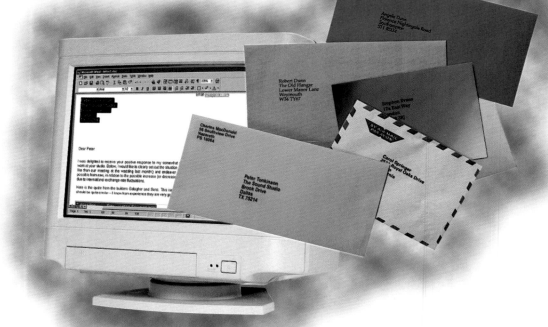

You don't need any extra software, a special printer or computer-compatible stationery to have your envelopes printed by your PC. In fact, Word helps you produce them quickly and easily. You can even select the address from your finished letter and have Word place it in position on the envelope. Word will also print your own address (the return address) in the top-left corner of the envelope, which looks neat and professional. Let's have a look at how easy it is to get Word to help you print great looking envelopes.

## LET THE WIZARD HELP

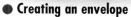

You may find that it's fun to use Word's Envelope Wizard, which you'll find by going to the File menu, clicking New and selecting the Letters and faxes tab, then clicking on the Envelope Wizard.wiz icon (left).

The Wizard is useful if you need to print an envelope for something you didn't use Word to produce, but it is similar to Word's other method of producing envelopes (see opposite), where you highlight the address in a letter you have written. When using the Wizard, you don't have an address to copy, so you enter the recipient's address in one window, the return address in the window below and then click on Print. You have the same options that we feature opposite, as well as the paper clip icon (right) which you can click on for help.

## ● Creating an envelope

There are two methods of using Word to print envelopes. There is the Envelope Wizard (see left, 'Let The Wizard Help') or you may prefer to employ Word to do some of the work. You do this by going to the option in Word's Tools menu called Envelopes and Labels. With this method, Word copies the recipient's address straight from your letter and positions and prints it onto the envelope.

## ● Laying out your letter

We have already seen how to lay out a formal letter using Word (see Stage 1, pages 34-35). You place your address in the top-right corner of the letter, and the name and address of the person to whom you are sending it on the left, above the 'Dear …' line. All you have to do is highlight this name and address, so when you go to the Tools menu and click on Envelopes and Labels, the recipient's details are ready and waiting for you in the window that appears.

*There are lots of different sizes and shapes of envelopes, but Word can handle anything you can fit into your printer and has ready-made templates for most common sizes.*

*You can produce such clear and well laid-out letters that it would be a shame to send them in hand-printed envelopes.*

# *Producing professional envelopes*

**Sending mail in clearly printed envelopes is a good idea for everyone, not just business people. Here's our guide to making that great first impression every time.**

**1** Here is our sample letter and, as you can see, the name and address of the person to whom the letter is being sent appears on the left of the page below the date.

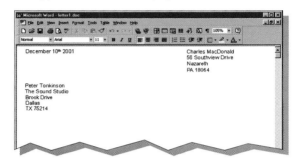

**2** To let Word know the recipient's address, you highlight both the name and address. Do this by holding down the left mouse button at the start of the name and dragging the cursor to the end of the address. Then release the mouse button.

**3** Move the mouse pointer to the Tools menu and select the Envelopes and Labels option.

**4** You will see a dialog box displayed in the center of your screen. The address you highlighted has been transferred to the Delivery address panel. The first time you do this, the bottom panel (the Return address box) may be empty. When you enter a Return address, Word remembers it and uses it in future letters.

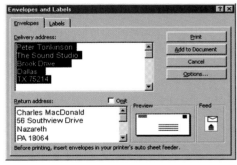

**5** You need to check the size of your envelope. A common business-size envelope is 4⅛ x 9½ in. Click on Options in the Envelopes and Labels window and you'll see an Envelope size option (above right). It has a pull-down menu (right) with various envelope sizes. Click on the envelope size you want and then click OK.

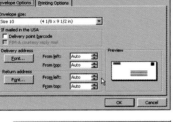

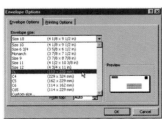

**6** Reduce the size of the font for the return address to avoid confusion with the main address. In the Envelope Options window, click on Font under Return address and use the Size scroll bar to select a smaller font size. You can also change the font style by clicking any of the 11 Effects boxes. You can create shadows behind the address or have an outline drawn around it. Some of these effects could make life harder for the mail carrier – so use them sparingly.

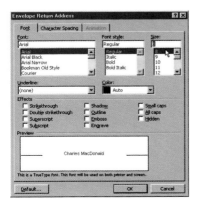

**7** Some printers accept only envelopes fed into them in a certain way, but with most inkjet printers you'll have some say in the matter. Click the Printing Options tab in the Envelope Options window (above) to check the orientation of the envelope and which way up it goes into the printer (below left).

If the setup is correct, click OK, which returns you to the Envelope Options window, and then click Print (above right). You must be sure that your envelope is placed in the printer in the right way (see Stage 2, page 97).

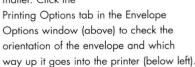

# Putting text in columns

**W**henever large amounts of information have to be presented in an easy-to-read format, or several different items need to appear near one another, you'll find text divided into columns.

Newspapers and magazines, for example, rely heavily on this format. Both need to display lengthy articles alongside shorter stories in a way that lets the readers find their way around the page with the minimum of fuss and confusion.

Since these columns are narrower than a single page (usually 2–3 inches wide), you can scan the page and take in the information far more quickly than if the line extended to the full width of an 8½ x 11 inch page.

With text spread over longer lines, readers risk losing their way; at least with columns, they know where they are.

● **When to use columns**

In Word you can easily format your documents into columns, although this will probably not be appropriate for all the documents you write. A single-page letter, for example, would look silly and confusing spread over two or more columns.

*Big blocks of text running from one edge of a page to the other are hard to read and look far from enticing to the casual browser. So liven up documents and make them user friendly by putting text into columns.*

However, there are many occasions when placing text in columns can give a document a more professional appearance. Business reports and club or organization newsletters would all benefit from being put into a more accessible column format. We'll take an in-depth look at such documents on pages 30–33. For the time being, however, we'll concentrate on how to format a section of a longish document into columns.

*Structured columns of words are far more pleasing to the eye, and easier to read, than large blocks of text that are visually daunting and psychologically tiring.*

## EASY READING

It is quicker and easier to absorb large amounts of information when it is presented in short lines. When text is printed across a wide measure, the eye finds it hard to follow the story from one line to the next, and it becomes all too easy to lose your place on the page. For example, see how much easier it is to read the main text on this page, compared to the words in this box. Another big advantage of using columns of text is that they can be arranged around a picture if required and the reader will still have no difficulty in following the order. Pictures of any shape and size can be used without disrupting the flow of text. Notice the example in the picture above.

# Formatting into columns

You can use any document with a reasonable amount of text for this exercise. Ideally, you need three or four pages to see the true benefits. If you don't have a longish document, simply copy and paste blocks of text to make up the length.

**1** Highlight all the text that you wish to format into columns.

**2** Go to the Format menu and select the Columns command.

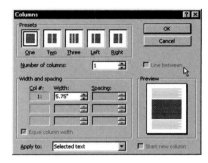

**3** The Columns dialog box now appears, as shown below.

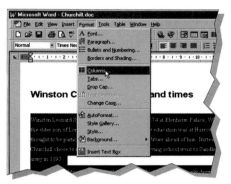

**4** At the top of the box are thumbnail images of a number of preset column styles. Click on them and you can see what they will look like in the Preview panel. The two right-hand images, labeled Left and Right give you the option of imposing unequal column widths, although these are very rarely used.

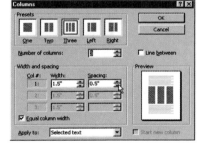

**5** You can easily alter the column width and the space between the columns by clicking on the arrows next to the relevant figures to increase or decrease the measurements of column width or spacing. Word will automatically adjust the other measurement so that the total fits inside the page. Click on the up arrow to make a slight increase of 0.25 in. in the space between the columns.

**6** Above the Preview panel is a box labeled Line between. If you click here to select it, Word will automatically draw a thin vertical line between the columns to emphasize the division between them.

**7** Now press the OK button to see the columns in your document. The heading for our document is not affected by the Column command because we did not highlight it in Step 1.

**8** If you need to get an overall view of how these pages will look now that they are formatted in columns, select Full Screen view from the View menu. Now select a smaller percentage view – say, 50% – from the Zoom window at the top right of the toolbar.

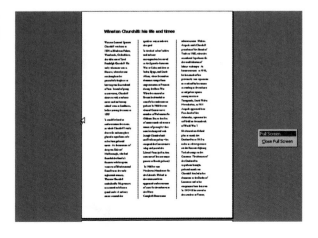

## DISAPPEARING COLUMNS

You will notice that columns disappear from view when you select Normal from the View menu. This is because in Normal View, Word tries to display the document as quickly as possible. By using a single column on the left, it can show line breaks without taking time to show all the columns.

*Microsoft® Word*

# Creating a newsletter

**Newsletters for the local youth club or school PTA don't have to be dull, typed pages. Here we show you how to make your club look like it means business.**

W e've seen in Stages 1 and 2 how to change fonts and add pictures and, in the previous pages, how to use multiple columns to make large blocks of text more interesting. Now we are going to use all these tricks – and a few more – to create a newsletter.

Of course, not everyone needs to produce a newsletter. Yet it's amazing how the same principles – captioned photos, headlines and box rules, for instance – can make a world of difference to many everyday Word documents. Homework essays and term papers, résumés and even basic memos or lists to be posted on a bulletin board can all be enhanced with these simple tricks.

### ● Make your own

It used to be the case that if you wanted to create anything livelier than the most basic document, you would use your word processor only to input and check the text, then transfer the words to an expensive and complex desktop publishing package to create the finished article. But nowadays, with a modern version of Word, you can achieve impressive results in one program, and save yourself a good deal of time and money in the process.

You could even create something similar to *PCs made easy* in Word. All you have to do is get to grips with the necessary tools and you're in the publishing business!

The newsletter we're going to create is based on a Word Wizard-created document – but don't be afraid to experiment, because it would be a very dull world if every publication had the same design.

Finally, an important design tip: don't be afraid to borrow ideas from the pros. Flick through magazines and choose the design features you like. Mix these ideas to create your own newsletters. It may sound like cutting corners, but it will save you several years at design school!

**Hold the front page! Create your own news with Word's Newsletter Wizard.**

# Adding floating text boxes

**Once you start using text boxes in more adventurous layouts, you'll discover just how versatile they can be.**

THE KEY TO any newsletter layout is using boxes for the different elements, particularly text. It gives you the flexibility to create columns of text that flow between different parts of the page.

You need only link two text boxes together: when one box is full, the excess text flows over to continue into the next box.

You can change the size of the boxes at any time, and you can easily move them around until you get a balance that you like. When you alter the size or shape of the boxes the text automatically reflows. As text boxes are the most important elements of any newsletter-type layout, we'll show you how to use them in your Word documents.

**Microsoft® Word**

## FLOATING BOXES

All boxes, including those we are adding in the exercise on this page, 'float' on top of the normal Word page. The space where you would normally type text sits underneath these boxes.

If you type without selecting one of the text boxes, the new text will appear at the current cursor position in the underlying Word text. If your document is blank (as it is here, underneath the text boxes), this text will appear at the top left of the page.

**1** The text box tool is part of Word's drawing tools, so click on the Drawing button on the toolbar. When you do so, Word changes from Normal View to Page Layout View.

**2** The view can change so that the whole page is visible on the screen. This is usually a 40 percent view. To see more detail, make sure the view is set to 100 percent.

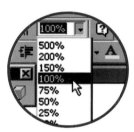

**3** Click on the Text Box icon on the Drawing toolbar. It's in the center of the toolbar below.

**4** Now click and drag the mouse to create a rectangular text box on the Word page.

**5** Click on the new text box, and type in a paragraph or two of text. To produce enough for this exercise, cut and paste it several times within the box until the text overflows at the end of the box.

**6** Now create a second text box, to the right of the first, by using the text box tool as you did in step 4.

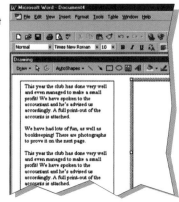

**7** Click on the first text box to select it, then click on the chain icon on the Text Box toolbar. You will see the cursor change into a pitcher icon.

**8** Move your cursor over the second (empty) text box – it will change into a pouring pitcher – and click. The text will then overflow from the first box to the second.

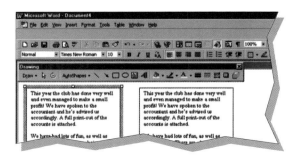

# Using the Newsletter Wizard

**Let's look at how we would go about creating a newsletter for a local football team. Word helps us start by providing the Newsletter Wizard.**

**1** Create a new Word document by selecting New from the File menu. The New dialog box will appear.

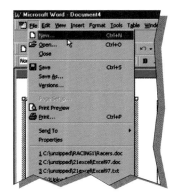

**2** Now click on the Other Documents tab and double-click on the Newsletter Wizard icon.

**3** When the Newsletter Wizard has started up, displaying the screen below, click Next.

**4** The flow chart on the left of the window will show that you have moved to the next stage, where you are presented with a choice of three styles of newsletter: Professional, Contemporary and Elegant. We're using Professional because it is the most clean-cut in design and the easiest to use. Leave the other settings exactly as they are and click Next.

**5** The next screen lets us type in the name of our newsletter, and add a date and issue number. You can either accept Word's suggestions or type in your own. If you don't want any details at all, click on the boxes to remove the check marks. Then click Next.

**6** The following screen allows you to print mailing labels. Click No, as our newsletters are going to be handed out at the stadium. Then click Next.

**7** The final screen will tell you that the Newsletter Wizard has everything it needs. Press the Finish button.

**8** Word will create a newsletter with your title at the top, plus lots of dummy elements for holding text and pictures. At present, the boxes hold instructive dummy text. On the next page, we'll swap these dummy elements for our club newsletter information. But first check the paper size and change it if necessary (see PC Tips, below).

---

## WHERE IS IT?

It's possible that you won't find Newsletter Wizard in the Other Documents tab of Word's New dialog box (Step 2). If it's missing, add it from your Word CD-ROM. Simply insert the CD-ROM and select Find from the Start menu.

Type Newsletter into the text box, select the CD-ROM drive in the Look in option and click the Find Now button. Windows will search the CD-ROM for the Newsletter Wizard. If it finds more than one file, select the one that says Microsoft Word Wizard under the Type menu icon.

| Name | In Folder |
|---|---|
| Newsletter.doc | C:\My Documents |
| Newsletter Wizard | C:\Program Files\Mi... |
| Newsletter.doc | C:\WINDOWS\Rec... |

3 file(s) found

## PC TIPS

The Newsletter Wizard creates documents based on letter-size paper. If you are using another size, such as legal (8½ x 14 in.), you might have problems printing it. To change the page size, click on the File menu and select Page Setup. Click on the Paper Size tab and change from Letter to Legal. Click Apply to: whole document and then click OK.

Letter 8 1/2 x 11 in
Legal 8 1/2 x 14 in
Executive 7 1/4 x 10 1/2 in
210 x 297 mm

# Customizing your newsletter

**The Newsletter Wizard does a lot of the work for you as it has the pages already laid out – all you have to do is insert text over what's currently there.**

ONCE WORD has created your basic newsletter with dummy text and pictures, it's a good idea to print it out. This will give you a ready reference for the layout – just in case you accidentally delete something you may want later. What's more, the text on the page is a handy reference guide to creating the different items used and a breakdown of all the preset customized text styles, such as headlines, body text and quotes. There are two ways of adding and formatting your own text in the newsletter. You can either select and delete the document text, paste in your own and then format it afterward, or you can change it bit by bit so that it keeps the styles already applied. The second method gives you more control and is suitable for creating text from scratch.

**1** Replace the dummy text in the newsletter by simply highlighting it and typing over it. You can select complete paragraphs by triple-clicking (three rapid clicks of the left mouse button).

**2** You could just replace all the text in the newsletter, but we want to jazz up a few of the headings as well. Highlight the heading in the first column and type in a new one. Then, from the Format menu, select Font. Choose a suitable font, size and color, and check how it will appear in the Preview panel. Be careful not to make the font too big, however, as it will put the page out of balance.

**3** Once you are happy with the heading style you have chosen, go to the Styles pull-down menu (with the heading still highlighted) and select Heading 1 – Professional, which is the preset style for this kind of heading.

**4** Word knows that you have changed the font of one of the headings, and asks you whether you want to modify the other headings to match the change. Choose Update the style to reflect recent changes? and Automatically update the style from now on, then click OK. You will see other headings that use the same style automatically change to match the one you changed in Step 2.

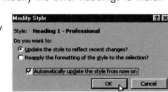

**5** Now we're going to insert a picture. You could do this by selecting Picture from the Insert menu but as there is a picture already on the page, click on that and then select Insert Picture from the pop-up Picture toolbar.

**6** Choose a picture – we found this example on the Microsoft Office CD–ROM. It's called 1stplace.wmf and appears in the Clipart folder.

**7** The size of the picture is not quite right for our newsletter, but we can resize and trim it to fit. Click on the Crop button on the Picture toolbar and then click on one of the picture handles and move it in. Repeat this until you are satisfied. If you want to move the picture to a different point in the text, use Cut and Paste.

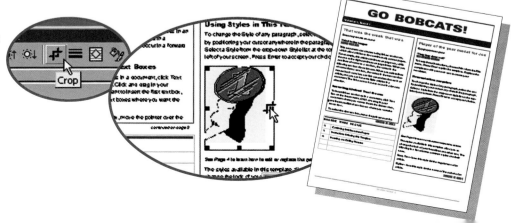

# Talking tabs

The [Tab] key is useful for moving text across the page, but it can be customized to do so much more. Set up as many invisible stops as you wish, wherever you want, to create professional lists and documents.

I n an earlier example (see Stage 1, pages 32-33) we used the [Tab] key in Word to make some simple indents in a letter. By pressing the [Tab] key several times at the beginning of each line of our address, we moved it to the right of our page to create a very simple letterhead layout.

Using tabs could be limited to just that, or they might simply be used for indenting the first line of each paragraph to make a letter look more presentable. However, tabs are far more versatile than that. They have many other easy-to-use applications that can be utilized on a wide variety of documents.

● **Tab behavior**

If you press the [Tab] key when the text insertion point is at the beginning of a line of text, Word shifts the text to the right. Try it again on another line of text and you will see that Word shifts the text by exactly the same amount. Press it again and your second line of text will be indented to twice the distance of the first.

Now try typing the following on a blank line: 1 [Tab] 2 [Tab] 3 [Tab] Four [Tab] 5. You will notice that Word doesn't space the entries evenly – the distance between the 'r' in the word 'Four' and the number '5'

*The [Tab] key will enable you to place words exactly where you want them on the page, making lists and documents neater and easier to read.*

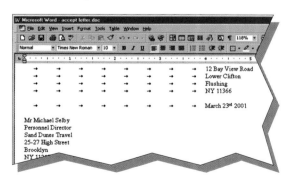

*Here you can see the dozens of tabs we've had to use to move our address to the right of our letterhead. Once you've mastered tabs, you can do this with a single tab for each line.*

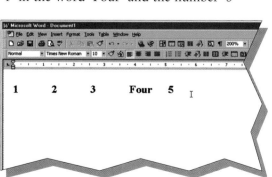

*Despite initial appearances, tabs don't actually add any space. Instead they just shift text to the next invisible tab stop on the page; that's why the 'Four' appears to be closer to the '5' than the '3'.*

is shorter than between the '1' and the '2'. This demonstrates an important facet of tabs: a tab doesn't actually add space; instead, Word shifts text to the next of a series of invisible tab stops (which are placed at half-inch intervals).

## MEASUREMENTS

When setting tab stops or working with Word's ruler, you might have a preference for either inches or centimeters. Fortunately, Word lets you switch between these units as often as you like.

Click on the Tools menu and select Options. You will see a dialog box. Click on the General tab and at the bottom of the dialog box a drop-down list box will appear.

Select whichever measurement unit you want to use and then press the OK button. You will usually need to use the Inches or Centimeters choices. The Picas and Points options are measurements that are used in the publishing and printing industries.

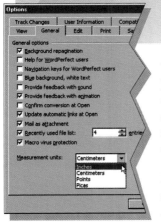

### ● Changing settings

While these default tab stops are usually fine, there might be times when you require different settings. For example, Word can normally fit 11 tab stops across a standard page. Therefore, if you ever wanted to line up 12 columns of text, you would run out of space. To overcome this kind of problem, Word lets you specify both the position and number of tab stops.

### ● Alignment options

There's another way in which Word's normal behavior might not be quite right for creating neatly aligned tables of information in your documents. If you press the [Tab] key to move to the next tab stop in a document, Word will align the text so that it starts at the tab. This is called left alignment. Type more text and you'll find it starts at the tab stop. As usual, this is the default – because it is the most popular choice. However, you may want to align your text differently. Word places other useful options at your disposal, such as creating special tab stops that help align each piece of text in subtly different ways.

For example, if you were creating a price list, you might use a tab to separate the item name and its price. Normally the table would look like this:

| | |
|---|---|
| New engine | $695.00 |
| Air filter | $5.99 |
| Oil filter | $17.95 |

However, it's not clear at first glance that there's a big difference between the prices of these three components. It's a lot easier to see the difference when they are aligned on the decimal point:

| | |
|---|---|
| New engine | $695.00 |
| Air filter | $5.99 |
| Oil filter | $17.95 |

Now it's easy to see the prices in relation to each other. By using a special decimal tab stop, you can get Word to line up information just like this. There are also right and center tab-stop options that can help to clarify the entries in other tables.

### ● Professional results

Other options can help make your tables of information look professional. Most table of contents of books and magazines lay out the list of chapters or articles with their title, a tab and a page number. However, to make it easier to read across a wide column, the designer will often fill the space between the titles and page numbers with a continuous line of periods.

Word lets you achieve the same results through its tab options. If you're creating a newsletter (see pages 30-33), adding a contents list as described above can help give it a polished and professional look.

### ● Following the rules

Adjusting the tab stops and choosing different alignment options is a very simple matter. By using the ruler (located just under Word's toolbars) you can add and remove any tab stop with a few clicks.

You can also use the Tab's dialog box to add lines of periods, or any other characters, to your contents lists. On the following pages we'll show you how to do all of this.

## PC TIPS

You don't have to use tabs to indent the first line of paragraphs in your documents. If you want every paragraph to have an indented first line, you can save yourself time and trouble by applying this command as a default setting. Start with a new Word document and, before typing any text, click on the Format menu. Choose the Paragraph command and select the Indents and Spacing tab from the dialog box that appears.

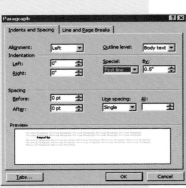

Find the Special box on the right-hand side and choose First line from the options. Use the By number box to choose the amount of indentation that you need, and click OK.

As you type, you'll find that the first line of each paragraph is indented. However, if you want to apply indents to individual paragraphs, click the text insertion point in the paragraph you want before choosing the Paragraph command from the Format menu, as shown above.

# Setting tabs using the ruler

**The simplest way to add, change and remove tabs is to use Word's ruler. With a few clicks you can align your text and see the effects immediately.**

**1** We've started with a simple shopping list as an example of something that would look better with the item name and price in two columns. If we used Word's normal tab stops, we'd have to use a different number of tabs for each line, depending on the text length of each item. For example, we'd need just one for the long 'Nails, screws, tacks' item, but several for the short 'Paint' item.

**2** However, it's possible to do all this with one tab. Start by using the Select All command on the Edit menu.

**3** Now that all the text is selected, we can apply our tab settings to it. Move the mouse pointer over the ruler. When you're roughly in the position you'd like your tab to be, click and hold down the mouse button.

**4** A dotted line will show you the position of your new tab stop. With your cursor, move it left or right and, when it is in the desired position, release the mouse button. Word will indicate your tab stop with a small L-shape on the ruler.

**5** Click once again to remove the highlighting. Now click just in front of the price for the first item in the list (3 tubes carpet glue). Press the [Tab] key once and you will see the price move to the right, aligning its left edge directly under the tab stop.

**6** Now do the same with the other prices. Only one tab will be needed each time.

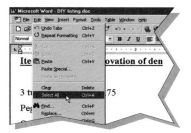

**7** The table looks OK, but it would be even better if the prices lined up on their decimal points. Start by selecting all the text again. Now remove the tab stop we put in by clicking on its L-shape on the ruler and dragging it onto the document; as you do, it will change from black to gray. Release it and it will disappear. The prices in the table will move and appear even more ragged than they did before, but don't panic – we'll soon fix that.

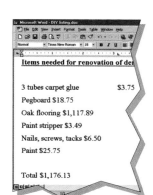

**8** Change your style of tab stop by clicking on the square on the ruler's left side. Each time you click, it changes: left, right, center, decimal and then back to left again. Click on it until the Decimal Tab is displayed.

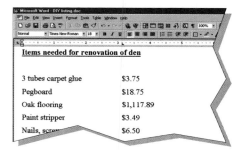

**9** Now, making sure that all the text in the document is still selected, move the mouse pointer to the position on the ruler where you placed the first tab. Click the mouse to position the decimal tab in the same place.

**10** When you release the mouse button, the prices in the table will immediately realign from their ragged state. Word looks at the items and positions them so that their decimal points line up directly below the decimal tab stop.

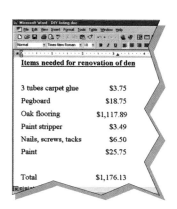

## MIXING YOUR TABS WITH WORD'S TABS

If you had already used tabs to format your list or table – with Word's normal half-inch tab stops – you will probably find that there are now too many tabs in your table. With Word's normal tab stops you often have to add several tabs to make things line up. Now your single tab does the job, but any extra tab characters in the table make it look ragged. You can delete unwanted tab characters one by one until the table lines up under your own tab stop. To see the tab characters, click on the Show/Hide button on the Toolbar (right).

# Fine-tuning your tab settings

**Now we have worked with tab settings, let's make some changes to improve the look of the document we created in the previous exercise.**

**1** You can create and alter tabs via the Tabs window in the Format menu. This has all the options of the ruler – and more besides. Start with a new Word document. Click on the Format menu and choose the Tabs command.

**2** A dialog box will appear. At the top, you will see a box that you can use to change the Default tab stops. As you can see here, Word is set to a half-inch (1.27cm).

**3** You set tabs by typing a figure into the Tab stop position box. Type 2" into the space provided and press the Set button below.

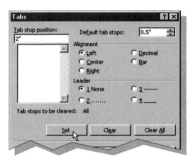

**4** You'll see this tab stop position appear in the box just underneath. You can add more tab stops by repeating Step 3. As you press the Set button, each tab position appears in the list.

**5** Deleting a tab stop is simple. Just highlight it in the list, then press the Clear button. Clear all the extra tabs until you have only the 2" tab remaining.

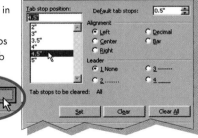

**6** You can also select the type of alignment for each tab stop in the Alignment section. Highlight the 2" tab stop and you'll see that the Left alignment option is selected. Here, we've chosen to align by the decimal point and so have selected Decimal.

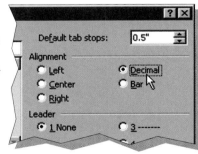

**7** The other section of the dialog box is called Leader, and it's here that you can tell Word to fill in the space between tabs with characters. There are four options, the second one of which uses periods and is often seen in contents and price listings. When you add a tab stop, Word doesn't normally use leader characters: the '1 None' option is selected by default. Select our 2" tab stop and then click on the periods option. Press the Set button.

**8** We can apply this new tab trick to the list that we made on the previous page. When you have finished that exercise, select all the text by clicking on Select All in the Edit menu. Go to the Tabs box and clear the tab you set previously, as we did in Step 5. Change the tab stop settings by adding an aligned tab at 2" and selecting the second option from the Leader options. Press the Set button and then press the OK button. You'll now see a neat and easy-to-read list.

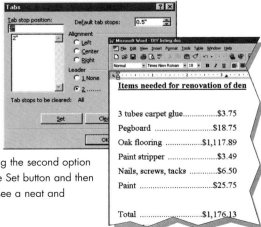

Items needed for renovation of den

3 tubes carpet glue...............$3.75
Pegboard .........................$18.75
Oak flooring .................$1,117.89
Paint stripper .....................$3.49
Nails, screws, tacks ............$6.50
Paint ................................$25.75

Total ......................$1,176.13

# Inserting special characters in text

**Word doesn't limit you to just ordinary letters and numbers in your text documents. You can also add foreign characters and a whole range of useful symbols and icons to create the right effect for your intended message.**

One of the advantages of a personal computer over a typewriter is that it allows you to use all sorts of extra characters as well as the ordinary alphabet letters and numbers. This makes it as easy to produce an informal letter, adorned with little doodles and pictures, as it does to write a letter in a foreign language with accents, or a business letter with symbols.

Most of these special characters don't appear on your computer keyboard, apart from the punctuation and currency symbols. But, by using special commands, Word puts as many as 200 different characters at your disposal – and even more can be added with extra fonts.

### ● Improving letters and documents

This versatility gives you the ability to produce documents with a professional finish or with a large element of fun and creativity.

Special characters can be divided into three main categories: foreign characters (such as ç and é); business symbols (such as © and ™); and fun symbols (❤ and ✗). There are two ways to insert these characters. The first is to pick them out from a grid, via the Symbol command on the Insert menu. Some characters can also be entered using the keyboard. This is done by pressing a combination of keys.

Although this method is quicker if you use foreign characters a lot, it is harder to remember.

It's easy to see how different types of letters and documents can benefit from these additions. A foreign-language letter, for example, would be impossible to write correctly without these characters. Equally, business letters can be made to look more professional if you use ready-made symbols, such as those for copyright or trademark. Fun symbols may not be as important, but they can enliven a letter or party invitation.

*Your keyboard can contain up to 200 hidden characters and symbols – all you have to do is find them!*

# Adding symbols

**Use foreign characters and fun symbols to enhance your letter writing.**

TO ILLUSTRATE HOW special characters can be both useful and fun, we'll write a love letter to an absent girlfriend. Here is an example using both accented characters and symbols:

My Dear Gisèle,

Was it only yesterday we said goodbye? Je pense à toi. Les feuilles mortes sont tombées des arbres, mais mon amour reste toujours vivant. Ça me soulage que tu reçoive ma lettre. Je serai encore une fois avec toi, ô mon trésor éternel.

♥ Je t'embrasse ♥

*Christian* ✗✗✗✗✗  ☺

**1** Type in the text until you reach a special character. Then select the Insert menu and choose Symbol.

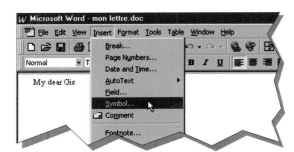

**2** When the Symbol window opens, select the Symbols tab and choose (normal text) from the Font drop-down menu.

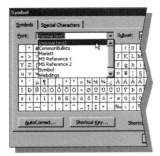

**3** Now look at the grid and select the character you are looking for, in this case è, by clicking on it with the left mouse button. A large version of the character will be displayed on a blue background. When you click on the Insert button, the character will appear in the text document (inset).

My Dear Gisè

**4** Close the Symbol window and continue with the letter, entering all the letters with accents in the same way. The next special character is the heart symbol. This is entered in a similar way, but is part of the Symbol font, so select Symbol from the Font drop-down menu.

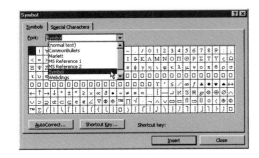

**5** Click on the heart in the Symbol characters grid, then click on the Insert button. When you come to insert the second heart, save time by copying and pasting the first one. Have a look at all the symbols in this grid to see the variety available for use in different types of document.

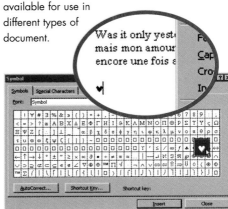

**6** If you want to add other embellishments, try an '✗' for kisses after the signature. This is part of the Wingdings font, so select this font and choose from the grid as before. Again, you don't need to insert each '✗' separately, just copy and paste the first one.

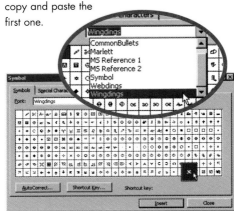

**7** Another symbol is the 'smiley' face. This is also one of the Wingdings font characters. Insert this at the end of the document. All the special characters appear in the font size you are using to write your letter, but this time, let's make it bigger. You do this in exactly the same way as with an ordinary character. Select the 'smiley' and put up the font size to 48.

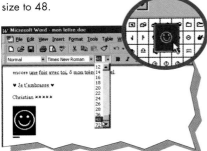

# Finding and replacing text

*Are you looking for a quick way to get to the right part of your document, to add some formatting to frequently occurring words or to correct a name misspelled throughout? If so, Word's powerful Find/Replace tool is what you need. It will even search for 'sound-alike' words.*

It can sometimes be difficult to find exactly the part of a Word document that you want to work on, especially if it is a long document. The most obvious, but cumbersome, way is to scroll through the document until you find what you're looking for. However, Word provides a much simpler way of dealing with this.

Word includes a Find tool that allows you to search for occurrences of words or phrases within your document. This means you only have to remember a relevant word from the part of the document you want to work on, then you can use the Find tool to skip to the places that this word occurs in the document until you reach the instance you want. This tool can also be handy when you want to find certain key words or phrases in documents with which you are unfamiliar.

● **Changing words and phrases**
Word's Find tool is not just a search tool for locating words and phrases – you can also use it to replace them with different words or phrases. For instance, you could replace all the occurrences in a document of National Broadcasting Corporation with NBC in one swift operation. Or you could correct all the occurrences of somebody's name if you discover that you've spelled it incorrectly.

In fact, it's not just words and phrases you can replace – you can actually replace any sequence of characters. For instance, many typists were originally taught to add two spaces after a period. If this is a habit you just can't break, you can search for two consecutive spaces and replace them with one.

There are also other special characters that you can replace, such as paragraph marks, tab characters and page breaks. The Word Find/Replace tool has some other advanced features. For example, if you're not sure of the spelling of a word you need to look for, you can ask Word to search for a word that sounds like the one you type in. You can also get the Find/Replace tool to look for words that appear in a particular format (for example, typeface, size, bold, italics and so on). You can instruct Word to replace these words with different words in the same format or the same words in another format.

Word also lets you match case. This means that if you want to replace the name of a company called 'FAST', but leave the ordinary word 'fast' as it is, Word can oblige.

National Broadcasting Corporation is programming a production of Oscar Wild's A Picture of Dorien Grey at 9.0(

NBC is programming a production of Oscar Wilde's *A Picture of Dorian G... 0.00 pm* this evening.

There are man... ...en you want to make the same changes to w... ...hat occur throughout a l... text docume... ...t to put some w... such as NB... ...o word... **bold** or *it...* ...elling... person's f...

NBC
*Pictur...*

NBC ...
*Pictur...* ...evening.

There ... change s... text docum...

**PC TIPS**

**Searching for words that sound similar**
You can use the Find/Replace tool to look for words that sound like the word you type in. For example, you can ask Word to search for all words that sound like 'there'. This will locate each instance of both 'there' and 'their', as well as common misspellings, such as 'thier'.

# Using Word's find and replace tool

**The Find and Replace tool helps you locate and change any sequence of text, including numbers and special characters. It makes it easy to move around long documents and correct misspelled words in a single action.**

**1** Here's a letter that we've been working on. There's a mistake in one of the names – the first George Smith should be Andrew Smith. Let's use Word's Find/Replace tool to make things right.

**2** Position the text cursor at the start of the letter so that Word will search through the whole document from the beginning. Now select Replace from the Edit menu.

**3** The Find and Replace dialog box appears: type the word George in the Find what text box at the top of the dialog box. Then type in the word Andrew in the Replace with text box. If we wanted to change all the occurrences of the name George to Andrew, we would just press the Replace All button. However, we won't do this here because we want to show more advanced replace options.

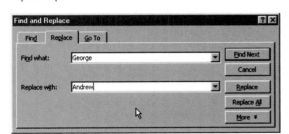

**4** Let's exploit the difference in format between the two occurrences of the name George (one is in italics, the other is not). Click on the More button and the Find and Replace dialog box will extend to reveal more options. Click once in the Find what text box, then click the Format button and choose the Font option.

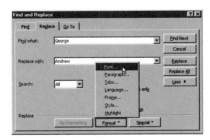

**5** Use this dialog box to specify the format of the word to replace. We chose 10 pt. Arial with an italic style (to find George in italics). Select suitable settings for your document and click on the OK button.

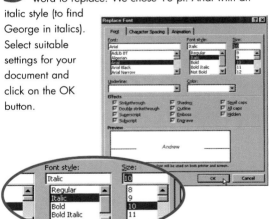

**6** Position the cursor in the Replace with text box, click on the Format button and select Font again. Repeat the choices we made in Step 5 and click OK. Notice how both text boxes have identical Format lines below them.

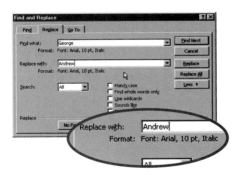

**7** Click on the Replace button and Word will locate all words in the style specified in Step 5 and ask you to confirm each replacement as you go. For this exercise, click on the Replace All button. Word makes all the replacements (one in this case) and reports back to you. Click on the OK button in the dialog box that reports the number of changes (below).

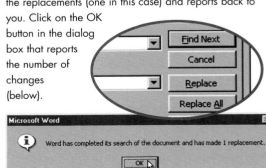

**8** Click on the Close button in the Find and Replace dialog box and you'll see your modified document with only the one George changed to Andrew, as intended.

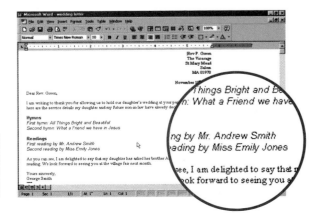

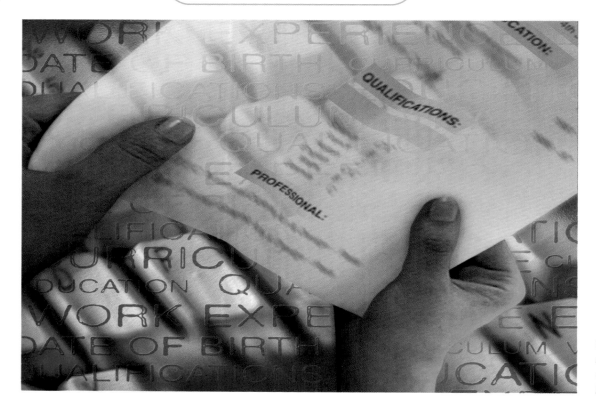

*If you're applying for a job, why not take advantage of your PC's capabilities to make your résumé look as good as possible?*

# Borders and shading

**Adding borders and highlights to give your résumé a really professional look couldn't be easier when you're using Word.**

If there is one document you just have to have professionally presented, it is your résumé – your employment and educational history. The résumé is the document that clinches an interview for a job or college place – or ruins your chances – and it is absolutely vital that it create the right impression.

### ● The computer advantage

All too many résumés are simply typed out in a haphazard way or, worse still, handwritten. With a PC and a printer, however, you have at your fingertips the power to produce a clean, neat document that will make the most of your chances. Even better, by spending a little time making your résumé as clear, concise and attractive as you can, you will increase the chance that yours will stand out from the rest of the pile and help get you that interview and, ultimately, the job.

With a PC, it is easy to make last-minute corrections to your résumé to make sure every detail is right. You can also update it to incorporate your most recent work experience or each new qualification – no more handwritten corrections that make your résumé look sloppy. You can modify it to suit different types of job that you may want to apply for. Perhaps most importantly, you have complete control over the way it looks.

In the next few pages, we give you a few tips on preparing a résumé. In particular, we'll show you how to use Microsoft Word's tools to create a professional look – adding borders and shading to emphasize specific features to draw the eye to important sections.

Microsoft® Word

## CHECKPOINT ✓

### MAKING THE MOST OF YOUR RESUME

As well as the formatting ideas covered in the step-by-step examples (see pages 44-45), there are a few general principles to consider when creating a résumé. Follow the tips here and your résumé is less likely to end up in the reject pile because of poor presentation.

☑ Try to avoid using capital letters and italics for large blocks of text. Both make your information harder to read than normal text.

☑ Avoid the temptation to use decorative typefaces. They might be fun for the odd letter or jokey poster, but most potential employers are looking for efficient, businesslike employees.

☑ Be wary of using humor in your text – it's not what the résumé is for.

☑ Always get permission from your references before putting them on the résumé. Neither they nor a potential employer will be impressed if you haven't.

☑ Keep your résumé to a maximum of two pages, unless you are asked to do otherwise.

It is vital with a résumé to present everything in clear, easy-to-understand sections so that the reader can see at a glance what your education was, what your recent employment history has been, and so on.

Borders are an excellent way of sectioning off different parts of your résumé, making it look bold and interesting. This helps a lightweight résumé look more substantial, without distorting the facts.

### ● Dividing your life up

You should always start your résumé with your name, address and contact numbers (phone, fax, email and so on). Some people prefer to put this information in the center of the page, using the center text control. Others prefer it on the far left of the page, which is known as flush left text. The rest of the résumé then divides into three main areas: job objective, employment history and qualifications and education.

The idea is to give the reader a clear outline of your life. Each entry in the employment history begins with the relevant dates. Keep entries brief and to the point, but make sure it is clear what you were doing in each job, listing in order: dates, your job title, your employer's name and address, and what your job entailed.

### ● The right order for you

Recruitment experts advise putting your employment history in reverse order. That means that you begin with the most recent job. Remember, when potential employers are reading through lots of résumés, they probably want to see what you're currently doing, without having to wade through your entire career of part-time, summer and temporary jobs.

It is really up to you to decide what works best with your life history and also shows potential employers most clearly the important facts, such as where you have lived.

The final sections should cover your personal affiliations, which can be surprisingly helpful at getting you that interview. You may also want to offer to give the names and contact details of two people who will give you good references. These are usually work-related, but some employers also like a personal reference. Many people simply put the phrase 'References on request'.

## WHEN TO USE UNDERLINE AND WHEN TO USE BORDERS

Most of the time you will use the Borders tool to add horizontal lines under some text in your documents. But you might also have been using Word's Underline tool (below) to achieve the same effect. Which one is better?

### Underlining

In Word, you can emphasize any amount of text, from a single word to the whole document, by using the underline command, which places a single line under the selected text. Some people also use the Underline tool to add a horizontal rule across a page, by adding a whole

*Once you've got used to adding borders, you'll probably only use Word's Underline button for adding a single underline to individual words and short phrases.*

line of spaces, selecting them and then clicking on the Underline button. While this might look fine, it's a time-consuming approach. There are other potential problems, too: for example, if you increase the size of the text used in the document, you will find that the line of space continues onto the next line – and so does the underline.

### Borders

When you use borders for such lines, you'll find you have much more flexibility available at the press of a few buttons. For example, you have a wide choice of different line widths and you can choose from a variety of styles, including solid, dotted and even wavy lines. When you work with borders, you'll discover

that you can use them on any side of your text. You can put lines on one, two or three sides of the text, or even completely enclose it.

As you experiment with the borders options, you'll find that in most cases they're more suitable than the Underline tool. On the whole, underlining is the best option for emphasizing a word or phrase in formal letters and documents, but the borders options are much more suitable for making paragraphs or longer sections stand out.

*Special effects, such as wavy lines and 3-D edges, won't suit all of your documents, but they illustrate the flexibility of Word's border options.*

# Adding borders to sections of your résumé

**To show you the basic steps of producing a résumé, we've created an imaginary example for someone applying for the job of supermarket manager. Either copy the format of this résumé or create your own.**

**1** Type in the text of your résumé, following the guidelines given (see Checkpoint on the previous page). For the moment, don't add any formatting other than tabs to create columns. All the formatting commands will be added later on.

**2** To divide the résumé into clear sections, you can create lines across the page under each separate heading with the Borders and Shading option. Start by clicking on the line beneath Personal Details (or whatever your first heading is).

**3** Now go to the Format menu at the top of the screen and pull down the menu. Select the Borders and Shading option and click on it to bring up the Borders and Shading window on the screen.

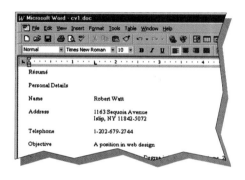
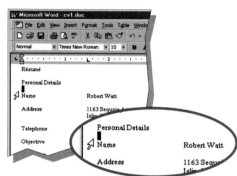
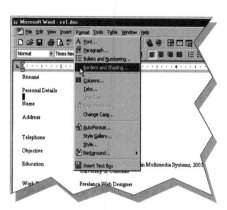

**4** The Borders and Shading window shows a Preview, plus a choice of Style, including hatched, dotted and solid border options. We shall choose the default option, which is a simple solid line.

**5** Click on the button that shows a top border and a line will appear across the top of the text in the preview panel. Click OK to put this in your résumé.

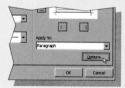

## PC TIPS

### Spacing borders

When you add a border to a section of your text, you will see that Word leaves a standard distance between the text and the border. Usually this distance will look fine, but you might find that you need the border a little closer or farther away from the text. In fact, Word lets you change the distance in any of four directions. First, open up the Borders and Shading window as before and click on the Options button in the bottom right-hand corner (top). Another window pops up with a number of options (right). In the From Text section, you will be able to set the distance you want the border to appear from your text, at the top, bottom and both sides. The easiest way to adjust these settings is to click on the up and down arrows next to each figure (left).

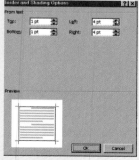

**6** The Personal Details section should begin with a neat line (inset). Now go through the rest of the document adding a border at the beginning of each section in turn – Summary of Qualifications, Work Experience and so on.

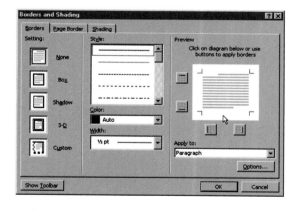
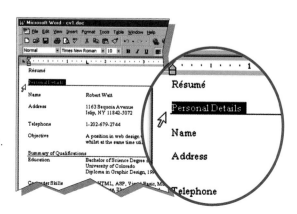

# Adding emphasis

**Shading is a great way of making words stand out.**

TO MAKE each of the section headings stand out clearly, you can use Word's shading option. One way to use this is to reverse the normal colors so that the headings are white text on a black background. For our fictitious résumé, we want to make all the section headings, such as Personal Details, Education and Qualifications and Employment, stand out to make the résumé easier to read.

**1** Click just to the left of the heading you want to highlight, in this case, Personal Details. Choose Borders and Shading from the Format menu as you did for Borders (see page 44, Step 3).

**2** When the Borders and Shading window comes up on the screen, look for the Shading tab at the top of the window and click on it. This brings up a box with colored squares in the Fill section.

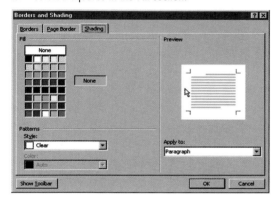

## PC TIPS

Like many of the features in Word, you can also access most of the Border commands from the toolbar. Press the Outside Border button (right) and the current paragraph will be bordered or you can highlight the text you want to border and then press the button. Choose the border type you want by clicking the bar to the right of the Outside Border button and selecting your choice from the pop-up box (below, right).

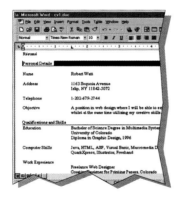

**3** The Fill section allows you to select the color of the shading. This is white by default. To make it black, click on the black square. The Preview on the right will now change to black to show you the effect. If you like it, click on OK.

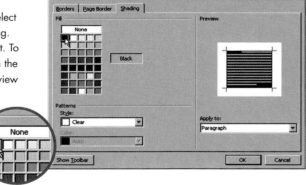

**4** The whole line now goes black. To shade only the words in the section heading, click on the Right Indent marker on the ruler and drag it to the left.

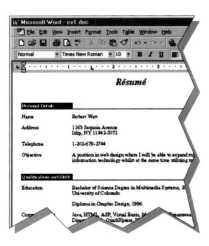

**5** As you drag the Right Indent marker to the left, the dotted line shows the width. Release it when it corresponds with the inner margin.

**6** To see the effect, click anywhere in the document. Notice that the line beneath the shading is visible again and the text is white on black.

**7** Repeat the procedure outlined in Steps 1–6 for all the other section headings in your résumé. To finish the document, you could embellish the text by selecting an attractive, but businesslike, typeface, such as Arial.

# Using Word's drawing tools

*If a picture paints a thousand words, then why not make the most of the possibilities offered by Word's drawing tools? Use them to liven up documents such as letters, résumés and newsletters.*

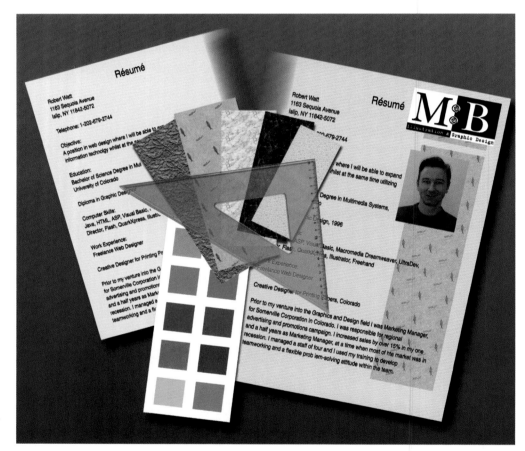

W e have already touched on how you can add photographs and illustrations to text (see Stage 1, pages 44-47). However, both of these exercises assume that you have access to the type of graphics you want to use. The examples we used were perfectly acceptable but when you want to do something specific, such as create a professional looking logo, they may not necessarily be a great deal of help. Not only will they probably not look quite right, but other Word users will recognize them for what they are right away.

### ● Better graphics
Fortunately, Word has a number of advanced tools with which you can create all manner of individual graphics. In fact, it not only has some of the fundamental tools of a drawing package, such as CorelDRAW, but also contains some rather clever and fun-to-use three-dimensional features.

Combining these tools with the basic options, such as colored fills, colored lines, patterned rules and customizable preset shapes

(to name just a few), will give you more than enough scope to create some highly impressive graphics, and it will be quicker than working with a completely separate graphics program.

### ● Personalized portfolio
Another extremely useful facet is that all the graphics you create can be edited. This means that you can gather together a portfolio of graphics, each one of which is slightly different, to create a theme in a large document or to make variations on your logo for use on letterhead or note paper.

This also allows you to come back to the designs whenever you like so you can create further variations as your needs change.

*Stand out from the crowd. Use Word's drawing tools to give documents a professional look.*

# The drawing tools

**Word has an impressive selection of tools hidden in its Drawing toolbar. When you know where to find them, your Word documents could take on a whole new shape.**

THE DRAWING tools can be broken down into a few broad categories. There are buttons you can see on the Drawing toolbar, then tools and commands that are available through drop-down lists.

Look along the toolbar (shown below) and you'll see buttons that look, and work, like those in other programs: lines, arrows, rectangles and circles, plus line style and color options. Using these could not be simpler. Just click on the appropriate button, then move the mouse to the page and click and hold the mouse to draw the object on the page. Add more detail by clicking on other buttons which allow you to change the color of the objects and alter their outlines.

### ● For Word's next trick...

Word also has some tricks of its own, one of which is AutoShapes – shapes and lines that you draw in much the same way as the simple drawing tools but which have a built-in intelligence, which makes them very easy to customize to your exact requirements. Finally, there are shadow and 3-D commands that you can apply to boxes on the page.

*Microsoft® Word*

**Select Objects**
Lets you select one or more objects

**Draw**
A drop-down list of advanced commands (see box below)

**Fill Color**
Fills an object with a solid color

**Free Rotate**
Rotates any object with the mouse

**AutoShapes**
Adds Word's ready-made shapes

**Line**
Draws simple lines

**Arrow**
Draws arrows

**Rectangle**
Draws squares and rectangles

**Oval**
Draws circles and ellipses

**Text Box**
Adds a box for text

**Insert WordArt**
For special effects with text

**Line Color**
Specifies line and outline color

**Text Color**
Chooses a color for text

**Line Style**
Chooses a thickness for lines

**Dash Style**
Specifies outline appearance

**Arrow Style**
Specifies arrow's appearance

**Shadow**
Adds a drop-shadow to an object

**3-D**
Adds a 3-D look to an object

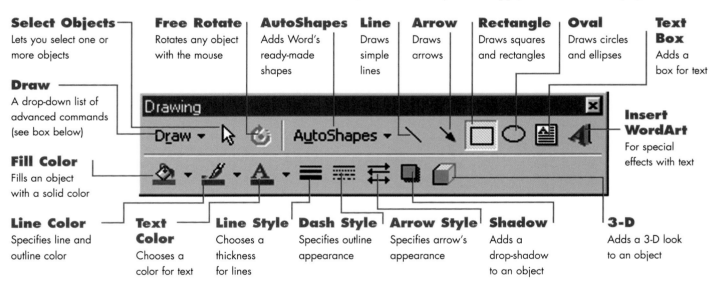

## ADVANCED DRAWING TOOLS AND OPTIONS IN THE TOOLBAR

The drop-down list of options in the toolbar's Draw menu is concerned with how the objects 'sit' on the page and how they relate to each other. The grouping options let you combine or separate objects. Group combines them; Ungroup breaks them up again.

The options under the Order menu let you move objects in front of, or behind, each other. Bring Forward and Send Back shift the object, one level at a time; Bring to Front or Send to Back moves the element to the front or to the back of an overlapping stack of objects.

Objects you draw usually float on top of the Word document you are working on. However, the Send Behind Text command puts an object under the Word text. This is useful for adding a colored panel behind the text.

Word usually helps you line up objects on the page when you draw or move them by aligning them to an invisible grid. Grid lets you turn this facility off if you want to line objects up by hand.

Nudge commands shift objects by tiny amounts. With the Align or Distribute commands you can get Word to position objects. You can choose whether to line them up or have them evenly separated. The Rotate

and Flip commands allow you to rotate an item by exact amounts or flip it to make a mirror image (you can do this horizontally or vertically). By using the Edit Points command you can subtly alter the shape of special AutoShapes, such as smooth curved lines.

Change AutoShape lets you change one AutoShape into another – a circle into a multipointed star, for example.

Set AutoShape Defaults allows you to customize a shape so it is exactly how you want it each time you draw it. For example, draw a square and change the thickness of its outline to 6 pt. By clicking on Set AutoShape Defaults, any shape you subsequently draw will also have a 6 pt. border.

# Drawing simple pictures in a letter

**Word's drawing tools should not be underestimated. Not only are they powerful enough to allow you to be creative, but they are also available at the click of a mouse button.**

**1** Let's set up an imaginary example, adding some simple pictures to a letter explaining some work to be done on the garden. Once you've entered your letter text, click on the Drawing button on the toolbar.

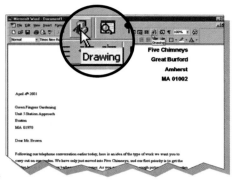

**2** Now select the Rectangle tool and draw a rectangle on the page. We'll use this as our garden outline. Unfortunately, the text of the letter runs under the rectangle.

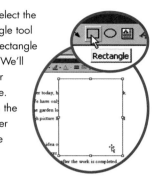

**3** Click on the rectangle with the right mouse button and select the Format AutoShape option from the menu that pops up.

**4** Click on the Wrapping tab from the Format AutoShape dialog box that appears. Click on the Square option and then click the OK button. You will now see that the text wraps to create a new line, instead of disappearing under the rectangle.

**5** Now we'll change the color of the garden. Make sure the rectangle is selected, click on the Fill Color button and then select a suitable square from the drop-down palette. The rectangle will fill with your chosen color. Now we want the green to look patchier, so that it reflects its poor state.

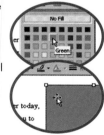

**6** Click the Fill Color button and select Fill Effects. This dialog box lets you add many different types of effect. Click on the Pattern tab.

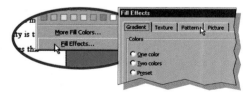

**7** You'll see a variety of patterns. Choose one that looks a little patchy. Press the OK button and your rectangle will then change.

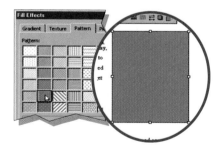

## PC TIPS

### Sticky buttons

You'll notice that when you use the tools on the Drawing toolbar, the buttons 'unclick' themselves after you have drawn each object. This can be very inconvenient when it's necessary for you to draw several lines or shapes one after the other.

To get around this problem, double-click on the button. This will make it remain selected; you can now draw several shapes in a row.

When you want to use another tool, just click on the selected button to unstick it.

**8** Now we want to add a shed using the same steps. Choose a roof color and pattern.

**9** We used the horizontal lines for our pattern, but now we want brown planks with white lines – not the other way around. To do this, bring up the Pattern tab of the Fill Effects dialog box (Steps 6 and 7) and switch the Foreground and Background colors. Press the OK button to see the effect on your garden shed.

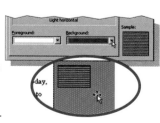

**10** We're going to finish our first plan by adding the paved walk from the back of the house to the garden shed. Now we're ready to use Word's more advanced drawing tools to draw a diagram that will show how we want the garden to look (opposite).

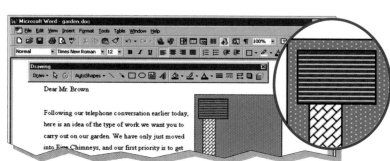

# Using advanced drawing tools

**We can use some more of Word's drawing capabilities to finish the garden plan started on the opposite page. Here we'll show you how to add some fine details.**

**1** Start with the letter we created opposite. Use this to make a similar garden layout to which you need to add several small dark green circles (using the circle tool) to indicate small shrubs.

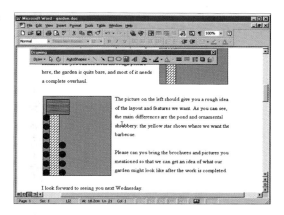

**2** We want to add a special object that will draw the attention of our gardener to an area for a barbecue. Click on the AutoShapes button, select the Stars and Banners list and then click on the first shape: Explosion 1. Use the mouse to drag the shape to the top of the garden (inset right).

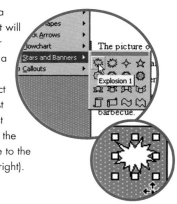

## AUTO SHAPES

Word's basic shapes are easy to add to your documents, but there are times when you will need more complex shapes, which Word supplies. You can select one of these and then tweak it to form the exact outline you need.

Click on the AutoShapes button and you'll see that Word has six categories. For example, there are ready-made star shapes, arrowheads and speech bubbles.

AutoShapes' Lines options are also very useful when you need more than straight lines. The Scribble tool lets you draw lines by hand and will follow the exact path your mouse takes on the mouse pad. Use the Curve tool to smooth the line or try the Freeform tool to combine Curve and Scribble.

**3** Use the Fill Color palette to color in the explosion shape. Make sure it's a shade that will be easily noticed to avoid it being confused with the other existing garden objects.

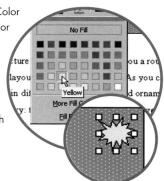

**4** Now we'll use another of Word's AutoShapes to create an ornamental pond. Select the Moon shape from the Basic Shapes collection and drag the crescent into the blank area of the garden.

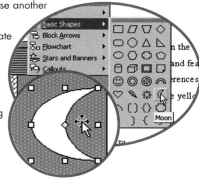

**5** The Moon is a special kind of shape: there's an extra handle (the small yellow diamond) in addition to the usual handles along the edge. AutoShapes with these special handles can be tweaked. Click and drag this handle to the right.

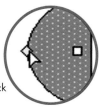

**6** This handle controls the curvature of the concave side of the Moon, making it more or less bowed (experiment with other AutoShapes to see other ways these diamond handles work).

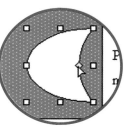

**7** Use the patterns tab of the Fill Effects dialog box to fill the pond. Choose suitable blue colors and the wavy-lines option to represent the water surface.

**8** Here we've added the final touches (right) – some more shrubs by the pond and a patio area. Use the rectangle and oval tools to add these. Such simple diagrams give you an idea of what you can achieve in a few minutes, without even firing up another graphics program.

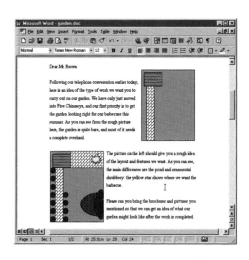

# Using mail merge

**Sending the same circular letter to a group of people can be extremely time-consuming if you have to personalize each one. Fortunately, Word can lend a helping hand, with a special feature called mail merge.**

*Professional, personalized and relatively painless...mail merge can save you time and effort.*

There are various occasions when you need to send similar letters to several people. Sometimes, a basic form letter will do. Often, most of the text can remain the same, but it is much better if each letter is personalized. For example, party invitations or feeler letters to potential employers look much better when they are individualized.

### ● Changing information

You can amend each letter by hand but Word's mail merge facility makes the job much easier. With mail merge you need only write the document once and then tell Word what you want changed, so you can print hundreds of personalized letters with a single operation.

The principle behind mail merging is that you store the parts of a letter that change (such as the name, address, and so forth) in a separate database. This information can then be incorporated into a letter (or other document) in positions that you specify. All you need to do is create the basic letter, inserting special codewords in the places where you want the variable information to be inserted from the database, and then merge the two together.

You've probably seen examples of 'junk mail' created this way. Such letters usually set the data up in another program, which is one reason you sometimes see letters addressed to 'Dear Mr. 10 Park Rd'. Thankfully, Word makes everything far simpler.

This is partly because you do everything in one program, although Word still creates two documents: a form letter and a data source. It also has an easy-to-follow dialog box – called the Mail Merge Helper – to take you through the whole process in detail.

### ● A simple example

For our first step-by-step exercise, we are going to take the example of a school notice to tell parents about the forthcoming sports day. This is a very simple mail merge and requires only basic data to be entered. But even this example illustrates another advantage of mail merging. If you want to send another letter to the same people – providing the sports day

results, perhaps – you can reuse the names and addresses from the database without having to retype them.

● **Setting up mailing data**

Although this example uses only simple data to create a brief letter, the same principles apply no matter how complicated the data or how long the Word document is that you want to generate. All you have to do is insert meaningful markers, or fields, in the document that correspond to the entries in your database.

You can have as many fields as you like. You can even sort or filter the mailing according to the data that appears in them. In our first example, we want everyone on the list to get the same letter. But in the second example (see page 53), we will see how to use more

advanced options to ensure that only members of the PTA committee get a letter.

Mail merges can be as complex as you want, depending on the details in the database. For instance, when mailing a club membership, you could include information on whether or not a subscription has been renewed and write only to those who haven't paid up!

The mail merge facility is so efficient that it can incorporate many different types of variable information in the same document. For example, a self-employed home PC user could use a database of customers and create different sets of letters for good customers and late payers on a monthly basis.

When you start mail merging, you go right into setting up your database, but don't feel nervous – there is lots of hand-holding to guarantee quick results.

## WHAT IT MEANS

**FIELDS**

*In a mail-merge document, a field is a block of data that is held in a database. When you are preparing a mail merge, Word automatically sets up your data in separate fields that might include entries for, say: title (Mr., Ms., Dr., etc); first name; last name; first line of address (company or building name); second line of address (house number and street); city; state; and Zip code.*

*Word also uses fields as special place markers in a document. These fields indicate places that are reserved for information, which Word automatically adds, e.g. a field can automatically insert current date or time.*

*In the case of a mail merge, when you prepare the letter for merging you can include fields that correspond to the blocks of data in your database. The fields in the letter can then draw upon the data and place the correct details in the document when you complete your merge.*

# *Creating data for your mail merge*

**The mail merge process is divided into two main parts; creating fields to use in your mail merge and adding the fields to the letter or document you want to merge.**

**1** Start with a new blank Word document, then select the Mail Merge command from the Tools menu.

**2** The Mail Merge Helper appears. Click on the Create button and select Form Letters from the pop-up menu (top right). A dialog box pops up asking which document to use (below right). Click Active Window.

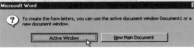

**3** Now we will start creating a database to hold the parents' information, such as names and addresses. Click the Get Data button and then select the Create Data Source option.

**4** You will now see a dialog box that helps you create the fields for your mail-merge letter. Word suggests many different types of fields in a list on the right-hand side. For our mailing to parents, we don't need all the fields offered.

You can delete irrelevant fields by clicking on them and then pressing the Remove Field Name button (below left). Change the list so that it reads: Title, FirstName, LastName, Address1, Address2, City, State and Zip Code (below right). Then press the OK button.

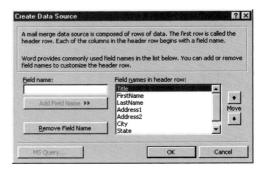

**5** Before you can add names and addresses of parents to your mail merge database, you will be prompted to save it. Use the Save As dialog box to locate a suitable folder (we've used a folder called My Files), then give the file a name and save it.

**6** Word now lets you know that your mail merge database (the data source) is still empty. It gives you a choice of adding names and addresses by clicking the Edit Data Source button or writing your mail merge letter by clicking on the Edit Main Document button.

We'll add the names and addresses first, so click the Edit Data Source button.

**7** You now see the Data Form dialog box. This looks like an index card in which you add parents' details one at a time by typing into the boxes next to the field names you set up. Fill in dummy entries for the first person, then click Add New to add another set of information. The Record box (bottom left) shows how many people you have entered. Repeat until you have three or four examples, then press the OK button to create your letter.

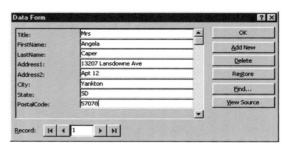

# Creating a merge letter

**1** After Step 7 (above) the first thing to notice as you switch back to your letter document is the special mail-merge toolbar (see below). This is used to enter the merge fields, which, for this example, will all be located at the top of the letter (right), where you'd normally put the recipient's name and address.

**2** At the top of the document, place the mouse in the position where you want to add the first field (the Title). Press the Insert Merge Field button. A drop-down list of fields appears. Select Title. The word Title will appear in the document between special markers to show that it is a field (inset).

**3** Continue adding fields until the letter looks like the one shown. If you are writing to people you know well, you could use FirstName. Note that wherever you have two fields next to one another, you must put spaces between them (inset) or the data will print with no spaces.

**4** Now type the rest of your letter as usual, making up a few lines about the sports day. When you finish, save it as Sports letter and select the Mail Merge Helper from the Tools menu (above). When the dialog box (right) pops up, click the Merge button to start merging the data with the letter.

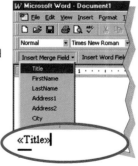

**5** Now the Merge dialog box pops up. Leave the settings as they are and click the Merge button. Word now inserts the data into the letter to create a new document, with one page for each person typed into the Data Form dialog box (inset).

## PRINTING MAIL MERGES

In Step 5 of our example, we created a long document with one page for each letter to see the results of the mail merge.

By selecting Printer instead of New Document in the Merge to: drop-down list box, you can print the letters directly without needing to use this intermediate step.

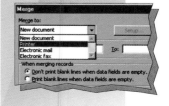

# Advanced mail-merge techniques

THE FIRST step-by-step exercise demonstrates how a mail merge consists of two documents, the form letter and the data source. These combine to create the finished document, which can then be printed out (or faxed or emailed). We've explained the essence of the form letter, so now we're going to look in more detail at the data source to show how you can sort your records and customize your mailing. For this example, we're going to create a new field, specifying whether or not parents are members of the school PTA, and then create a mailing that goes only to those who are.

**1** Open the data source document (saved opposite as Parents). You will see your database of names and addresses displayed as a Word table, with field names across the top and one row for each person.

**2** Word has a special Database toolbar you can use with your mail-merge data. Click on the View menu, then Toolbars and select the Database option.

**3** When the toolbar appears, click on the Manage Fields button to bring up a dialog box that allows you to change the fields in the database.

**4** Now add extra fields: type a new field name into the box at the top left and press the Add button (we've added 'PTA members'). Click on the OK button.

**5** You'll see the PTA members field appear as a new column in your table of information. Add the word 'Yes' to a couple of the rows in your names and addresses database. When you have made these changes, save the document.

**6** Now open the Sports letter you created opposite. Click on the Mail Merge Helper button on the Mail Merge toolbar.

**7** In the dialog box that pops up, click the Query Options button in the bottom section.

**8** The Query Options dialog box has two tabs that allow for advanced mail-merge options. Select the Filter Records tab and use the first drop-down list box to locate the PTA_members field.

Note: Word needs to add the underscore character (_) between 'PTA' and 'members' in order to use it. You can ignore it for now.

**9** Click on the Comparison box and select the Is not blank option from the list. Then click the OK button.

**10** Now click the Merge button in the Mail Merge Helper. When the dialog box pops up, leave the default settings as they are and click Merge. As before, Word will create a new document containing all your letters – but this time you won't have a letter for those people for whom the PTA members field is blank.

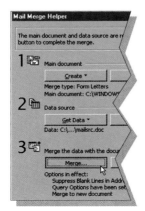

## CENTRALIZING YOUR DATA

As you start to use your computer for making small databases, such as the names and addresses in this example, you may find that the information overlaps with other databases – perhaps a basic address book that you use. The best idea is to put all the information into a central pool. The information can then be used for letters, invitations and newsletters – in fact, any mail merge document that you wish. This means that you don't have to type in the same details several times.

# Working with percentages

*Percentages are used in all sorts of calculations, from personal finance to a detailed business plan. So whether you are trying to sort out your tax or help with math homework, here's how Excel can help you get the right answers.*

Working out percentages is one of the most common mathematical operations after basic addition, subtraction, multiplication and division. That's why many calculators have a special percentage key. In a similar way, Excel makes it very easy to calculate a percentage.

On the next page, we'll work through some simple instances to see how to do this. In practice, it's probably quicker to use a calculator for such simple examples. But as with other tasks, the beauty of learning how to use Excel is that you can set up a detailed worksheet containing large numbers of figures that will be recalculated automatically every time the data changes. This is the basis of tables that can be used for calculating things, such as the profit on a small business venture or even the odds on a series of bets.

Many common sums are expressed as percentages. Obvious examples are the sales tax (e.g. 8.5%), interest rates (6% a year,

perhaps), or a business profit margin (20%, say). All these factors can be included in a spreadsheet calculation and are easy to enter into Excel.

All you need to do is to use the % symbol together with the percentage factor and type this into the cell where it applies. Suppose you want to find the sales tax on a purchase costing $63. This can be written out in the form of a simple calculation: $63 x 8.5%. To input this into Excel, you would write it out as =63*8.5%. If you type this into an empty cell in Excel, it will work out the result for you and display the answer: 5.36. Opposite, we show how to set up some percentage calculations in your worksheet.

*Excel automates the calculation of percentages with a special percent button, so you will be able to plow through your work in no time at all.*

## CALCULATING PERCENTAGES

The word percentage comes from Latin and means 'out of a hundred'. It's used as a simple way of showing how any two numbers are related by referring them to the single standard number 100.

The advantage of this is that it makes it very easy to compare wildly different sums. For example, it can be hard to say whether 9/13 is bigger than 747/1189 without working them out, until you are told that one figure is roughly 69 percent and the other 62 percent. These figures are worked out by calculating the fraction (e.g. 9/13 is 1 ÷ 13 x 9 which equals 0.6923) and multiplying by 100 (to get 69.23%).

Any fraction can be expressed in this way. If it is less than 1, it will be expressed as a percentage less than 100 (so a half is 50%, three-fourths is 75%). If it is more than 1, it will be a percentage more than 100 (so 2 is 200% and 4½ is 450%).

# Calculating percentage increases

**One of the most common uses for a percentage calculation is to add a factor to an existing sum and display the result. Here we show you how.**

**1** It's your lucky day! You have been given a pay rise of 8.5%, at your part-time job and you want to find out what difference this will make to your yearly salary. Start your worksheet by typing in some simple text labels in three consecutive cells (A1, B1 and C1) for Salary, Increase and New Salary. The cells underneath these headings will be used for our figures and calculations.

**2** Type your salary, say $18,000, into cell A2 and then move to the next cell across to type in the percentage increase of 8.5%.

**3** Move to the New Salary column and enter the formula that will calculate your new salary. Multiply the old salary by the percentage increase and add the answer to the old salary. Type the formula =A2*B2+A2. This works without brackets because Excel does the multiplication before the addition.

**4** When you press the [Enter] key, Excel will calculate the correct answer. Now, if you change the number in cell B2 – perhaps you negotiated a better pay rise – the result will change automatically.

| | C |
|---|---|
| | **New Salary** |
| | 19530 |

---

# Calculating a percentage discount

**1** You are considering specifying 10 friends and family telephone numbers to save 15% off your bill. However, as the plan costs $5 every month, you need to know whether this would be of benefit to you. Type in four column headers, and enter your estimated monthly bill and discount.

**2** Move to the Saving column and enter the formula to calculate the expected savings: =A2*B2. Press the [Enter] key to see the result.

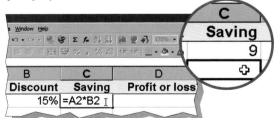

| | C |
|---|---|
| | **Saving** |
| | 9 |

**3** Now move to the Profit or loss? column and enter a formula to see if you will save or lose money. Type in = C2-5, which is the saving less the $5 monthly charge. You will save $4. Now try changing the monthly bill. If the answer is positive, this is how much you save every month. If it is negative, the plan costs you money.

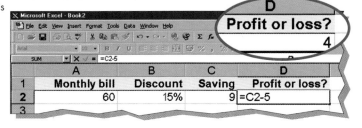

## HOW TO SUBTRACT A DISCOUNT

A common problem is to find out how much is left after applying a discount. One easy way to do this is to take the percentage discount away from 100, which shows the percentage remaining. For example, a 15% discount would leave 85%. Type = 60*85% into a cell and check that the new bill is $51.

# Excel at mini-databases

*So far, we have used Excel for accounts and financial purposes, but Excel can handle text as well as numbers and will help you organize anything from a Christmas card address list to a gem collection.*

xcel's worksheet is made up of rows and columns of cells. So far, we have mostly put numbers into these cells, but Excel is designed to organize text information as well as numbers. In fact, Excel can be used to create what is called a database, which is basically a list of items organized into different categories. There are other full-scale database programs, but Excel is capable of doing the work just as well for small-scale jobs.

For example, a database makes the perfect electronic address book. Opposite, we show you how to set up a database address book in Excel. You can use it for tasks such as making Christmas card or wedding invitation lists or any other occasion where you might need separate lists for separate events.

### ● At your fingertips

Excel's database has many other useful functions. If you are involved in a club, for example, you'll find it a great way to store a membership list. Or if you collect things such as stamps or minerals, you can use the Excel database to catalogue and label them.

What makes an Excel database so useful is that it makes lists easy to sift through, even when they have become long and involved. One way it does this is with a facility called Form view, which lets you see one record, or entry, at a time. To look at data in Form view,

first click on any record within your list. Next, select the Form option from the Data menu. You will see a new window pop up in the middle of your Excel screen. It also shows one record at a time, starting with the first one. Each field is shown in its own box. A set of buttons on the right-hand side allows you to flick backward or forward through your list, one record at a time. Other options let you add new ones and delete old ones. This way of viewing information is extremely efficient and easier to work with as you have only to concentrate on one record at a time.

*Using an Excel database for an address book helps you get rid of all those scraps of paper on which you have jotted down new addresses, names and so on.*

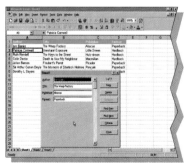

*If you have a large book collection stored in an Excel database, Form view will show you the complete record you have made for each book – author, title, publisher and format.*

*With an address book, Form view will bring up the complete name and address, plus any other information you have put in the record.*

## WHAT IT MEANS

**RECORD**

*A record is one entry in a database. For example, in an address book, you would probably have one record for each person. The information within a record is split into fields. In a list of items in an Excel worksheet, these fields are the individual columns you use for separate pieces of information, such as the name, address and telephone number.*

# Making an address book

**A record of names and addresses is useful to have on your computer. Here we show you how to make one.**

**1** The first task is to choose the headings you want to use. We've started with first names, last names and addresses in the first four columns, adding other headings for telephone numbers or email addresses. You could even put headings for anniversaries such as birthdays, or people to go on your Christmas card list.

**2** The next job is to enter all the names, addresses and other details. Here we've typed lots of names and addresses straight into the Excel worksheet. As you can see, the worksheet soon becomes a confusing way to look at lots of names and addresses.

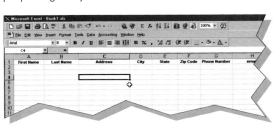

## PC TIPS

### Keeping zeros at the start of telephone numbers

If you type a foreign telephone number into Excel and press the [Enter] key, you will often find that a zero at the start of the number disappears. Excel thinks you are entering a normal number and removes leading zeros.

To avoid this, select the column containing the telephone numbers and choose Cells from the Format menu. In the Format Cells dialog box that pops up, click on the Number tab at the top of the box, select Text from the list of categories and press the OK button. Excel will now interpret all information in this column as text and leave the leading zeros in place.

**3** Let's try switching to a more convenient way of viewing the names and addresses. First, highlight any one of the cells containing information by clicking over it. Now go to the Data menu and select the Form command.

**4** This is what Form view looks like. Notice how it displays our list one record at a time, with each piece of data (or field) in its own text box. The buttons on the right let us step backward and forward through records, add new ones and delete old ones. To begin, click on Find Next.

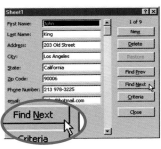

**5** Now we're looking at the second record in our address book. We can repeat the process by pressing the Find Next button until we reach the last record. We can also work backward through the records. To go back to the first record, simply press the Find Prev button.

**6** To add a new record to our address book, press the New button, type the new information into the text boxes and press the [Enter] key. You will see the new record appear in the worksheet and the Form view empty, ready for you to add another new record.

**7** Now let's delete an old record we don't need any more. Use the Find Prev and Find Next buttons to locate the right record and press the Delete button.

**8** As a safety precaution, Excel asks you if you're sure you want to delete the record. Press the OK button to confirm your decision and you will see that the record disappears from the Form and also from the table of information in the worksheet. To close the Form view and return to the worksheet, just click on the Close button. Save your changes as usual, using the Save command in the File menu.

# Conditional formatting

**We've already seen how you can apply formatting to make cells more noticeable. Excel can also be set up to apply formatting automatically to draw your attention to important developments.**

Making cells stand out from the rest of a worksheet – by changing their text style and background color, for example – is a handy feature of Excel. We know that Excel makes it easy to add such simple formatting (see Stage 1, pages 56-57), but wouldn't it be useful if you could use the formatting to make a cell stand out, depending on the value of the data in it? You can do this by hand, but it would be especially valuable to get Excel to do this automatically.

For example, you might use a worksheet to keep track of your bank account payments. Wouldn't it be great if your checking account balance cell automatically turned red whenever it was overdrawn? Well, Excel can do this using a process known as conditional formatting.

● **Balancing the books**
Conditional formatting allows you to set a condition at which Excel will automatically format a cell. In the example (left), the conditional formatting applies only

| | Item | Date | Payments | Receipts | Balance |
|---|---|---|---|---|---|
| 1 | Item | Date | Payments | Receipts | Balance |
| 2 | January Salary | 01/02/01 | | $800.00 | |
| 3 | Rent | 01/03/01 | $220.00 | | |
| 4 | Supermarket | 01/06/01 | $35.66 | | |
| 5 | Gas | 01/11/01 | $15.02 | | |
| 6 | Supermarket | 01/14/01 | $31.45 | | |
| 7 | | | | | |
| 8 | Totals | | $302.13 | $800.00 | $497.87 |
| 9 | | | | | |
| 10 | | | | | |

| | Item | Date | Payments | Receipts | Balance |
|---|---|---|---|---|---|
| 1 | Item | Date | Payments | Receipts | Balance |
| 2 | January Salary | 01/02/01 | | $800.00 | |
| 3 | Rent | 01/03/01 | $220.00 | | |
| 4 | Supermarket | 01/06/01 | $35.66 | | |
| 5 | Gas | 01/11/01 | $15.02 | | |
| 6 | Supermarket | 01/14/01 | $31.45 | | |
| 7 | Vacation deposit | 01/21/01 | $500.00 | | |
| 8 | | | | | |
| 9 | Totals | | $802.13 | $800.00 | -$2.13 |
| 10 | | | | | |

*To start with, our checking account balance in cell E8 is healthy and Excel displays it (top). However, as soon as we add our vacation deposit payment, the account becomes overdrawn. Attention is focused on it by making Excel turn the cell red.*

when your checking account balance cell reaches a condition of less than zero.

Every time a new entry is made on your worksheet, Excel automatically checks the checking account balance cell's value to see if the set condition has been reached. Of course, you don't have to set the condition at zero, you can choose any figure you wish and apply it to any cell. For example, you might get Excel to turn the checking account balance cell orange if it falls below $50, to warn you that you could be in danger of overdrawing.

You can use conditional formatting for different types of worksheet. If you are doing a research project on mountains and have entered details of the heights of various peaks on your worksheet, you can set up Excel to highlight any mountains that exceed or fall short of your desired conditions. You could get it to show all the mountains that are over 23,000 ft. (7,000 meters) in one color and those that are below 16,500 ft. (5,000 meters) in another.

# Applying conditional formatting

**We are going to use the example of a worksheet containing a list of the tallest mountains in different countries to show how to apply conditional formatting.**

## PC TIPS

To locate which cells have conditional formats, choose Go To in the Edit menu and click Special in the dialog box. Click Conditional formats and then click OK.

**1** This worksheet lists mountains by their country and height. Glancing at the worksheet it is hard to tell which mountains are over 7,000 meters or under 5,000 meters. However, conditional formatting picks them out.

**2** Let's start by trying to give the mountains rising to over 7,000 meters a different background color. Use the mouse to highlight all the cells that contain mountain heights and then go to the Format menu and select the Conditional Formatting option.

**3** This will bring up the Conditional Formatting dialog box. You set conditions and actions by changing the text in each box and using the Format button.

**4** The first box contains 'Cell Value Is', which is OK, so click on the down arrow at the right end of the second drop-down box and select greater than.

**5** The dialog box changes to provide a window in which you enter your condition. Type 7000 and click on the Format button.

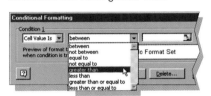

**6** Use the Font tab in the Format Cells dialog box (left) to change the text to yellow and the Patterns tab to change cell shading to red. Click on OK to close. To return to the worksheet, click on OK in the Conditional Formatting dialog box. Heights over 7,000 meters show up as yellow on red (right).

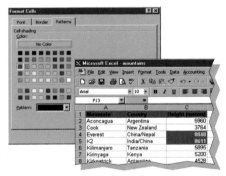

**7** While this gets the point across, we'd prefer to emphasize the names of the mountains rather than their heights. To do this, first remove the conditional formatting that you originally set up. Highlight the same cells as in Step 2, then bring up the Conditional Formatting dialog box and click on Delete. Excel asks you to confirm your choice. Select the Condition 1 checkbox, click on OK and return to the worksheet.

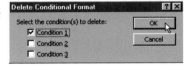

**8** Now select the cells containing the mountain names (cells A2 to A15 in our example) and bring up the Conditional Formatting dialog box. Choose the Formula Is option in the first drop-down box and type =$C2>7000 in the new text box. Use the Format button to set the cell formatting as in Step 6.

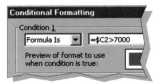

**10** You can now see how the worksheet reflects two sets of conditions. By using formulas in conditions, you'll find that you can give your worksheets more built-in intelligence.

**9** Click the Add button and the dialog box expands to let you apply another condition. Use the Formula Is option, type in the formula =$C2<5000 and use the Format button to set a different format (left). Press the OK button.

# Advanced cell formatting

*Detailed entries on a worksheet can take up too much space if they are kept on a single line. Excel includes several tools that help you format text and keep your worksheet neat, tidy and readable.*

So far, you have seen how to apply simple formatting effects to worksheet cells in Excel and how to change the background color of cells and the color, size and font of text by using the Formatting toolbar (see Stage 1, pages 56-57). Now you'll see how you can add all sorts of text alignment options to your formatting skills to make your worksheets much easier to read and understand.

## ● When the text won't fit

These options are a great help when you have a few cells that contain very long lines of text. Normally this text overlaps into the cells next to them. If you want to constrain some text to fit the width of the cell it's in, you can get Excel to 'wrap' it. This converts it into a miniature paragraph (bottom left).

Excel even makes it a simple drag-and-drop affair to change the angle of text in a cell (as shown inset right). You can even specify an exact angle for the rotation. Alternatively, you can make text appear in a vertical stack, which is very useful if you need a narrow column.

Another advanced formatting option is Merge cells. By joining adjacent cells into one cell you can make your worksheet easier to use. For example, if you have a three-column table, you can combine the three cells above the table into a single cell for a heading using the alignment commands.

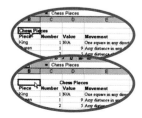

*By using Excel's advanced – but simple – formatting options, you can rid yourself of many awkward text problems. You can make a long line of text wrap as a mini paragraph (above left) and make a table heading sit in the center of a range of cells (above right).*

## ● Formatting cells

While you can carry out some of Excel's alignment options directly from the toolbar, the more powerful commands are only available through the Format Cells dialog box. This has an Alignment tab which includes all the alignment options.

You need only select the cells you want to format and bring up this dialog box to use the commands. After you follow the exercise on the next page, you will soon get the hang of even the most advanced options. Don't be afraid to experiment. Practice with a dummy worksheet if you are worried about your data.

## WHAT IT MEANS

**MERGE CELLS**

*Until now, all our Excel examples have used a regular grid of cells – with all cells in a column the same width and all cells in a row the same height. Excel also allows you to merge adjacent cells so one cell spans more than one column or row.*

# Formatting text in cells

**You can use the Cells command from the Format menu to align text in cells and make your worksheets not only more attractive, but also easier to read. Here's an example of a worksheet containing text only. We'll improve its overall legibility by formatting.**

## INDENTED LISTS

You may find that for some types of tables, a small indent helps readability. By using the Indent option, you can specify the exact amount. First select the cells you want to indent, bring up the Alignment tab and increase the Indent setting. This is a quick way to make lists with several sections easier to read – as shown in this example of fruit and vegetables.

**1** Enter an easy table like this. We've used simple formatting to widen column E and add color and emphasis.

**2** We want to make our title 'Chess Pieces' sit across the four columns of our table. Select the four cells, B2 to E2. A simple click of Excel's Merge and Center button will merge these four cells into one and allow us to use the 'Chess Pieces' text as the centered title.

**3** Highlight the four subheadings from B3 to E3. Select Cells from the Format menu (or see PC Tips, below). Click on the Alignment tab in the Format Cells dialog box and use the mouse to rotate the Text pointer below Orientation to roughly 45 degrees. Click the OK button to see the result (inset).

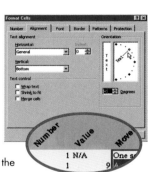

**4** Now we want to make sure the long text entries in the Movement column don't run outside our colored columns. Highlight the cells (E4 to E9 in our example) and go to the Alignment options again. On the left of the dialog box you will see three Text control options: check the Wrap text box and press the OK button. You'll see the long text lines wrap into paragraphs within the cells.

**5** When cells have become taller to allow the text to fit, text in the rest of the row stays at the bottom of the cells. This looks a little odd (right inset), but it can be altered. First, select all the cells in the table (B4 to E9 in this example).

**6** Bring up the Alignment tab again. Under the Text alignment section, you will see two drop-down boxes that control the position of text in cells. Click on the drop-down list box under the Vertical label. Select the Top option and press the OK button to apply this change.

## PC TIPS

You can also bring up the Format Cells dialog box by using the right mouse button. Once you've got used to it, you'll find this is a lot quicker than using Excel's menu bar. First select the cells you want to format, then click once on the highlighted cells with the right mouse button. You will see a small pop-up menu; one of its options is the Format Cells command. Select this and you will see the usual dialog box.

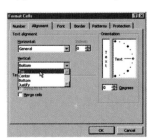

**7** For the final touch, we'll use a simpler alignment option to center the text in the cells under the Number and Value subheadings. First, highlight the cells (C4 to D9 in our table on the right), then press the Center button on Excel's formatting toolbar.

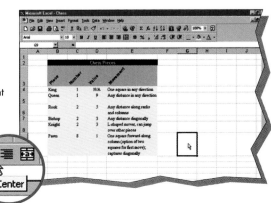

# Understanding cell references

*We have seen how Excel puts references into formulas so that it can make calculations. It's not essential to know exactly how this works but, as usual, an understanding of the basics helps avoid mistakes.*

Performing calculations is incredibly easy when you use Excel. For example, if you want to add the contents of cells A1 and A2, with the result appearing in A3, just type =A1+A2 in cell A3. You can change the numbers in cells A1 and A2 and Excel still updates the result in cell A3.

The key to all this is the way Excel allows you to refer to cells by their row (as a number) and column (as a letter) coordinates. These cell references (A1, B3, X86, etc.) are a fundamental part of Excel, so it's well worth spending some time getting comfortable with how cell references work if you want to get the most out of Excel.

In particular, Excel also uses these cell references to keep your calculations up-to-date when you move cells around.

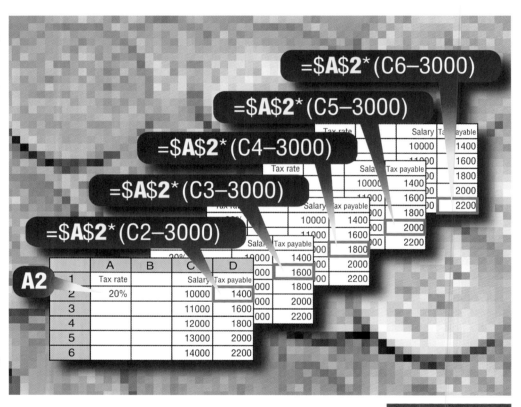

### ● Automatic updating
Type some numbers into cells A1 and A2 and the formula =A1+A2 into cell A3. Now insert a line before row 1 by clicking on cell A1 and selecting Rows from the Insert menu: you will see the numbers shift down one row.

The numbers and the sum are still the same, but surely the answer to the sum should be different as A1 and A2 have now both changed. Double click on cell A4, though, and you will see that Excel has changed your formula to =A2+A3.

Most of the time this automatic updating will prove extremely helpful because it saves time and effort. For example, if you have set up lots of calculations in your worksheet, you don't want to go through manually updating them all just because you have added a new row or column.

### ● Relative and absolute cell references
In our simple example, Excel changes the formula. This is because the references we originally typed (the 'A1' and 'A2' in =A1+A2) are relative cell references and can change according to the cell in which they appear. As another example, type some numbers into cells B2 and B3. Now copy the formula from cell A4 (select Copy from the Edit menu) and paste it into B4 (select Paste from the Edit menu). Excel guesses that you want to add the figures in the B column and changes the cell references in the calculation: the formula it puts in cell B4 is =B2+B3.

However, for some calculations, you won't want Excel to change the cell references. In order to do this you need to use an absolute cell reference instead of a relative one. We show you how to do this on the facing page.

**WHAT IT MEANS**

ABSOLUTE CELL REFERENCE
*An absolute cell reference in a formula always refers to exactly the same cell coordinates. If you copy the formula to other cells, it will always be the same.*

*Absolute cell references look just like relative cell references, but use $ signs – so you would use $A$1 instead of A1 and $B$4 in place of B4 in such references.*

# Using absolute cell references

**Working through this exercise will pay off in the long run. Absolute cell references have many uses – especially for constant factors, such as the one set up here.**

**1** We'll start with a simplified hypothetical tax calculator. Type the information shown here into a blank worksheet. Unlike our previous worksheet (see Stage 2, pages 66-67), we've brought the tax rate out to a separate cell (B1) so we can take advantage of absolute cell referencing.

This basic layout now allows us to calculate the salary after taxes for more than one person, but requires the tax rate to be entered only once.

**2** The first step is to add a formula to calculate Jane Green's salary after taxes. This formula must work out the taxable salary after allowances (e.g. deductions and exemptions), calculate the tax payable and deduct it from the salary to produce the salary after taxes. It sounds complicated, but a single formula can do it. In cell B6, type =B4-(B4-B5)*B1/100 and press the [Enter] key. Excel calculates the net salary.

## Cells in other worksheets

We have shown you how to set up workbooks that consist of several worksheets. Excel also lets you create formulas that refer to cells in other worksheets, by using an exclamation mark with the worksheet name and the cell. All you need to do is include the name of the worksheet as part of the cell reference. For example: to multiply the contents of cell A1 in Sheet1 by cell A2's contents in Sheet2 and have the result placed in a cell in Sheet3, you would type =Sheet1!A1 *Sheet2!A2 into any of Sheet3's cells.

**3** Now let's see what happens when we copy this formula into cell C6 to calculate Mary Green's salary after taxes. Click on cell B6, choose Copy from the Edit menu, move to cell C6 and then select Paste from the Edit menu to paste in the formula.

**4** Excel has automatically updated the relative cell references in our formula, so the cells B1, B4 and B5 have been replaced with C1, C4 and C5. Unfortunately, in this case it has updated the B1 reference to C1, which is blank, so the calculation is wrong. We need to keep the reference to cell B1.

**5** Let's replace the relative reference in the original formula. Click on cell B6, move to the formula bar and change B1 to $B$1. When you press the [Enter] key, you'll see the result is still the same.

=B4-(B4-B5)*$B$1/100

**6** Copy the formula from cell B6 into cell C6. You'll notice that Excel now gets the calculation right.

= =C4-(C4-C5)*$B$1/100

**7** Now, let's imagine we want to add another row of information to this worksheet, such as details of another taxation rate. Right-click on the gray square at the left end of row 1 on the worksheet and choose Insert from the menu that appears. Then type in the information in cells A1 and B1.

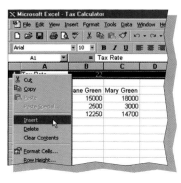

**8** Notice how the formulas in cells B7 and C7 still calculate the correct result. This is because Excel can automatically update absolute cell references as well as relative cell references when you modify a worksheet. Click on cell C7 and look at the formula that's displayed in the Formula Bar. You can see that the absolute references to cell B1 have been updated to those for cell B2.

# Hiding rows and columns

*What do you do when you don't want to be distracted from important parts of your worksheet by masses of other information? The simple answer is to hide the sections that you don't need.*

As you become more experienced with Excel, you're likely to start constructing more complex worksheets containing larger tables of information. Sometimes this will make it difficult to pick out important facts and figures – such as annual or monthly totals – from a mass of unwanted detail.

As we've already seen, we can use cell formatting to make important cells stand out in another color or font (see pages 58-59). But what do you do if you want to see the really important figures on-screen without having to scroll backward and forward through a large worksheet?

### ● Concealing information

The solution is to conceal all the detailed information when you aren't using it. Excel lets you do this by hiding complete rows and columns of a worksheet. Don't worry about accessing the data. When you hide a row or column, all the figures and formulas contained within its cells are remembered and used by Excel. And it is just as simple to unhide this information as it is to hide it.

All you have to do to hide a row of figures on a worksheet is to select it, click on the Format menu, click on the Row option and select Hide from the submenu that appears. You can use the same technique to hide a column, too.

Of course, Excel also makes it possible for you to retrieve any rows or columns that you

have hidden. You might be wondering how it's possible to do this if you can't see a hidden row to select it. The answer is easy: you just highlight the two rows on each side of the hidden one. Then go to the Format menu, position the mouse pointer on the Row option and choose Unhide from the submenu that appears.

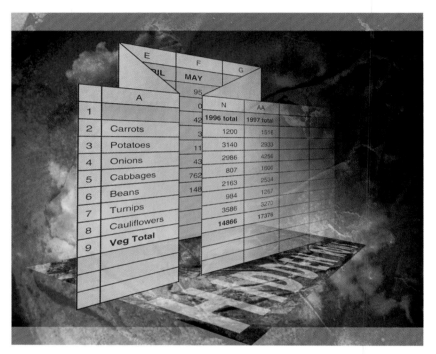

*Here's a typical table of information (left) relating to a family grocery business. The monthly sales totals contain lots of detailed figures for individual items, but it's quite hard to see the 'big picture'. By hiding the rows of individual fruit and vegetable figures (below) it's a lot easier to see how overall fruit and vegetable sales vary from one month to the next.*

*Show only the main rows or columns in your document by hiding unnecessary text.*

### WHAT IT MEANS

**UNHIDE**
*The Unhide option is the reverse of the Hide option and is used to make hidden rows or columns visible again. If you want to reveal all the hidden rows and columns in a worksheet at once, click on the gray button in the top-left corner of the worksheet before choosing the Unhide option.*

---

**Microsoft Excel - Brown's Grocers**
File Edit View Insert Format Tools Data Window Help

Arial — 10 — B I U

A1 =

| | A | B | C | D | E | F | G |
|---|---|---|---|---|---|---|---|
| 1 | | Jan | Feb | Mar | Apr | May | Jun |
| 2 | Carrots | 34 | 96 | 22 | 5 | 6 | 11 |
| 3 | Potatoes | 656 | 56 | 43 | 44 | 95 | 324 |
| 4 | Onions | 88 | 34 | 65 | 21 | 0 | 65 |
| 5 | Cabbages | 78 | 23 | 68 | 11 | 42 | 24 |
| 6 | Beans | 23 | 667 | 432 | 43 | 3 | 77 |
| 7 | Turnips | 675 | 35 | 57 | 762 | 11 | 33 |
| 8 | Cauliflowers | 345 | 657 | 9 | 148 | 612 | 668 |
| 9 | Veg Total | 1899 | 1568 | 696 | 1034 | 769 | 1202 |
| 10 | Apples | 55 | 0 | 67 | 1 | 11 | 88 |
| 11 | Pears | 3 | 67 | 53 | 62 | 565 | 45 |

---

**Microsoft Excel - Brown's Grocers**
File Edit View Insert Format Tools Data Window Help

Arial — 10 — B I U $ % ,

A1 =

| | A | B | C | D | E | F | G | H | I | |
|---|---|---|---|---|---|---|---|---|---|---|
| 1 | | Jan | Feb | Mar | Apr | May | Jun | Jul | Aug | Sep |
| 9 | Veg Total | 1899 | 1568 | 696 | 1034 | 769 | 1202 | 1618 | 1705 | 319 |
| 19 | Fruit Total | 582 | 1198 | 625 | 285 | 813 | 685 | 672 | 2876 | 37 |

# How to conceal unwanted data

**With continued use, a worksheet can grow in size. Hiding the greater part of the information it contains can make it easier to see the overall picture.**

**1** To illustrate how hiding rows and columns works, we've set up a table of sales figures for a family grocery business, but you can use any worksheet for the following steps. In our worksheet, we want to make it easier to see how the overall monthly fruit and vegetable sales compare.

**2** Let's hide the row of figures for carrots. Select the Carrots row by clicking on the gray button at the left end of the row. Click on the Format menu and then select Hide from the Row options. You'll see that Row 2 disappears from view, but the row below is unaltered.

**3** Even though Row 2 can't be seen, its data is still present and calculations that include the carrot sales figures are still correct. For example, the totals in the Veg Total row stay the same.

| | | |
|---|---|---|
| 8 | Cauliflowers | 345 |
| 9 | Veg Total | 1899 |
| 10 | Apples | 55 |

**4** Hide the other rows of individual vegetables by selecting them all at once and using the same menu selection as in Step 2.

**5** Here's how to restore the hidden rows whenever you want to look at, or update, any of the detailed figures. Use the mouse to highlight the first two rows of the worksheet, where Rows 2 to 8 are hidden. Then go to the Format menu and select Unhide from the Row options.

## PC TIPS

### A Quicker Way to Hide

There's a quicker way to hide rows and columns than going through the Format menu and submenus. Once you've selected your rows or columns by clicking on the gray buttons, simply click the right mouse button and then choose the Hide option from the menu. Unhide works in the same way.

**6** You can also hide a column of a worksheet. Let's use this to pick out the February sales figures. Highlight the January column, go to the Format menu and position the mouse pointer on the Column option. Then select Hide from the submenu that appears.

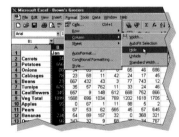

**7** As with the rows, it's also possible to hide more than one column at a time. Use the mouse to select all the other columns of monthly figures after February. Go to the Format menu and choose Hide from the Column submenu.

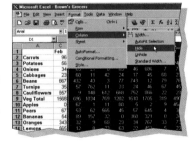

**8** You can restore hidden columns when you want to see the other monthly figures again. Start by highlighting the first three columns of the worksheet with the mouse. Go to the Format menu, position the mouse pointer over the Column option and choose Unhide from the submenu.

**9** Of course, you can combine hiding columns with hiding rows at the same time. We've used the options on the Row and Column submenus of the Format menu so that only the annual totals for the veg and fruit tables are visible.

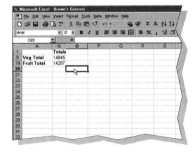

# Make charts look great

***Do you want to give your charts and graphs a more professional image?***
***Here are the secrets of how to make great looking charts with Excel.***

We have already seen how to use Excel to create graphs and charts from the data stored in your worksheets (see Stage 1, pages 58-59). But, with a little extra effort, you can make your graphs and charts really leap off the page.

Once Excel has created a chart, customizing it is as simple as clicking on the part you want to change with the right mouse button. For example, you can choose to work on the chart's title, its legend (or key) or the data points that make up the actual chart.

You can format a graph or chart element in much the same way as you would a worksheet cell. This means you can apply font, alignment and background-pattern formats to the chart's title, add special effects to the bars or pie segments in your graphs and charts, and much more. As you experiment with the techniques shown opposite, you'll find that different options for varying elements are available, depending on whether you're editing a pie chart, bar graph or line graph.

● **Quick results**
You can select individual elements by clicking on them in the chart itself. A right click will bring up a menu of the formatting tools. For example, if you're working on a segment of a pie chart, you can apply a wide range of colors, patterns and fills. As an even more impressive fill, you can use any photograph or drawing that you have stored as a graphics file. Opposite, we show how to enhance a pie chart comparing school sports by using pictures of the activities themselves.

We know how to make individual elements of graphs and charts colorful, but with a little extra knowledge, customized colors and pictures can also be incorporated.

## WHAT IT MEANS

DATA POINTS

*A data point is the element of a chart that represents a particular value in your worksheet. For example, in a pie chart, each section is a data point. In a bar graph, each bar of the graph is a data point. In a line graph each point plotted on the line is a data point.*

# Making more attractive pie charts

**You can use some of Excel's advanced charting tools to give a simple pie chart a unique and much more impressive look. Below we show you how.**

FOR THIS example, we have entered some data and created a pie chart using Excel's Chart Wizard. We followed the basic method covered in Stage 1, pages 58-59, in order to set up an imaginary chart of a school class's favorite sports.

Microsoft® Excel

**1** Use the mouse to select the segment of the pie chart that represents soccer.

**2** Right-click on the segment and then choose Format Data Point from the menu that appears.

**3** In the Format Data Point dialog box, make sure the Patterns tab is selected, then press the Fill Effects button.

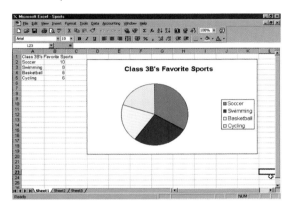

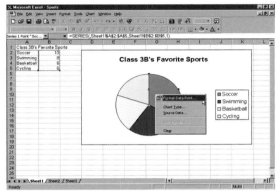

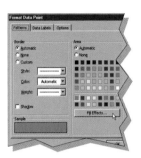

---

## PC TIPS

We've used the right mouse button to jazz up the sections of the pie chart here, but you can also use it to customize many other elements in the chart. The text can be formatted just like text in any worksheet cell. For example, right-click on the chart title.

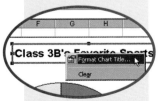

You will see a pop-up menu with a Format Chart Title option. If you select this, you'll see a dialog box that lets you change the font, color and alignment. Try experimenting with other chart objects.

**4** The Fill Effects window gives us an impressive choice of ways to fill this slice of the pie chart with color gradients, patterns and textures. However, we're going to use an image of a soccer player – so go for the Picture tab and click on Select Picture.

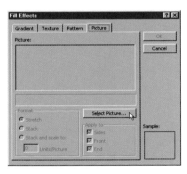

**5** Use the Select Picture dialog box to find the picture you want. We have selected this clip-art image from the CorelDRAW CD-ROM.

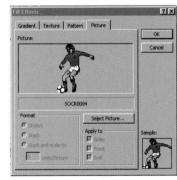

**6** Click the OK button in the Fill Effects window and then the OK button. The soccer segment of the pie chart should now look like this.

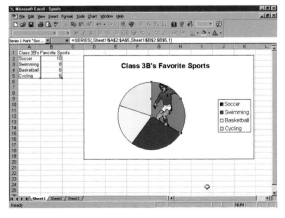

**7** Now repeat the process for the remaining three segments to fill them with appropriate pictures. The final result should look as professional as this.

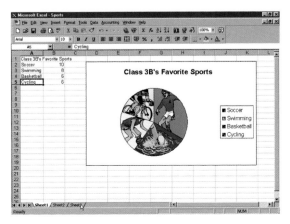

# The smart way to fill cells

*Creating a useful worksheet can be quite arduous. However, Excel can lend a hand and save time – even when copying and pasting cells isn't appropriate.*

Excel provides you with more than one way of filling cells with the same type of data. For example, rather than having to copy and paste the same information repeatedly, Excel allows you to highlight specific cells, which can then be filled from the Edit menu. For adjacent cells, you can even drag the contents of one cell and drop them into another (see Stage 1, pages 54-55).

However, so far we have only used this feature to fill in cells using identical data. Now we are going to discover how to fill a range of cells automatically with, for example, ascending or descending numbers.

### ● Smart fills

You could fill cells A1 to A5 on a worksheet with the ascending numbers 100, 200, 300, 400 and 500. Excel also provides ways for you to fill cells with successive days, months or years. Most of these automated fills can be accomplished with a simple drag of the mouse. These so-called 'smart fills' are controlled from the Series option on the Fill submenu. If you select this, it opens a dialog box that offers you a choice of four fill types: Linear, Growth, Date and AutoFill.

### ● The four options

The Linear option is used to increase (or decrease) the values between cells by a fixed amount each time.

Growth works in a similar way, but by increasing the values between each cell exponentially – 1, 2, 4, 8, 16 and so on, for example. Date obviously refers to date-related data fills, allowing you to choose from day, month and year.

The fourth and final option, AutoFill, will assess the data already keyed into the first few highlighted cells and then automatically decide on which type of fill is necessary for the remaining cells.

*Producing labor-intensive documents that incorporate long lists of headings can be made easy with Excel's AutoFill option. This makes preparing a complex workbook, based around a calendar perhaps, far less time-consuming.*

## PC TIPS

Excel will also let you add your own customized fill options. For example, you can set up a series of atomic elements to help with a science project. To do this, choose Options from the Tools menu and select the Custom Lists tab from the dialog box. Then, all you have to do is type in your list of elements and click on the Add button.

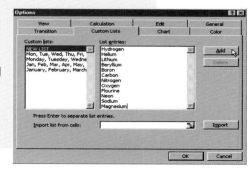

# Saving time with smart fills

*Here, as an example of how useful smart fills can be, we show you how quickly you can make a calendar for the whole year.*

**1** Start by consulting a calendar, then type in a few days and dates in January. As you can imagine, it would take ages to finish the calendar if we had to type in everything manually. Instead, we'll use Excel's smart fill tool.

## PC TIPS

There is a special mouse technique to help you use smart fills more efficiently.

Start with two adjacent cells in your series, say January in cell A1 and February in cell A2. Now highlight these two cells and drag the small black square downward.

As you do, Excel spots that January and February are part of a series and a small yellow tip pops up to show you successive months. Release the mouse button and Excel will fill the cells. This works for numbers and the days of the week.

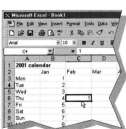

**2** First, we will fill in the month names. Highlight the cell containing Jan (cell B2 in our example) and the 11 cells to its right. Now select Fill from the Edit menu and choose Series from the submenu. Choose AutoFill from the Type section of the window and click OK.

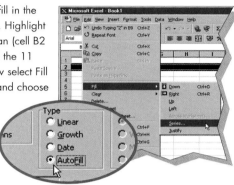

**3** The names of the months have appeared in the highlighted cells. Next, we'll add the remaining days of the month. Highlight the cell containing Sun (in our example, cell A9) and the 31 cells below it. Again, select Fill from the Edit menu and choose Series from the submenu. As before, choose AutoFill and then click OK.

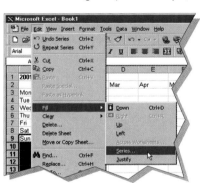

**4** The next job is to fill in the dates for January. Highlight the 31 cells that will contain the dates and bring up the Series dialog box again. Excel looks at the numbers that were already entered (Step 1) and suggests a linear series with a Step value of one between cells. Press the OK button.

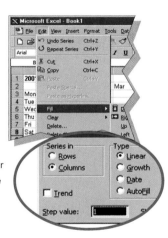

**5** Scroll to the bottom of the January dates. You can see that the 31st falls on a Wednesday. Scroll back up the worksheet and find the first Thursday in the February column. Type the number 1 and repeat Step 4, selecting this cell and the 28 cells below it.

**6** Repeat Step 5 for the remaining months of the year, remembering to change the number of cells you highlight to reflect the number of days in each month.

**7** Now apply some cell and text formatting to add the finishing touches to your calendar and make it easier to read. Gray out the weekends and official holidays and add a colored fill to indicate the unused days at the top of the calendar.

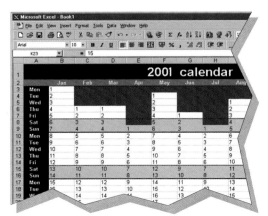

# Modifying text styles

**With CorelDRAW, you aren't stuck with the basic typefaces that come with Windows. You can create new letters with striking, original shapes – even ones that look as if they are cut from solid granite.**

If you normally work with text using a program such as Word, you might think of type as pretty much a fixed element. Once you have chosen a font, you can change its size, style or color, but not the basic shape of the characters.

With CorelDRAW, on the other hand, this is anything but the case. Type can be edited like any other object you create. In fact, CorelDRAW goes out of its way to provide tools to help with everything from basics, such as changing the color and texture of text, to sophisticated options, such as creating your own customized typefaces.

### ● A choice of text styles

CorelDRAW is able to do this because of the way it handles vector-based images. It still uses ordinary fonts – exactly the same ones as you find in Word – but it allows you to convert them into shapes so that they behave like any other object drawn on the worksheet. From there, you can do with them what you will.

There are two types of text available in CorelDRAW: Paragraph Text and Artistic Text. Paragraph Text works in exactly the same way

as in Word. In fact, the text Property Bar looks very similar to the Formatting toolbar in Microsoft Word. It has all the same functions, allowing you to choose the font, alter the size, and add basic formatting commands such as Bold, Italic and Underline. And, of course, you can choose to align your text to the left, center or middle, or to justify it. To make things easier, CorelDRAW uses the same icon symbols as Word for all these functions.

Artistic Text is most useful when you want to start playing around with text, by doing such things as adding special effects or altering its shape. It is the tool of choice for anyone who wants to create interesting logos or would like to produce more imaginative or decorative text effects.

## WHAT IT MEANS

**ARTISTIC TEXT**
*This is CorelDRAW's term for text to which you can apply special effects – distortion, extrusion, blending and so on (see Stage 2, pages 84-87). Artistic Text is created from the Text Tool.*

**CorelDRAW ™**

### ● Creating imaginative effects

When text is first typed in using CorelDRAW's Text Tool, it is a fixed shape that can be changed only in basic ways, such as shrinking, moving and rotating it. However, you can convert the text into curved objects very easily. This adds object nodes to each character, which lets you change its shape and edit it as if it were an ordinary CorelDRAW object.

Once text has been changed into curved objects, you can start applying a number of special effects to the text. Essentially, these are the same as the effects that can be used with any ordinary object, such as distortion, adding a texture or other pictorial effect and merging with other objects. However, by bringing a little imagination to the special effects you choose, and the way that you apply them, you can create some exciting images.

### ● First steps with Artistic Text

In the examples shown on the next page, we use the Envelope special effect to distort the text into dramatic shapes, using preset envelope designs and your own creations. We also look at how the use of color effects can suddenly make text appear much more interesting and dynamic, either by using the

## CREATING YOUR OWN TYPEFACE

Perhaps the most impressive thing you can do with text in CorelDRAW is to create your own typefaces. This is quite an involved process, but allows you the ultimate freedom when using text.

Instead of changing letters every time you want them to look different, you can define a set of characters for your own alphabet. This can then be saved and selected and used at any time in the future.

Of course, this will take some time, so if you don't relish creating your own complete typeface from scratch, you can simply alter an existing one, which allows you to edit or replace only the existing letter shapes that you need.

Fountain fills from previous exercises or the amazing clip-art-like fills that come with CorelDRAW.

Finally, if you're really adventurous, you can start experimenting with the shapes of the letters. You've already learned how to move and use nodes, and this works in exactly the same way.

# Some advanced effects

**CorelDRAW offers enormous scope for experimenting with Artistic Text. Here we show some of the most popular effects you can achieve in addition to the main examples that are shown in the step-by-step exercises.**

As well as the examples on the following pages, you can produce many other effects. These include making text run around a shape or outline, as is often seen on badges and labels. Fitting text to a fixed path or outline (top) is easy, as you simply draw a curved line for the bottom of the letters to follow.

Beveled text (middle), which looks as though it has been carved out of a solid material, is also easy to create using the built-in Beveled tool and just a little bit of tweaking to make sure the text stays readable.

Realistic shadows can also be created from a copy of your original shape, which is then distorted and blurred to look as if the letters are solid and the shadow is being cast by a real light source (bottom).

Even features such as large, dropped capitals at the start of paragraphs, or text specially fitted inside irregularly shaped objects are relatively easy. The only real limit is your imagination, as you learn to use CorelDRAW's tools to create an infinite variety of effects.

# Using Envelopes and Fills

**A number of CorelDRAW's basic graphic effects work particularly well with text, and provide interesting results. Here we take a look at Envelopes and Fills.**

**1** Select the Text Tool from the toolbox. Click once with the mouse in the drawing area. A vertical bar will appear, which shows you where your text will begin to appear.

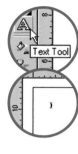

**2** Before typing anything, use the Property Bar options. We'll start with a bold typeface. Click on the drop-down font list and scroll down to select Arial Black. You can also use the size drop-down box to choose a bigger size (24 pt.).

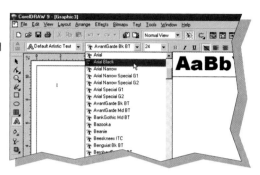

In this sequence we use a preset Envelope shape, but if you prefer, you can create your own shape for your text to follow. Select the Interactive Envelope Tool and then drag the nodes that appear on your text box. The text shape now changes and fills the box's altered shape.

**3** Now type your text. For the time being, keep the line of text quite short, as we have done here.

**4** Select the text box and then click on the Interactive Envelope Tool that appears when you click on the small black arrowhead on the fourth tool from the bottom of the toolbox.

**5** The Envelope toolbar appears. It includes several ready-made shapes for you to use. Click the Add Preset button and a drop-down list of shapes appears. Select one by clicking on it. You'll now see the text change to reflect the shape you chose.

**6** Now use some color effects to add more interest. Select the text box again and choose Favorite Fills and Outlines from the Scrapbook submenu of the Tools menu.

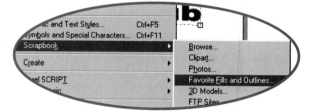

**7** A folder containing small icons that represent the different texture patterns available appears. Double-click on one of them.

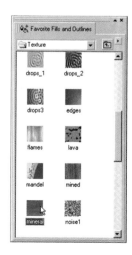

**8** You will instantly see your line of text fill with the pattern you selected. If you want a different pattern, use the Fill Tool's Pattern Fill option to locate and select your bitmap pattern.

# Changing the shapes of letters

We've given these letters a special twist to suit a Halloween party, but you can easily choose an example that will be more useful to you – perhaps using Artistic Text to create a personal logo.

**1** Select the Text Tool from the toolbox. Once again we have chosen Arial Black and set it to 24 pt. (see Step 2 on the previous page). Click the cursor into the middle of the screen and type in your text.

**2** In order to edit the letters with the Shape Tool, you must first convert them to curves. Select the text with the Pick Tool and press the Convert To Curves button on the Property Bar.

**3** At first, the text will look the same as before, but click on the Shape Tool and you'll see a large number of nodes appear around the two words.

## PC TIPS

As you edit the nodes of a character, remember that it is now just like any other CorelDRAW shape. This means you can add and delete nodes as necessary.

To add a node, click on the outline with the Shape tool where you want the node to appear and then use the large plus button that appears at the far left of the Property Bar whenever you have the Shape Tool selected. The minus button can be used to remove a selected node.

**4** Try altering the shape of some of the letters. Use the Shape Tool as normal to move the nodes (inset). You'll probably have to zoom in using the Zoom Levels drop-down menu on the toolbar to see them clearly. If you need an extra node, see PC Tips.

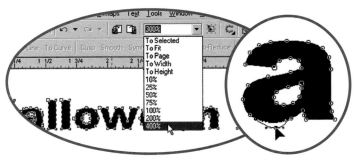

**5** Remember that if things go wrong you can use the Undo button to go back and erase one action at a time. CorelDRAW, unlike Microsoft Paint, remembers all the actions you do, so you can undo your edits all the way back to the initial blank page. You can also reinstate them if you use Redo.

**6** Now that the text has been converted to curves, you can use any ordinary object tool on the text in the same way as the Shape Tool. For example, you can change its color. Try using a simple fill or, as we have done here, apply a Fountain fill (see Stage 2, page 83) to create the result shown below.

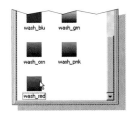

# Halloween

# Introducing Corel PHOTO-PAINT

**When you buy the CorelDRAW package, you also get lots of handy graphic extras. One of the most useful of them is PHOTO-PAINT.**

PHOTO-PAINT is one of the two main programs supplied in the CorelDRAW package. However, unlike CorelDRAW, which is vector-based, PHOTO-PAINT is a bitmap-based paint package. This means that you work with pictures made up of thousands of dots, much as you do in Microsoft Paint (see Stage 1, pages 62-63). However, PHOTO-PAINT is far more advanced than Microsoft Paint and offers a much bigger range of features for creating and editing bitmap pictures.

### Menu Bar
Nearly all Windows programs share the same basic features, and the menu bar is one of the most important. PHOTO-PAINT is no exception, although its bar does contain a number of special options.

### Standard Toolbar
This contains buttons for various common commands, such as File Open and File Save.

### Property Bar
The basic layout of PHOTO-PAINT is very similar to that of CorelDRAW; in both programs the Property Bar changes according to which option or tool has been selected. The default setting shows information relating to the pick tool.

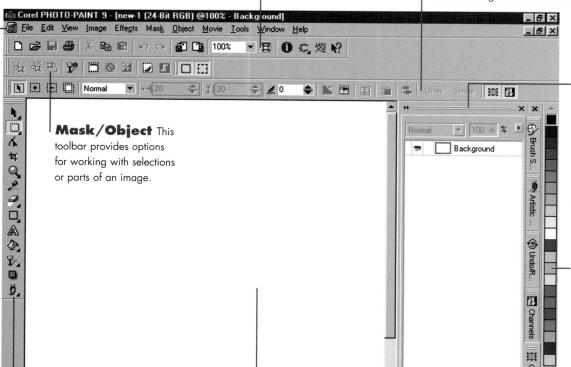

### Mask/Object
This toolbar provides options for working with selections or parts of an image.

### Docker
PHOTO-PAINT uses a docker window, which can be hidden, to provide access to many different options. You can hide or show parts of images, tweak the paint brush settings and undo or redo past actions with this docker.

### Palette
The palette is extremely versatile, and although it displays only a small number of colors by default, you can pick any color that the human eye can distinguish, via one of four types of color picker.

### Toolbox
PHOTO-PAINT's toolbox is in a similar position to the one in CorelDRAW, but the tools available here are very different. Most are not object-based, and there is a wide variety of brushes and editing tools.

### Canvas
This is where all the actual work and drawing is done. The default canvas size is quite small, but you can change it to any size you choose and to any color or pattern.

### Colors Used
This series of displays indicates the particular color of paint you are using, the page you are painting on and the fill, if you choose to use it.

**WHAT IT MEANS**

**OPACITY**
*The term 'opacity' refers to the degree to which an object or paint is transparent. Paint that is 100% opaque completely covers the background. Paint that is just 5% opaque is almost transparent.*

● **Advantages**
If you've followed the Microsoft Paint exercises, you'll have realized that while it's adequate for simple pictures, even the most accomplished computer artist can create only rather basic and cartoonlike pictures with it. This is because it lacks any advanced tools and relies almost entirely on a few brushstrokes, plus the steadiness of the user's hand.

PHOTO-PAINT, however, is much easier to use, because it provides a greater degree of accuracy and has many additional features, such as safety nets, colorful fills, more realistic brush strokes and opacity. These tools help you to add more subtlety to your pictures than Microsoft Paint allows. For example, you can use softer, merging shading on a background, rather than having abrupt changes of color. You can also soften the edges of an object.

● **Realistic pictures**
PHOTO-PAINT comes into its own when you are working with photographic images from a scanner or digital camera. The program allows you to adjust or edit the images in several different and important ways; for example, you can adjust the brightness and contrast to help make the picture clearer.

# *Get started with PHOTO-PAINT*

**How to start up PHOTO-PAINT and set up a blank window in which to work.**

**1** You will find the Corel PHOTO-PAINT program in the CorelDRAW folder.

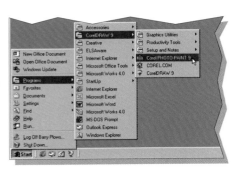

**2** When you start PHOTO-PAINT, you will see a welcome screen very similar to that used in CorelDRAW (see Stage 2, pages 68-69). You have six icons to choose from. For this exercise, click on the one at the top left, which is called New Image.

**3** You will see a large dialog box with several sections. The options here control the following:
**Color mode:** This lets you choose how many colors your image should be displayed in. Usually, 24-bit RGB gives the best display quality.
**Paper color:** PHOTO-PAINT lets you choose any color you like.
**Image size:** Think of this as 'paper size'. You can pick almost any size you wish.
**Resolution:** This lets you select how many pixels (dots) will be used for each inch (or centimeter) of your painting. The more dots that are used, the finer the detail in the image will be. The final parts include options for very advanced users.

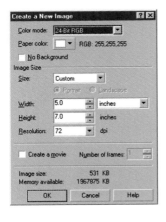

**4** For our first exercise we want to choose the exact number of pixels to use in our picture. Click on the box in Image size that currently says 'inches' (if a PC is set up to work in metric units, it will specify 'centimeters'), and select pixels from the drop-down list.

**5** Still in Image size, change the numbers used for the width and height to 400 and 300 and then press the OK button.

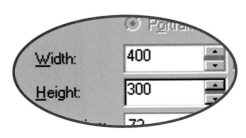

**6** You will now see your blank image ready to use (right). PHOTO-PAINT shows your image in its own window inside the main PHOTO-PAINT window. This allows you to work on several pictures at once (unlike Microsoft Paint).

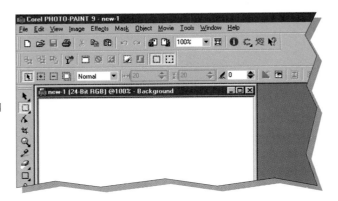

# PHOTO-PAINT basics

**Start by getting used to the main tools available in PHOTO-PAINT. Other tools can be added later as you become more familiar with the program.**

IF THE HUGE number and variety of tools used in PHOTO-PAINT looks intimidating after the simple appearance of Microsoft Paint, it's worth trying some basic tools to see how they work. If you look down the toolbox you will see that some, such as the Rectangle Tool and Eraser, look the same as those in Paint. However, after a few minutes of experimentation, you'll soon see that these tools are much more powerful than Paint's.

**1** We'll start by drawing a simple colored shape on our blank image. First, select the Rectangle Tool from the toolbox on the left.

**2** Now click with the right mouse button on a square in the color palette on the right side of the screen. You will see the Fill box at the bottom of the screen change to indicate the color you have chosen.

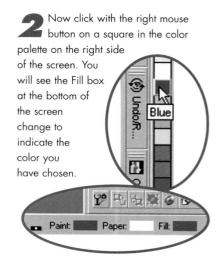

**3** Draw a rectangle using the same click-and-drag technique you have used in Microsoft Paint and CorelDRAW (see Stage 1, page 63 and Stage 2, page 71). When you release the mouse button, PHOTO-PAINT immediately draws and fills in the rectangle.

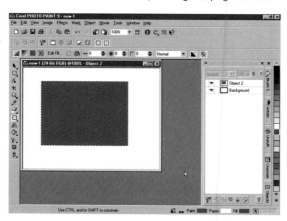

**4** Now try the Eraser Tool. Click once on the tool in the toolbox and then drag it through the blue rectangle. As you do so, you'll see that the path it has cleared through the blue rectangle has soft edges. This contrasts with Microsoft Paint's eraser, which leaves hard edges when it erases.

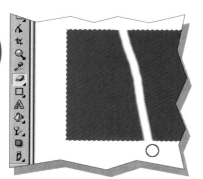

**5** Now let's save this example. PHOTO-PAINT saves files in the same way as other Windows programs, so select Save As from the File menu (right).

**6** Use the Save in drop-down box to find your PC's My Files folder, then type in a name for this picture and press the Save button. Note: PHOTO-PAINT uses its own file format (with the CPT extension), but it can also export pictures in many different formats for use in other programs (see PC Tips, right).

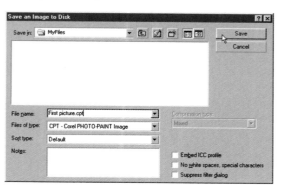

## PC TIPS

### Saving in different formats

PHOTO-PAINT can export your images in many formats. Among the most useful is the Bitmap (BMP) format used by several Windows programs, including Microsoft Paint.

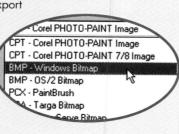

# PHOTO-PAINT's advanced tools

**Extend your graphics capabilities using PHOTO-PAINT's advanced tools.**

PHOTO-PAINT has many more advanced tools and options than the Microsoft Paint program. Although the tools are more sophisticated, they are easy to use once you have experimented a little. To give you some idea of how these tools can help you to create better pictures, we'll introduce you to some of the most commonly used ones below.

## Brush Types

PHOTO-PAINT has a huge number of brush types and styles – far more than Paint. You can specify just about every aspect of the brush, including its type (airbrush, paintbrush, and many more). You can also choose from several options that change the way 'paint' goes onto your 'canvas', such as its thickness.

## Image Sprayer

This amazing tool paints with images; as you drag the pointer over your blank page, it leaves a trail of mini pictures. PHOTO-PAINT has several ready-made image brushes: for this picture we've simply drawn an X on a blank screen using the foliage image brush. You can also create your own image brushes.

## Fills

PHOTO-PAINT also provides you with many different fill options, just like CorelDRAW. While Microsoft Paint has just one solid fill, PHOTO-PAINT has fountain fills, texture fills and bitmap fills.

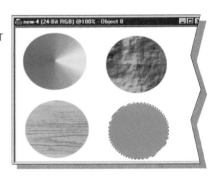

## Smearing, smudging and blending

PHOTO-PAINT has other tools to edit your pictures, once you begin drawing them. The tools are able to smear, smudge or blend parts of your drawings. This helps to give them a more realistic and noncomputerized look. You can also use these tools to customize the images stored on the CorelDRAW CD-ROMs for use in your own pictures.

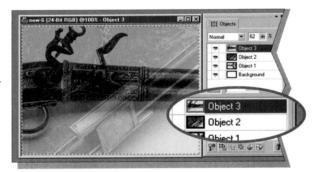

## Safety Nets

Where Microsoft Paint can undo only the last three commands, PHOTO-PAINT has a system of 'Safety Nets', which allows you to undo any number of commands. It presents the commands that you have carried out as a list, allowing you to see exactly what has happened in your painting.

## Objects

PHOTO-PAINT can also use some of CorelDRAW's object-based drawing capabilities. Objects can be made to 'float' behind or in front of the bitmap image you are painting. You can also make objects transparent to create composite pictures.

## Masks

You can create and edit masks for your pictures. These masks allow you to mark off parts of your picture to protect them from paint – just like masking tape does when you are painting a window frame. The difference is that PHOTO-PAINT masks can be absolutely any shape you like.

## Editing Movies

You can even use PHOTO-PAINT to create and edit video movie files that you can play on your computer. You can use any of PHOTO-PAINT's tools on individual frames of a movie and then reassemble them into a complete film of your own making.

*In addition to having lots of fun with PHOTO-PAINT effects, you can also bring old photos – and the memories that they inspire – back to life.*

# Simple photo editing

**Whether you have access to a scanner or not, the ability to alter photographs and other images is extremely useful – and exceedingly easy in Corel PHOTO-PAINT.**

We have already seen how photographs and images can be reproduced on letters and documents (see Stage 1, pages 44-47), converted into background wallpaper for the Windows Desktop (see Stage 1, pages 68-69) or used in other paint packages.

But with the right software, you can do so much more with your images. Once a photo has been scanned and saved on your computer, you can use a program such as Corel PHOTO-PAINT to retouch it, to change the brightness and color, to cut out parts of the picture or to add 2-D and 3-D effects.

### ● A change for the better

There are usually two reasons for making such changes. First, for example, you might want to improve the quality of your photograph before you use it again by enriching the color and light. Alternatively, you might want to add some fun effects to

alter the picture – from something as simple (and fun) as changing the color of your pet dog, to cutting out and pasting the heads of relatives onto other bodies!

### ● For greater effect

There is a wide range of effects available and all work in a similar, easy-to-understand way. Often, all you have to do is select the effect and apply it to your picture. You can even undo the effect if you don't like it and want to start again. Once you've learned how to brighten an image, it's very easy to learn how to sharpen or blur it. If the original quality of the photo that was scanned is poor, you can even compensate for that as well by revitalizing faded areas or removing scratch marks and blemishes.

Whatever the task, serious or fun, PHOTO-PAINT should be able to help – and without a camera or darkroom in sight. We show you how to make a start on the opposite page.

## WHAT IT MEANS

**RETOUCH**
*This term refers to any alteration made to a completed picture, usually a scanned photograph. Retouching can be a minor process, such as making the picture slightly brighter, or a more substantial change, such as cutting out part of the picture and replacing it with a new image.*

# Retouching photographs

Here we show you how easy it is to make a number of amendments to a photograph – from simple contrast changes to more complex two-dimensional special effects.

**1** The photo we are going to retouch is a picture of a macaw. As you can see, the scan hasn't been done very well and the image is a bit too dark.

**2** To change the brightness and contrast, click on the Image menu. Choose the Adjust option and select the Brightness-Contrast-Intensity option.

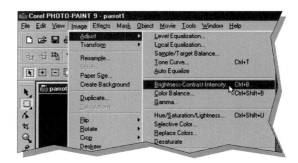

## PC TIPS

You don't need a scanner if you want to practice retouching photos. There are plenty of photo images on the CorelDRAW CD-ROMs for you to use, or you can import a photo image from someone else's PC or the Internet.

You will find plenty of photo images on disk three of the CorelDRAW CD-ROMs. Use PHOTO-PAINT's Open command to retrieve the photos directly from the CD-ROM.

**3** A new window appears, containing several controls. The Brightness, Contrast and Intensity slider bars work much like the controls of a television set or PC monitor. To change the brightness, move the slider bar to the left for a darker image or to the right for lighter one. If the Preview button (inset) is pressed, you can see the effect of your changes to the image.

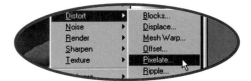

**4** You can change the Contrast and Intensity in the same way. Experiment and check your changes with the Preview button. If your changes make the picture worse, simply press the Cancel button or move the sliders to a new position and preview the result. Click the OK button when you're happy with your changes.

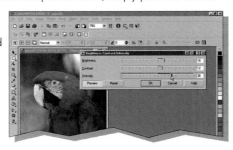

**5** If you want to try something more exciting, there are lots of special effects you can apply to the picture. We'll try one of the Distort effects, called Pixelate. This will stylize your picture so that it is composed of much larger blocks of color. From the Effects menu, select the Distorts option and choose the Pixelate option.

**6** The Pixelate dialog box works similarly to the Brightness-Contrast-Intensity box. You can change the shape of the pixels with Pixelate mode. We've selected Radial, so the color blocks seem to revolve around the center of the picture. Use the sliders in the Adjust section to alter their width and height. The smaller the pixels are, the clearer the picture will be. We've chosen 5 to give a blurred effect. Use the Opacity slider to set how much the original picture shows through. When finished, click OK.

**7** You'll now see the difference you can make to any image with just a few mouse clicks. Try some of the other options under the Effects menu to see what other changes you can make. As always, don't be afraid to experiment.

# Resizing pictures

*You might have found exactly the right picture that you were looking for, but if it is five times larger than your screen or printer paper, you're going to have to learn how to shrink it to fit.*

Any computerized picture has its own specific shape and size, which can be measured using a number of different units. Programs such as Corel PHOTO-PAINT can tell you the size of an image in inches, centimeters or even millimeters. When working with computer images, though, it is often more useful to describe their size in pixels. These are dots that make up the images on your PC screen.

The number of pixels used to display Windows tells you the resolution of your screen – the more pixels there are, the more detailed the image is on screen. Most home computers are set at a resolution of 800 x 600; that's 800 pixels wide by 600 pixels tall (see Stage 2, pages 12-13).

Browse through photos on the CorelDRAW CD-ROMs and you will find pictures at many different sizes. A few might be 1024 x 768 pixels; others will be bigger, some might be smaller.

● **Wrong size pictures**
Sometimes you'll want to change the size of a picture. For example, Windows lets you display a picture on screen as your Desktop background. But if you're using an 800 x 600 display and you find a 1024 x 768 pixel picture, for example, it will be too big to fit on the screen.

Programs such as PHOTO-PAINT can solve this type of problem in several ways. You

*Whether it's for a special effect or just to make a picture the exact size you want, it's easy to fit a computerized picture into any space!*

*Distorting pictures can be a fun experiment and will add impact to page designs.*

could use the selection tool to choose an 800 x 600 pixel area of the picture and then get PHOTO-PAINT to cut everything outside this area out of the picture.

In addition, you can resize a picture to match your exact requirements, as if it has been stretched or squeezed from the edges. You can change a picture to almost any shape with PHOTO-PAINT, although this might result in distortion, as in the pictures shown above and left.

If you start with a portrait photo of 400 x 600 pixels and change it to 800 x 600 pixels, the subject's face will be stretched to twice its width. This can be fun to use for special effects. In the exercise opposite, we'll show you how to resize a picture that's too big so that it makes a better fit for the background wallpaper on your Desktop.

**PC TIPS**

**Graphics for the Web**
Resizing a picture is particularly useful when creating images for a website.
Use the exercise opposite to make sure your picture is the right size for your Web page. Bear in mind when designing Web pages that many visitors will be using a relatively small screen.

# Fitting a picture to the Desktop

**We've looked at different ways of customizing the Desktop (Stage 2, pages 10-11).
Now we'll make it unique by using our own choice of picture as wallpaper.**

**1** Start PHOTO-PAINT and choose Open from the File menu. Insert the second CorelDRAW CD-ROM and browse through the photos to find one you'd like as your new background. We've chosen 864069.wi in the water_ani folder. Select the photo and click on Open.

**2** When a picture loads from the CD-ROM, you see a dialog box reminding you that you cannot save the picture to the CD-ROM. However, you can save it to your hard disk. Click on OK.

**3** Now let's save the file: select the Save As option from PHOTO-PAINT's File menu. When the dialog box appears, use the Save in section to find the Windows folder. Click on the Files of type drop-down list and select BMP-Windows Bitmap. This is the format that Windows uses for Desktop wallpaper.

## WHAT IT MEANS

### ASPECT RATIO

*The aspect ratio is the ratio of a picture's width to its height. When resizing an image, it will look distorted (squeezed or stretched) if the aspect ratio changes.*

**4** The first thing you'll notice is that the photo is quite large – certainly larger than your computer screen. If you were to use it as wallpaper, you wouldn't be able to see it all. But this is where PHOTO-PAINT's ability to change the size of a picture comes into effect. From the Image menu choose the Resample option.

**5** From the Resample dialog box that appears you'll see that you are able to choose the exact size of the picture. Now click on the units drop-down list at the top right of the Image size selection. Select pixels from the list of options.

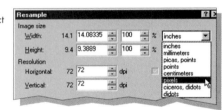

**6** First, type 800 into the Width box. As you do, the Height box below will automatically change to read 533 (the exact figure depends on the dimensions of your original picture – if you chose another one, it might be different).

**7** If you now try to type 600 into the Height box (the other dimension we want for this picture), you'll notice that the Width changes (it is 900 in our example). PHOTO-PAINT always tries to keep pictures in proportion when changing their size. This is because the Maintain **aspect ratio** box is ticked, but you can change the proportions if you want to make the picture exactly 800 x 600. First you will have to uncheck this box, then type in the correct Height and Width. PHOTO-PAINT will have to squeeze the photo to fit it into the width and, since 900 x 600 is enough to include most of the picture, we'll stick with this setting. Just press the OK button. Save the picture and exit CorelDRAW.

**8** To make this picture your Desktop wallpaper, right-click anywhere on the Desktop to bring up the Desktop pop-up menu. Select Properties.

**9** We've already used the Display Properties dialog box for changing the number of colors Windows uses (see Stage 2, pages 12-13), but you can also use it to choose pictures for the background. First click on the Background tab. This will show you a picture of what your display looks like. Press the Browse button and use the dialog box to find the file you saved in Step 3. Select it and press OK. Then press OK again to close the Display Properties dialog box.

**10** The picture will instantly appear as your Windows Desktop background wallpaper.

# PHOTO-PAINT's different brushes

**Artists who work with acrylic or water-base paints have a variety of different brush styles available to them. With PHOTO-PAINT, computer artists have just as many choices.**

*canvas*

*nibs*

One of the major benefits that CorelDRAW PHOTO-PAINT has over simple paint programs is the amount of control it gives you over brush types. You can choose from a huge range of brushes, brush nib shapes, and the type of 'paint' that is used.

You're not restricted to painting on perfectly smooth paper, either. You can choose the type of surface on which you are painting – such as thick drawing paper or expensive canvas, like that used by real artists to heighten the reality of the paint surface.

### ● Choosing your brushes
When you click on the Paint Tool button in the toolbox, you will see PHOTO-PAINT's Property Bar change to reflect the options available (below). These options let you choose the type of brush – from conventional brushes to pencils, airbrushes and even specialist brushes that mimic famous painting

styles, such as Impressionism and Pointillism. Some of the other popular options available include quick access to choice of brush size and nib shape (whether circular or square) directly from the Property Bar.

For full control over the huge variety of available brushes, you use the program's Docker windows. Like CorelDRAW, PHOTO-PAINT brings together related options into a single window. Corel calls these options Dockers because they 'dock' into position at the side of the PHOTO-PAINT window.

### ● Brushes and Nibs
Select Brush Settings from the Window menu's Dockers submenu. At the far right is the usual X button for closing the window, and in the

---

Property Bar : Paint/Clone Tool

| Custom Art Brush | Normal | | 25 | 65 | 0 | | |

Brush Type — PAINT Mode — Nib Shape — Nib Size — Transparency Value — Soft Edge — Repeat Stroke — Nibs Options — Brush Options

*When you are using the Paint Tool, the Property Bar changes to give you quick access to many brush choices.*

*The canvas effect can be used to make a photograph (top) look as though it's been painted on one of the materials used by artists, such as cotton (above), wood, paper or canvas.*

middle is the Roll-Up button. Click on this to make the contents of the window appear or disappear.

The main part of the Brush Settings Docker menu lets you choose from a wide variety of ready-made nib shapes and sizes. Here you'll find more than the simple circular and square options offered on the Property Bar. For example, there are stars, swirls, and even a collection of unusual shapes for a paintbrush, such as lions, birds and human figures. When you click on one of these, painting becomes as simple as selecting a color and clicking on the painting area you wish to fill with that color.

If you can't find the nib shape you want, you can create your own. Anything you can draw with the mouse can be made into a nib. This is one area of painting that is easier to do on a computer than with a real brush.

### ● Effects

As well as changing the properties of the brush, you can also change the type of paint you use. This is achieved via the Effects menu, which allows you to alter the thickness, 'wetness' and texture of the paint.

Effects works slightly differently from the brush options. When you alter the type of brush and nib, it affects the things you paint subsequently – your existing painting remains as it was before. When you use Effects, however, it affects your existing painting. For example, if you select part of your picture and use the Effects menu to add a wet paint look, it will affect only the selected area.

### ● Canvas effects

With all the options possible for the brushes and paint, it's no surprise that PHOTO-PAINT also allows you to alter the background of your 'paper' as well. This is done by using canvas filters, which can be added at any stage of your drawing to give a texture to the background.

If you want to give your picture the look of a painting created on canvas, for example, you simply apply a linen-type texture to the whole painting area. You can have lots of fun with your existing pictures by applying effects to them. For example, if you have a photograph of a relative, you can make it look like a painted image just by making use of a canvas effect. No extra painting work is necessary and when printed out on high-quality paper, you have an ideal gift!

# Advanced Paint Tool Settings

*By clicking on the small black arrows next to each section name, you reveal extra settings for the Paint Tool.*

IN ADDITION to changing the nib and brush types, you can also make a number of alterations to the way the brushstrokes are applied to the page.

At first, these will seem like minor changes, mostly because you simply have to change a percentage or move a slider bar. But they can have a profound effect on how your brush appears on the page.

You can access the brush options through the different sections of the Brush Settings Docker. The top part lets you change the angle of the brush and its size.

The Brush Texture section includes options for the way brushstrokes bleed into a painting. For example, you can simulate watercolor painting by tweaking the Bleed and Sustain Color settings so that as you paint in one color, it blends with the colors of paint already underneath.

The Dab Attributes option lets you control the way successive dabs of the brush are applied. You can change the spacing – making brushstrokes closer together or farther apart, depending on your specific needs – and you can also add some subtle (and not so subtle) color variations by moving the Hue Saturation and Lightness sliders away from their normal '0' settings.

# Choosing brushes and paint effects

**To get the best out of your own abilities (and those of your computer) try using the different brush styles PHOTO-PAINT has to offer. We look at some here.**

**1** Start a new picture and then click on the Paint Tool from the toolbox on the left of the PHOTO-PAINT screen.

**2** Select Brush Settings (far right) from the Dockers submenu on the Window menu (right).

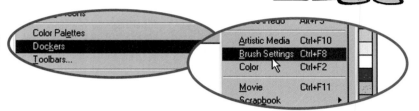

**3** Use the pop-up window's scroll bar to look through the different nibs. Pick one that would be useful for drawing a tree and single-click on it.

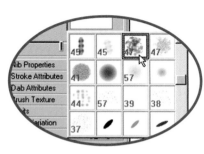

**4** Now select a shade of green from the color palette on the right and start to paint a tree. Feel free to experiment with different nibs for the trunk.

**5** For the second tree we shall use the same nib, but alter the texture of the paint so that it looks as if it has been applied wet. Start by painting a second tree next to the first.

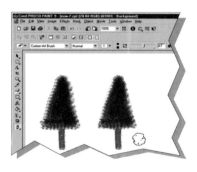

**6** Select the Rectangular Mask Tool from the toolbox and drag a rectangle over the second tree so that it completely encompasses it.

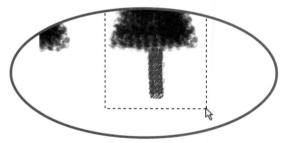

**7** From the Effects menu, select Distort and then choose the Wet Paint option.

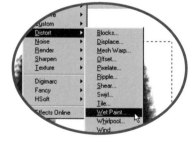

**8** A dialog box appears, with two sliders to control the effect. Alter the size of the drips (Percent) and the wetness of the paint (Wetness), and you can see your picture change to show the effects. Click the OK button when you are happy with it.

**9** For the final tree, try one of the preset brush types. Click on the Art Brush button (inset below) on the far left of the Property Bar and select the last brush. Then select Pointillism from the drop-down list box just to its right.

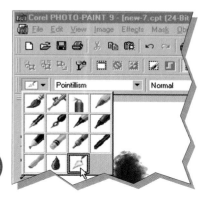

**10** Now as you paint your tree, you will find that it is built up from many small dots. However, the great thing is that you don't have to draw the individual dots yourself, because PHOTO-PAINT does it for you.

# Making your own brush nibs

**As you can see, there are many different ways you can alter your chosen brush in PHOTO-PAINT. If you still can't find exactly what you want, you can make your own.**

BESIDES CUSTOMIZING the brushes by using preset commands, you can also create a custom nib completely from scratch. In fact, the preset nibs are really just simple bitmap pictures, so you can easily create your own and specify it as a nib. Below, we do just that by drawing a picture of a leaf and then using it to paint a tree.

When drawing a new nib bitmap, you should remember that it will generally be used with one color at a time. Any holes you wish to include in the nib bitmap drawing will also have to be carefully drawn so that they have no gaps in them through which the brush fill color might seep.

When making any customization alterations to the nibs, it is best to do it at a high zoom magnification, because most brush nibs are, by necessity, fairly small when they appear on-screen.

**1** Start a new painting and create a simple shape with the Paint Tool. Take extra care to make sure the shape is clear and distinct. In our example we've used a leaf.

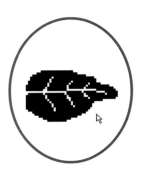

**2** Draw a Rectangle Mask around your design. Now select Create from Contents of Mask from the menu that appears when you check the Nib Options button.

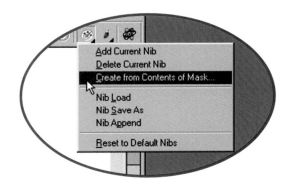

**3** Click OK in the box that appears (below) and the shape you want to use will immediately become a nib.

**4** Use your new nib to paint a picture. Notice how the black and white areas of your original nib control where the paint is applied.

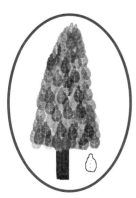

**5** Go to the Brush Settings window and click the Brush Texture heading. Change the Bleed setting to 50. Now use a star-shaped brush and drag it to create some fireworks.

**6** Use the Dab Attributes section to adjust the way successive dabs appear. Experiment with the Spacing, Spread and the settings. See how the star brush paints differently.

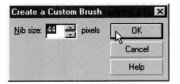

**7** By using these settings wisely, you can come up with many natural-looking effects, such as flocks of birds, that would otherwise take a long time to create with a single stroke.

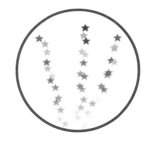

# Being creative with PHOTO-PAINT's filters

*Even if you're no good at painting with the mouse, you can use PHOTO-PAINT's many filters to edit and customize existing images so that you can create your own works of art.*

Despite having the help of PHOTO-PAINT'S huge number of brushes and nibs, not everyone is cut out to be a computer artist. Painting with a mouse needs the same creative and compositional skills as painting with real brushes and genuine oils or watercolors. The mouse and PHOTO-PAINT's many powerful features are no substitute for talent.

However, the companies that make graphics programs know that not everyone is a Van Gogh, so they pack plenty of features into their products to help make PC art relatively easy. In fact, many of the professional computer artists who buy advanced art programs, such as PHOTO-PAINT, don't intend to paint images from scratch. Instead they want to apply their programs' image-editing features to work on existing images.

### ● Filter features

By being creative with the dozens of powerful filters built into PHOTO-PAINT, you can manipulate any type of picture. Photo-retouching filters (see pages 78-79) let you adjust brightness, contrast and the amount of highlights, midtones and shadows in an image. Every media art department in the world uses such filters to make photos as clear as possible before publication.

Other filters have much more dramatic effects. You can apply PHOTO-PAINT's Squizz filter to warp a picture (see page 88). The effect is like looking through a distorting glass lens: as with all the filters, you can add as much distortion as you like and control which parts of the picture are changed.

*CorelDRAW's filters can turn your photograph into a Pointillist 'masterpiece' or a shimmering reflection.*

These filters are a great way to get youngsters interested in the world of computer image editing. It's fun to take photos of Mom and Dad and stretch their faces into crazy shapes. You can save the photo and print it out on a color printer to make a unique personalized greeting card.

### ● Instant artist

If you want to create the illusion of a painted image, PHOTO-PAINT's filters can help out. There is a special set called Art Strokes, that can turn any photo into a painting style of your choice (see opposite).

At first glance, the Art Strokes seem similar to the texture effects that PHOTO-PAINT can apply to an image (see page 83). By adding a texture to a photo, you can give the impression that it is printed on a surface, such as canvas, linen or even concrete. It's a great effect, but the image still

## PAINTING MADE EASY

By applying the Watercolor Art Strokes filter to a photograph, such as a row of trees, you can transform the photo into a stunning graphic that has the appearance of a watercolor painting, as shown below.

looks like a photo. By contrast, the Art Strokes filters are much more sophisticated and much more flexible. They actually repaint the whole picture by applying brushstrokes to a plain background.

The idea behind filter software is that it looks at the colors of the pixels in the original photo and uses them to choose paint colors. It then repaints the picture in a variety of different styles. For example, it can redraw the picture as if it were created with watercolors: the filter picks up the main colors from the photo, but when it creates the new picture, it simulates the delicacy of watercolor brushstrokes to give the typical wash effect of watercolor pictures. The original picture is hardly recognizable, because all the tiny details are washed out, leaving a more artistic version of the image (see Painting made easy box, opposite page).

### ● Customizing tools

There's almost always a lot more subtlety and flexibility in these effects than in the simpler texture ones. You can see just how the filter will affect your image and fine-tune it in many different ways. For example, in the Palette Knife filter, you can change the size of the knife itself, alter its angle or soften the edge of the paint stroke laid down by the knife.

# Combining filters

**PHOTO-PAINT's filters needn't be used in isolation – you can combine them for even better effects.**

To create a particularly realistic painting effect from a photograph, you can combine several filters in succession. For example, if you use the Impressionist Art Stroke filter (see page 89) and then the Canvas texture, you can turn a flat photograph into an image that looks like it has been painted on coarse fabric.

You're not restricted to realistic images – there are plenty of weird and wacky filters that can help you to create out-of-this-world images from your photos. For example, the Psychedelic command (in the Color Transform submenu) lets you create the wild color changes that you often see in pop videos. You can then use this with other filters to change the original beyond all recognition.

You can also use different filters on different parts of your image. Just select an area before choosing a filter from the Effects menu. Applying different filters to separate areas of an image is perfect for creating a composite look. You could, for example, create a 'painting' done half in oils and half in watercolors.

*The starting point for many a graphic adventure using PHOTO-PAINT's filters is an ordinary photograph.*

*Use the Impressionist Art Strokes filter and you can turn the photo into an Impressionist-style painting.*

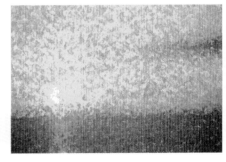
*Apply the Canvas texture to make the picture look even more like a real painting.*

*This poolside photo has had the Psychedelic filter applied to it, brightening its contrasts and colours.*

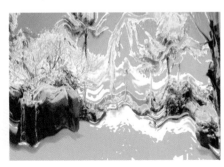
*Use the Ripple filter to add a watery look to the psychedelic poolside graphic.*

*Turn a single photo into an amazing composite painting, using as many filters as you need.*

# Fun with photos and filters

**Have fun with PHOTO-PAINT. Here we attack a portrait with the Squizz filter.**

**1** Start PHOTO-PAINT and open a portrait photograph. We've opted for 871014.wi from the People folder on the third of CorelDRAW's CD-ROMs, but you can use any image you happen to have on hand.

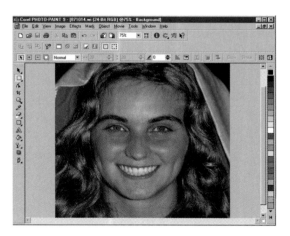

**2** Click the Effects menu and then select SQUIZZ 1.5 from the HSoft sub-menu. When the Squizz welcome screen appears, click the BRUSH button at the bottom of the screen.

**3** Your picture now appears on the left of the dialog box, with settings on the right. As your mouse passes over the picture, a circular outline shows the Squizz brush. If necessary, you can change the size of this brush in the Brush Properties section of the dialog box.

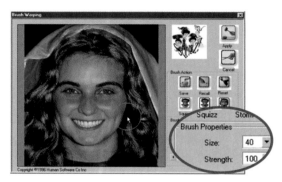

**4** To start Squizzing, drag the brush over any part of the portrait. Squizz drags the photo details around as if it is made of elastic. Notice how the colors are still as smoothly blended as in the original photo.

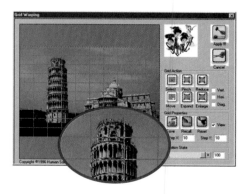

**5** When you've finished distorting your portrait, click the Apply button on the right to make these changes to your photo (or click Cancel to return the photo to the original).

**6** Squizz has two modes of working. The first is the brush you've already been using. The second is the Grid option, which helps create regular distortions. Open another photo and bring up Squizz again, this time clicking the Grid button when the welcome screen appears. The image appears with a rectangular grid overlying the picture (inset).

**7** Click and drag the corners where the lines intersect. When you release the mouse button, Squizz squeezes and stretches the pixels in the image to match the new shape of the grid.

**8** You can move as many of the corners as you like, gradually warping the image into a new shape. When you click the Apply button, PHOTO-PAINT makes the changes to your image. It's a great way to create a new slant on familiar images.

## PC TIPS

If you know what sort of distorting shape you want to make with the grid, you can drag as many of the corners as quickly as you like. Once you stop, PHOTO-PAINT will catch up and redraw the preview with your changes shown.

# Paintings from photographs

Create a painting by using PHOTO-PAINT's Art Strokes on a photograph.

**1** Open an existing photograph in PHOTO-PAINT. Select a picture that has very distinct shapes and outlines, such as this image of Khafre's pyramid. Click on Art Strokes in the Effects menu and select the Sketch Pad command from the submenu.

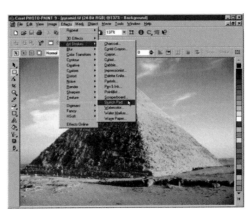

**2** As soon as the dialog box appears, PHOTO-PAINT applies the Sketch Pad filter to the image. It uses the default settings for this particular filter. In a few moments you see a black-and-white shaded sketch of your photograph.

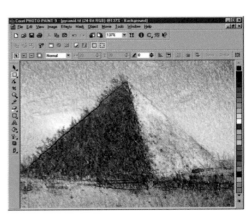

**3** The settings that give you control over the virtual pencil that PHOTO-PAINT has used are in the Sketch Pad dialog box. Try dragging the Style slider right to the Fine end and doing the same with the Outline slider.

**4** Your sketched photo is redrawn, with lots more detail added by the pencil. This shows the rough texture of the pyramid faces more clearly than the original Sketch Pad settings.

**5** PHOTO-PAINT also has a virtual set of colored pencils up its sleeve: click the Color option in the dialog box to access them. Make the sketch, then click the OK button when you are happy with the effect.

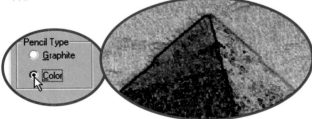

**6** PHOTO-PAINT is packed with great instant-art filters: open the photo again and try the Impressionist filter, listed in the Art Strokes menu. You get a superb result within a few seconds; painting this with a mouse would challenge even the best computer artist's abilities.

## PC TIPS

To view both the original photo and the altered picture, click the button with the two rectangles that appears on the dialog box title bar. This will show the images side by side.

**7** For a different Impressionist effect, select the Dabs option in the Impressionist dialog box. You can add more colors to the Impressionist palette by dragging the Coloration setting to the right.

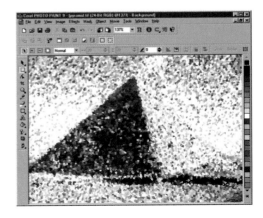

*Using CorelDRAW to combine photographs and drawings is lots of fun and very easy. It's a great chance to be really creative and make use of the advanced facilities of this program.*

# Adding photos to drawings

The real beauty of the CorelDRAW package is that it contains programs for creating and editing both bitmap images (such as photos and paintings) and vector images (such as drawings and illustrations). You'll be able to get even more out of the program, however, once you learn how to combine these two types of images. CorelDRAW makes it easy.

CorelDRAW itself is a drawing program (see Stage 2, pages 68-69) and Corel PHOTO-PAINT is a bitmap editor (see pages 74-77). So far, we've kept the two areas separate, but CorelDRAW can also use bitmap images created in other programs. It also lets you use bitmap pictures as patterns to fill objects in your drawings.

### ● More realism
Although you can create accurate pictures with CorelDRAW, nothing is as realistic as a photograph. And there are many occasions when using a bitmap image is preferable to using vectors, as CorelDRAW does.

Greeting cards, for example, can benefit from the personal touch. While you could simply use a photo editor to create and print

a bitmap picture, by using the picture in a drawing, you can add words and shapes in a manner that is not possible when you are using a photo editor.

The added benefit of importing bitmaps to your drawings is that you can edit them in the same way as vector objects. You can change the appearance of the picture and add special 2-D and 3-D effects. The possibilities are limited only by your imagination.

### ● Adding a bitmap to your drawing
The actual process of adding a bitmap picture to a drawing is easy. Browse through the CD-ROMs that came with CorelDRAW. One of them is stuffed full of photographs that you can use for any purpose. Remember, the manual shows small preview pictures of the images on the CD-ROM to help you find what you're looking for.

Once you've found a suitable picture, you can simply drag and drop it onto your drawing. In the following example, we'll create a composite picture using a photograph and some CorelDRAW shapes. We'll also show how to use a bitmap pattern to fill a CorelDRAW shape.

## PC TIPS

It's best to run Windows in 24-bit color mode (see Stage 2, pages 12-13) when using a graphics program such as CorelDRAW. This is because pictures look best when there are plenty of colors available to display them. If you would like to use a photo that contains thousands of colors, trying to display it on a computer that is set up to show only 256 colors at once will result in a poor on-screen image.

# Making a composite image

**CorelDRAW can combine drawings with photos. Here we use some of the images from the CorelDRAW CD-ROM.**

**CorelDRAW** ™

**1** Adding a photo to a vector drawing is very simple in CorelDRAW. For this example, we'll add a photograph to a frame. CorelDRAW has some ready-made frames in its clip-art collection, so we'll start by clicking on the Tools menu and selecting the Clipart option from the Scrapbook submenu.

**2** Choose a border from the second CorelDRAW CD-ROM. This one is in the Africa folder. You can load it into CorelDRAW simply by double-clicking on the icon.

**3** You'll see the frame appear on your page. You can now add a photo to use in the frame. Insert the third CorelDRAW CD-ROM. Choose Photos from the Scrapbook submenu.

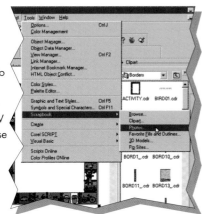

**4** Again, the choice of photo is up to you. Here, we've used 865067.wi, which is in the Ani_king folder within the Photos folder. Add the photo by dragging and dropping it onto the frame.

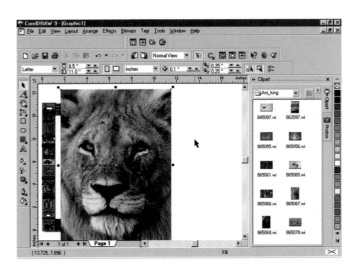

**5** To put the photograph behind the frame, click on it with the right mouse button, click on the Order options and select the To Back command. In this respect, the photograph you have added works just like any other object you would add to a picture.

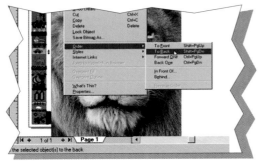

**6** The photo is a little large for the border, so we need to make it fit into the frame correctly. Now that it's behind the frame, we can use the Shape Tool (inset, below) to grab each corner of the picture and take it to the inside corner of the picture frame.

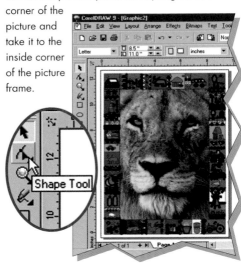

Shape Tool

## Filling shapes with bitmap patterns

**1** You can add bitmap patterns to any shape in your drawings. For this example, just start with a new shape. We've used the Polygon Tool to draw a simple pentagon. Click on the newly drawn shape with the right mouse button and select Properties from the pop-up menu that appears.

**2** Click on the Fill tab of the dialog box that appears. From the line of six buttons, click the third from the left and select Bitmap from the list of Pattern fill options.

**3** Click on the drop-down palette of bitmaps and choose one of the patterns. Press the Apply button and the bitmap pattern will fill the entire polygon.

# Hardware

# Adding more memory

*Adding more memory is one of the easiest and least expensive upgrades you can make to your computer – and it can also be one of the most effective.*

It's easy to think of your PC as a single box, much like a VCR or a CD player. However, unlike a VCR or a CD player – which you tamper with at your peril – a PC is built to be upgradable (see Stage 2, pages 110-111).

There are two reasons you might want to upgrade your computer system: to add new functions and capabilities (adding a larger monitor or plugging in a scanner, for example) or to make your PC work faster.

### ● Upgrading for performance

We've already covered some examples of adding new devices (see Stage 2, 104-107 and 108-109); here, we'll look at improving your PC's performance. It's a fact of computing life that once you've bought a PC,

newer, faster models will hit the market within months. It's also true that new software often works more slowly than previous versions because of all its new features. It's not unusual to find that upgrading your software seems to make your computer run slower! To counter this performance problem, you can change or add individual components

inside your computer. For example, changing to a better graphics card will make the software that uses it run faster. Without a doubt though, the best way to make your computer run much faster is to add more Random Access Memory (RAM) – and in all cases, the more the merrier.

### ● More memory

Windows likes memory – the more you've got, the more easily Windows can make space for the huge number of programs and files it uses. Many home computers were initially sold with 32 megabytes (MB) of RAM. This seems plenty – it's enough to store 33,554,432 bytes (see Stage 1, pages 96-97). However, many programs (including Windows) can use up many millions of bytes. When Windows runs out of memory for the programs and documents it is using, it stores them temporarily on the hard drive. You might notice your computer's hard drive light flashing from time to time, even when you're not opening or saving programs or documents on the hard drive. This is a sign that

*Here you can see how much faster a computer goes when more memory is added to its existing 32MB. The yellow bar shows the computer speed before adding memory, and the red, blue and green bars show the improvement with different amounts of memory.*

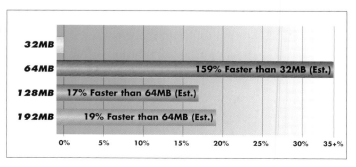

| | |
|---|---|
| **32MB** | |
| **64MB** | 159% Faster than 32MB (Est.) |
| **128MB** | 17% Faster than 64MB (Est.) |
| **192MB** | 19% Faster than 64MB (Est.) |

0%   5%   10%   15%   20%   25%   30%   35+%

## WHAT IT MEANS

### SIMM, DIMM

*Short for single and dual inline memory module, respectively, these are tiny circuit boards containing memory chips. They plug into matching slots on the PC's motherboard. Most PCs use either SIMMs or DIMMs, although a few can use both. Your PC's manual should tell you which your PC uses.*

Windows is swapping information between the memory and the computer's hard drive.

Unfortunately, the hard drive is much slower than the RAM memory, and swapping the information from one to the other is a slow process. With more memory – 64MB or 128MB – Windows has to do much less of this swapping, so its programs run more quickly and smoothly.

*RAM memory comes in strips called SIMMs and DIMMs and is simple to install, but it is fragile and should be handled only by an experienced technician.*

### ● Memory costs

Memory is the most cost-effective upgrade you can buy. Adding another 32MB to a computer that has only 32MB installed can increase performance by 159 percent and will cost you only about $20. Adding a further 128MB will only be around $50. However, due to the volatile nature of the computer business, the price is subject to fluctuation. As memory is supplied on SIMM or DIMM modules, adding memory is a simple, and therefore cheap, upgrade. Since computers normally have several slots for memory modules, you can sometimes add more without replacing your existing modules. It's still worth getting a dealer or computer expert to add more memory, as it's important to get exactly the right type (see Installing the right type of memory, below).

Try to track down a local dealer who either builds systems or does repairs – he or she may charge a little more for the memory than the big mail-order firms that advertise in the magazines, but will probably fit it free of charge.

How much memory you can add depends on how many free memory module slots there are on the motherboard. Older computers often have four SIMM slots on the motherboard. SIMMs must be fitted in matching pairs: two 8MB SIMMs for 16MB or four 16MB SIMMs for 64MB, for example. If there are empty SIMM slots, the dealer can use these to upgrade your memory, but if all four are used, upgrading memory means discarding the current SIMMs with higher-capacity modules (the dealer may accept the old ones as part of an exchange).

Newer PCs use DIMM slots – typically two or three. One of the main advantages of DIMMs is that they can be added singly. So if your PC has two 32MB DIMMs and one spare DIMM slot, you can add another 64MB DIMM to take the total RAM up to 128MB.

### ● No software installation

One of the best aspects of adding more memory compared with other computer add-ons is that there's no extra software to install or set up after the new memory has been added. Windows uses the extra memory right away so that each and every one of your programs can work more efficiently.

*Here are the two vacant slots for memory modules on the motherboard.*

*Here are the same two slots with two 32MB memory modules fitted in position.*

## INSTALLING THE RIGHT TYPE OF MEMORY

We don't recommend that you try installing new RAM yourself. This is partly because it's easy to cause irreparable damage – for example, it's all too easy to destroy memory chips with static electricity – and partly because it's just as easy to get the wrong kind of memory module.

There is a vast array of different types of memory, and this can be very confusing. Installing the wrong kind of memory module could damage the memory, your computer – or both.

You will see many abbreviations used: FPM RAM, EDO RAM, SDRAM, DDR SDRAM, Rambus, PC100 and so on. You might also see references to parity and nonparity. All this jargon refers to the various ways that the memory chips work.

Until a few years ago, FPM memory was used in all computers. However, more recent types of memory, such as EDO RAM and SDRAM, have been adopted because they work faster than FPM RAM.

If your computer will accept it, it is best to buy SDRAM type memory. SDRAM chips are commonly used in PCs that have DIMM slots. The fast pace of PC development means that there are several different variants. These subtle variations are based on the speed at which the PC's motherboard operates. For example, for motherboards that run at 66MHz, 66MHz DIMMs are required. Similarly, there are 100MHz DIMMs (known as PC100 DIMMs), and 133MHz DIMMs (known as PC133 DIMMs). DDR SDRAM is a new, faster variant but requires a different motherboard slot to original SDRAM bases. In newer PCs you may find Rambus memory. Generally speaking, the faster the chips run, the more expensive they are.

Your computer's manual should tell you which types of memory your computer can work with, but a computer dealer will be better able to check the type your computer has and, if necessary, install a similar type.

Screen space is always at a premium on a computer. Windows itself takes up a large amount of space with its Taskbar and Start menu, while programs, such as Word, also use up space with their menus and toolbars. The simplest solution to the space problem is a bigger monitor.

The first benefit you'll get is more screen area, which means the objects on the screen are easier to see and can be used at a bigger size. More important, larger monitors can run at a higher resolution than standard 14- or 15-inch monitors. This means that small text will be more readable and pictures will be both clearer and more detailed. One way in which the extra resolution can help is that, with the extra detail, you can see two documents side by side and easily

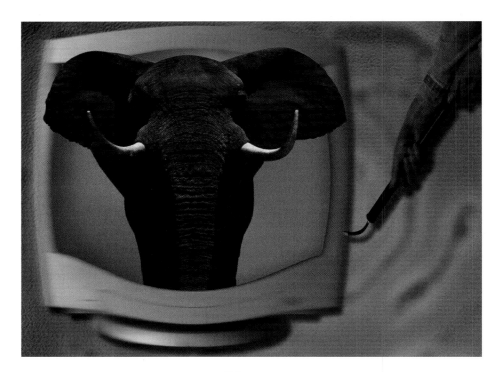

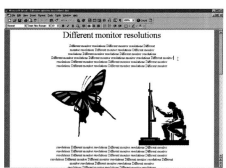

*Change to a bigger monitor and you'll get more information on screen. These pictures represent the difference, in both size and detail, between a 14-inch monitor (top) and a 17-inch monitor (bottom).*

# Upgrading to a 17-inch monitor

**Many new computers come with a 14- or 15-inch monitor, but there's much to be gained from buying a larger one.**

## WHAT IT MEANS

### REFRESH RATE

*Monitors work by drawing the image as a series of lines one after the other, from top to bottom. The speed at which this is done is called the refresh rate, and the faster it is, the better the image looks. If the refresh rate is too slow, the screen appears to flicker. This can lead to headaches.*

copy and paste information from one to the other.

We've used two screen images to demonstrate the difference between two resolutions (left). The top picture shows 800 x 600 pixels – a common setting used on 14- and 15-inch monitors; the bottom picture shows 1024 x 768, common for monitors one size bigger – 17-inch.

You can increase the resolution on any monitor, but it's unlikely that a 14- or 15-inch monitor will work very well at any resolution higher than 800 x 600 pixels. Some will try to show 1024 x 768 pixels, but text, icons and toolbar buttons appear very small without the extra screen size to show them. In addition, some 14- and 15-inch monitors can show a resolution

of only 1024 x 768 at a low refresh rate. If you really want to work at high resolutions, you will need a larger monitor. There are various sizes, but the next after the 15-inch is

## MEASURING MONITORS

Like TVs, monitors are measured across the screen diagonally. However, if you measure any monitor screen, you'll find that it's actually around an inch or so smaller than claimed. This is true for all screens except those built into laptop computers, which reflect the true measure of the screen diagonal. When looking at advertisements for monitors, look for 'Viewable Area' or 'Viewable Image Size' figures – these are the true screen size of the monitor.

the 17-inch. There are also monitors in the 19- to 21-inch range, but these are mainly aimed at professional computer users. Some of these large monitors are much more expensive. In addition, the longer cathode ray tube takes up a lot of space and is usually too long to fit conveniently on most desktops.

A 17-inch monitor is therefore a good compromise between size and cost; you can expect to pick one up for between $150 and $300. It's still a substantial purchase, but it is one that will last for many years. Even when you decide to replace your computer, you can continue to use your 17-inch monitor with the new system unit you purchase.

Installing a new monitor should prove no problem, since it has only two connecting cables – one for power and the other for carrying the signal from the computer's graphics card. Both of these will be supplied with the monitor.

## MONITOR DETECTION

If Windows doesn't detect your new monitor automatically, don't worry. Check the material that came with the monitor and you should find a floppy disk. This contains computer data files that make sure Windows knows how to get the best from your new monitor. If there's no floppy disk and no mention of how to set the monitor up correctly, call your supplier or the maker's helpline.

# Installing a new monitor

**Larger monitors enable you to see more information, more clearly. Here we show you how to make your computing easier on the eye.**

**1** The first thing to do when installing a new monitor is to remove the old one. Before doing so, make sure that both the monitor and computer are turned off

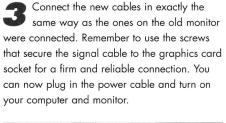

and the power cord is unplugged. That done, unplug the signal cable from the socket on the back of your computer. This cable might be screwed into place, so you will need to unscrew it before pulling it out.

**2** Here you can see the difference in screen size between the old and new monitors (the old monitor is in the background). You might also notice that your new monitor is much deeper than the old one. This is because the cathode ray tube used to display the image needs to be longer. As a general rule, the depth of monitors increases with their screen size, so considerable allowances need to be made for monitors with screens over 21 inches in size. You will also realize that the new monitor is heavier than the old one and so you might need help lifting it onto the desk.

**3** Connect the new cables in exactly the same way as the ones on the old monitor were connected. Remember to use the screws that secure the signal cable to the graphics card socket for a firm and reliable connection. You can now plug in the power cable and turn on your computer and monitor.

**4** Most new monitors are automatically detected by Windows, and as a result you will see messages appear on screen. You now need to tell Windows to use a higher resolution. Click the right-hand mouse button on an empty part of the Desktop and select Properties from the pop-up menu.

**5** When the Display Properties dialog box appears, click on the Settings tab. You will see a slider that allows you to change the size of the screen: click on the slider and drag it until 1024 by 768 pixels is shown. Press the OK button and Windows will change the screen to the new resolution.

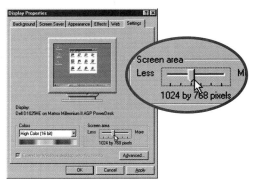

# Adding a Zip drive

Zip drives have been around for only a few years but they are now firmly established as a popular form of computer storage. And it's easy to see why.

Zip disks resemble a chunky floppy disk but they can hold up to 100MB or 250MB of information – 70 to 170 times more than an ordinary floppy. The drives cost between $100 and $150, while a 100MB disk costs around $15. The disks are also reusable, which means you can save and erase data as many times as you wish, just as you would with a floppy disk.

### ● Convenient storage
Zip disks are conveniently portable, too. You can easily fit two or three into a shirt pocket or bag, and the drive itself isn't a great deal bigger

*If your computer is starting to fill up with files or you're worried about losing data, why not add a Zip drive? For a small outlay and very little bother, you'll instantly gain lots of extra storage.*

*A Zip drive is a simple, plug-in device, and its high-capacity disks (right) are only a little larger than a conventional floppy.*

(about the size of a paperback book). In stark comparison to just about every other PC peripheral ever made, the Zip drive is quite a stylish addition to your desktop. Add all that up and you've got a very affordable, handy and desirable computer add-on.

In office use, the main function of Zip disks is to send big files from one place to another; at 100MB or 250MB each, they can take a lot of data – the text of several lengthy books, for example. But Zip disks have plenty of appeal for home computer users, too. They are very effective for backing up data (see box, left), being far bigger and far faster than the now old-fashioned floppies. You'd need 70 floppies to provide the same storage space as a 100MB Zip disk. Also, Zip disks are far more physically robust and less prone to magnetic corruption.

## ZIP DISK BACKUPS

While transferring data between computers might be the most common use of Zip disks, they also work extremely well as backup disks. Using Microsoft Backup (see Stage 2, pages 24-25) you simply work your way through the Wizard-style interface, choose the files, folders or entire drives you want to back up, and then select your Zip drive as the destination. If you're backing up a large amount of data, the software will simply prompt you to insert another disk when the current one is full. The software automatically splits large files across a number of disks (see below), so the process is almost entirely automatic.

It's so quick and easy that anyone with a Zip-equipped PC has no excuse for not performing regular backups.

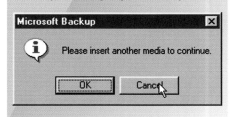

### ● A choice of drives
Zip drives come in various formats. The best type to buy as an add-on is an external type, which is connected to the computer by a cable. External Zip drives come in three versions.

A parallel port Zip drive connects to any PC via the parallel port socket. The SCSI (pronounced 'scuzzy') version needs a special SCSI connector, which typically takes the form of a card that plugs into a spare slot inside your PC and gives you a new socket at the back. The USB Zip Drive plugs into your PC's USB (Universal Serial Bus) socket.

When you've connected the drive and started the PC, the Zip drive icon will appear in the My Computer window. Its drive letter will depend on the devices fitted.

The main advantages of external Zip drives, whether parallel, SCSI or USB, are that they are a cinch to install and very portable. If you want to transfer big files to another computer which doesn't have a Zip, you can just take the drive along as well as the disk. A SCSI Zip drive is a lot faster than a parallel port one, but SCSI cards are tricky to install. The USB drive has the advantage of being 'hot-pluggable' – you can connect it without switching off your PC. You can also get an internal Zip drive, which occupies a 3½-inch bay at the front of your PC – the same size as a floppy drive. These tend to be a bit cheaper and will reduce the clutter on your desktop. But they aren't portable and can be quite tricky to install. You really need to get a professional to install an internal drive – which, of course, negates the saving of buying an external model.

### ● Using a Zip drive

Once your drive is installed (and, in the case of an external type, turned on), you can access it straight from the Desktop in the same way as for a floppy or CD-ROM drive. (You should always plug in the external drive before turning on the PC.)

The Zip drive icon will simply appear inside your My Computer folder, where it will automatically be assigned the next letter of the alphabet (following those used by devices such as your hard drive and CD-ROM drive) as its drive letter.

## PC TIPS

The original Zip drive does not have an on/off switch, so you must remember to unplug it after use to turn it off. Newer ZipPlus drives have an on/off switch and a smaller, more portable power unit. This is compatible with the original drive and can be bought separately.

# Installing an external, parallel port Zip drive

**Connecting this type of Zip drive takes a matter of minutes, but don't forget to turn off the PC before you begin and then restart afterward.**

**1** The Zip drive attaches to your computer's parallel port – if you already have a printer attached to this port, disconnect it.

**2** Connect the cable from the Zip drive to the parallel port, then tighten the plug's two security screws.

**3** If you had to disconnect your printer in Step 1, connect it to the parallel port on the back of the Zip drive.

**4** Plug the Zip drive's power adaptor into the power outlet and connect the small power cable to the side of the Zip drive.

**5** Switch on the power to the computer. Windows will detect the Zip drive. Follow the on-screen instructions – make sure you have your Windows CD-ROM and the Zip drive's setup disk handy.

**6** Once installation is complete, you can insert a Zip disk and copy files to and from it by using Windows' normal drag-and-drop procedures.

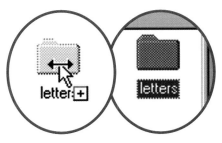

# Digital cameras

Digital cameras are the latest computer accessories to find their way into people's homes. A few years ago digital cameras cost over $2,000, but now a basic model sells at less than $100. So what do you get for your money?

A digital camera is similar to a traditional film-based camera, except that it stores your pictures electronically – that is, in a digital format that your PC can then use. Both traditional and digital cameras use a lens to focus the picture, an aperture to control how much light enters the camera, and a shutter to control the length of time the light enters. But that's where the similarities end.

In a film-based camera, the picture is projected onto a piece of plastic film with a light-sensitive coating. But in a digital camera, the picture is projected onto an electronic

*Imagine a camera that requires no film, has no processing costs, lets you send photographs around the world within a few minutes of taking the shot and even allows you to retouch the photograph using your computer. All this is possible with a digital camera.*

*From the front, digital cameras resemble conventional cameras but, unlike film cameras, the digital type has a screen on the back showing the picture you have captured. Shown here are the Kodak DC3400 and Canon PowerShot A10, which both have distinct styling.*

component called a charge-coupled device (CCD) that scans and converts the image into an electronic data file.

### ● Color by numbers
The file consists of numbers that represent the color and brightness of all the spots that make up the picture. This information is then stored in memory – like the memory in your PC – inside the camera.

Photographic film needs to be processed and developed. First, the film is chemically 'fixed' so that light does not affect it any further. And second, the pictures on the film are stored as negatives and have to be printed onto special photographic paper. Although this can be done

in as little as an hour, it's not cheap and it requires a laboratory.

With a digital camera, you simply connect it to your PC and 'download' the digital pictures. Transferring the pictures to your computer is quick and costs nothing, although if you print them with your color printer, you have to pay for the paper and colored inks.

### ● Private view
Many digital cameras include a built-in liquid crystal display (LCD) that allows you to view a picture as soon as you take it. This means that if you don't like it, you just erase it from the camera's memory and shoot it again. Later, with the appropriate software,

you can view the pictures instantly on your computer monitor.

For example, let's say you want to send a favorite aunt in Australia the latest family photos. Simply point your camera at the clan and shoot – within a fraction of a second, the picture is taken.

### ● Automatic settings

Like most 35mm cameras, everything is automatic, but it can take a little time for a digital camera to work out the light settings and automatically adjust the aperture size and shutter speed. Then there may be a further

## CHECKPOINT ✔

Here are some of the key features of digital cameras that you should consider before buying one:

☑ Resolution: the number of dots making up the image. The higher the resolution, the better. Very cheap (approximately $100) digital cameras may have a resolution as low as 640 x 480, while midrange, higher priced models should have 1024 x 768 as a minimum resolution.

☑ Image storage: the number of pictures the camera will store. On many cameras you can store more images if you choose a lower (worse) resolution. Standard storage ranges are around 50–200 pictures at low resolution (640 x 480 or thereabouts) and 5-20 pictures at maximum resolution.

☑ Memory cards: Nearly all digital cameras let you plug in a credit-card-sized memory card to store extra images. Check the capacity and price of these additional cards.

☑ Review panel: Nearly all digital cameras feature an LCD panel where you can check if the picture has come out correctly. Such panels are relatively small; others fold out to give a larger viewing area.

*If your digital camera has a viewing screen, you can check the picture as soon as you have taken it. Then, if you don't like the result, you can simply erase it.*

*After installing the software supplied, the pictures can be downloaded into a PC for viewing or printing. Each of them can be viewed in 'thumbnail' form (above). You can zoom in on any individual frame to see it in more detail (right). Some programs include extensive features for display, editing and printing out – as well as for changing the camera settings.*

4- to 8-second delay while the camera converts the photograph into a digital format. If your digital camera has a built-in LCD preview screen and you see, for example, that one of the family members wasn't smiling, you can simply erase the photo from the memory and take it again!

### ● Downloading

When you've taken your quota of photos or when the camera's memory is full, it's time to transfer your shots to your PC. To do this, simply plug the cord supplied into the camera, then plug the other end into your computer (see pages 102-103). You can then run the software supplied and transfer the photos.

Once the photos are copied to your computer, you can erase the originals from the camera and start shooting again. In the meantime, the

### ARE THEY AS GOOD AS THE REAL THING?

Yes and no...
If you're looking for award-winning, high-quality printed photographs, then a digital camera does not meet the same standards as a film camera. First, photographic film can record much more detail than even the best digital cameras. Digital pictures can sometimes appear 'fuzzy' when studied closely.

Second, the lenses fitted to most digital cameras are not as good as those on conventional cameras. This degrades the final image. Only the most sophisticated digital cameras have lenses as good as those on film cameras. But if you're looking for photos that are adequate for a range of jobs, perhaps for a newsletter, advertisement, photo-ID or to send a picture by email to a family member or friend, then a digital camera is ideal. There are no film and development costs, and you can duplicate the photographs by copying a file on your computer.

photographs can be viewed on your computer. If you have a color printer, you will be able to print copies – remembering that the higher the resolution of the printer, the better the quality of the printout.

Because the pictures are digital, you can even edit them with a graphics package. For example, you could brush out that spot on your nose or even copy the spot to a less deserving family member!

Also, if you have access to the Internet, your email software will let you attach a photograph to your message and send it to your aunt.

# Adding a digital camera

**A digital camera can be a useful addition or just a great gadget to play with. Either way, connecting it to your PC means you can view, edit and print your own pictures.**

During the past couple of years the digital camera has exploded onto the market, offering the user error-free photography and much, much more. The ability to take a picture, check it on a built-in LCD screen and then either save or retake it, is quite a draw for gadget-loving computer users. Add to that the ability to transfer pictures onto your PC – to include in a document, Web page or email – and they become almost essential buys.

In fact, for the would-be digital photographer, the only potential complication comes in the various ways that digital cameras connect to the computer. Most include all

*Connecting a digital camera to your computer is easy. You will then be able to download your own pictures and work on them with your favorite art package.*

## CHECKPOINT ✔

Before splurging on a digital camera, make sure to check the following for a trouble-free installation process:
✔ What sort of connecting cable does the camera come with?
✔ Does your PC have the appropriate socket, such as serial and/or USB?
✔ If the camera does not have a cable, does it have another means of transferring images to your computer?
✔ If so, is this method suitable for your computer?

If you're in any doubt over these questions, be sure to ask the dealer you are buying the camera from to confirm its compatibility with your computer, and ask for a money-back guarantee if the camera does not prove suitable.

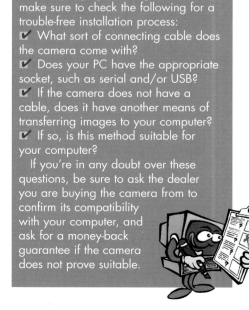

the cables and software disks or CD-ROMs that you will need, but you must still check that you can connect it to your computer with the minimal amount of fuss before deciding which one to buy.

● **Latest technology**
Digital cameras are evolving rapidly, but the most common way of connecting one to a PC is still by means of a serial cable. This is simple, as we show opposite, but relatively slow and it means you might have to switch the computer off before making the connection. The USB connection is becoming increasingly

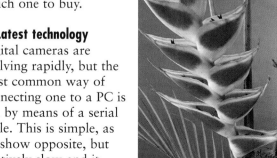

*With a digital camera, an inkjet printer and good quality paper, quite astonishing results can be achieved almost instantly.*

more common. This type of cable is much faster and you do not need to switch off your PC to make the connection. All modern PCs have USB capability, but with an older one you might have to use the serial connection.

In the exercise opposite, we show how uncomplicated it is to connect the camera to your computer by using a serial cable. Once this is done, you can use the camera's software to see thumbnail-sized previews of the photos you have taken and decide which ones to transfer to your computer's hard drive, and which ones you don't want to keep. Most cameras also come with photo-editing programs. Depending on the make and model of your camera, you might find that such software varies widely in capability. The simplest cameras allow you to vary the brightness and contrast in your photographs, but others include special effects which make it possible for you to twist and distort the photos in weird and wonderful ways.

It's also important to note that if you simply want to print out your photographs, then you can bypass the connection process and buy a simple photograph printer, such as the HP Photosmart. This allows you to connect your camera directly to the printer and print out high-quality prints of the traditional size.

# Connecting a camera to your PC

**Taking pictures with a digital camera is one thing – making the connection and downloading them to your computer is another. Here we show you how easy this can be.**

THE WAY that you connect your digital camera to a computer will vary from camera to camera. Most cameras use a serial cable. One end has a normal serial socket (like that from an external modem), and the other end has a special socket that fits into the camera. A USB connection is increasingly common. Some digital cameras, mainly those models aimed at users with notebook computers, use a PC Card, and a few have an infrared transmitter to send the signal. Obviously, the latter is only suitable if your computer is equipped with an infrared receiver.

In this exercise, we demonstrate how to connect a digital camera and then transfer its images using a serial cable connection.

**1** Most digital cameras require both the computer and camera to be switched off before the camera is attached (refer to your digital camera's manual).

**2** Locate a spare serial socket on the back of your computer and plug the digital camera's cable into this socket. Tighten the integral screws to secure the plug in place.

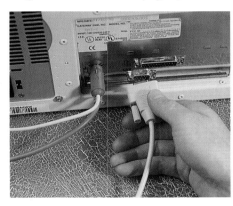

**3** Open the small plastic flap on the side of the camera to gain access to the sockets. Plug the other end of the cable into the socket on the camera. Make sure you are gentle with the camera, because its sockets can be delicate.

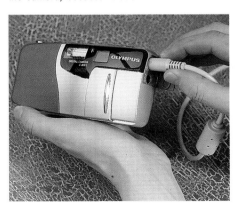

**4** You might be able to plug your camera into an electrical outlet (using a special adaptor supplied with it). This is a good idea when you are downloading pictures, because the camera can use batteries quickly.

## THE MOVING IMAGE OPTION

The Moving Image Option is an alternative to digital cameras for capturing photos to transfer to your PC. This comes in the form of digital video cameras – many of which can also capture still photographs. They compare well in price and features, and also provide the additional advantage of a video camera, including, of course, the benefit of sound recording.

**5** Cameras come with different programs for transferring photos to the computer. It's easy to preview the photos in the camera and select the ones you want.

# Understanding scanners

**A scanner is one of the most useful and exciting tools you can add to your computer. It enables you to copy pictures and photographs and incorporate them into your letters and documents.**

A scanner works like a photocopier but, instead of copying a picture onto another sheet of paper, it copies it onto your computer.

It works by passing a bright light over your picture. The light that is reflected back is picked up by the scanner's sensor. The brighter areas of the picture reflect lots of light and the darker areas reflect less.

The scanner converts the picture into data that your PC can understand and sends it down the cable to your computer. The scanning software running on your computer rebuilds the data into a picture you can see on your screen. You can then save the picture on your computer's hard drive and incorporate it into other documents on your PC.

### ● What could I use a scanner for?
Scanners have many uses. You can use them to copy photos, drawings, graphs or pages of text. Once you have scanned in your pictures, you can use software to do all sorts of useful and fun things to them, from

*The C Pen manual scanner is really a mini digital camera with memory. You pass it over the text to be scanned and transfer it to your PC via an infrared connection.*

changing their brightness and contrast to using special effects to make spectacular changes. If you have Internet access, you can send your scanned pictures across the world in seconds via email (see Stage 1, pages 154-156).

### ● Flatbed scanners
There are several varieties of scanner for the business and professional user, but for the home or small office, the flatbed scanner is the obvious and sensible choice. It is versatile, scans at high quality and is reasonably priced. The flatbed scanner looks and works in much the same way as a small photocopier. You lift the lid, place your original on a sheet of glass and the light sensor moves under the image. The flatbed scanner can also be used to scan books, magazines and mounted photographs.

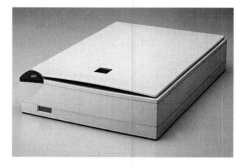

*Once found only in commercial offices, the flatbed scanner has now become a popular piece of equipment for many home PC owners.*

### ● Flatbed software
Most flatbed scanners are also supplied with a number of software packages that help you get the most out of the hardware. There is software that makes it easier to use the scanner and provides you with easy access to special effects for use in all kinds of documents.

Flatbed scanners used to be too expensive for all but the graphics professional. However, in recent years prices have fallen dramatically – to the extent that you can now

# The versatile scanner

**You may find that a scanner proves to be the best addition you've ever made to your computer system. Everyone in the family will find a way to use it – here are just a few ideas to get you started.**

*All-in-one devices like the one above, combine scanner, printer and fax/copier in the same casing. You can save a lot of space and minimize all the wires with such hardware.*

buy a good flatbed for as little as $100 and a superior, high-quality one for between $200 and $500.

### ● All-in-ones

Space is always at a premium in the home or office. A flatbed scanner is relatively small but it still takes up desk space – as do your printer and your fax/copier.

However, if you combine all three devices in one casing, you can give yourself some more much-needed elbow room. A wide range of such all-in-one devices is now available from leading manufacturers, such as Hewlett-Packard and Xerox. They cost between $500 and $600 – the quality rising with the price.

## OPTICAL CHARACTER RECOGNITION

This is the phrase, often shortened to OCR, given to software that can look at a page of text, 'read' it and convert it into text that you can edit in your word processor. This software can save lots of time-consuming retyping when text isn't available on disk.

It works by looking at the shape of the letters on the page and trying to match them against shapes it knows. This means that if the document it is reading is of poor quality, the OCR software often can't recognize the letter at all, or it makes a guess. For example, OCR software can easily confuse a slightly blurred 'cl' with a 'd'.

### School essays

Adding an illustration can make a world of difference to all sorts of documents, from school essays to business reports.

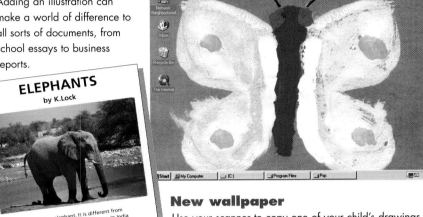

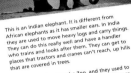

### New wallpaper

Use your scanner to copy one of your child's drawings and you can use it as your desktop wallpaper – it sure beats sticking the picture on the fridge!

### Newsletters

If you help publish a club newsletter, a church magazine or fanzine, use your scanner to bring it to life. 'Published' photos of events always prove popular.

### Personalized greeting cards

Scan family photos and print your own greeting cards; you'll find that a scanner is the ideal partner for a color ink-jet printer.

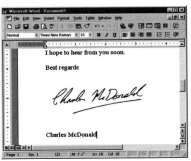

### Digitizing your signature

If you send many faxes directly from your PC, you can scan a copy of your signature and add it to your letters.

# Keeping it clean

*Due to static electricity, your computer acts as a magnet for dust. It's important to keep it clean, not just for appearance, but to avoid malfunctions that can easily be caused by dirt and grime.*

*A computer attracts dust and if neglected this can prevent it from working properly.*

**M**ost computers are a dull gray color that seems deliberately designed to look dirty quickly. There is a reason for this boring choice of color, however. International regulations previously stated that in order to limit eye strain there should be as little color contrast as possible between a monitor and its surrounding apparatus. But because computers are dull gray, they can look distinctly grimy unless they are kept clean. The effect is made even worse by the slightly textured surface of the plastic – again, it's designed to cut down reflections and reduce eye strain, but it also allows dirt to become engrained very easily. Dust and grime on the computer not only look unpleasant, but can also do real harm. Excess dirt on the fan or power sockets, for instance, can sometimes cause components to fail, while the inner mechanisms of the mouse will not work effectively if dust gets trapped inside and hampers smooth movement.

● **Grime prevention**

You can clean the outer casing of the computer with an everyday household cleaner and a dustfree cloth, but the PC's monitor, keyboard and back of the system unit need more gentle treatment.

For the screen and keyboard, you should use a special antistatic spray that reduces static and repels dust. You can buy these sprays, designed for stereo and computer equipment, from most electrical dealers. A can of pressurized air is also good for cleaning inaccessible areas, but you need to take care not to deliver the blast of air too close to delicate electronic components.

The caring computer user can buy a mini vacuum cleaner for sucking out dirt from between the keyboard keys. These are available from most computer stores for around $16.

Disk drives also benefit from regular cleaning. The best method is to use a head-cleaning diskette with cleaning fluid once a week. The diskette is available from computer stores for around $30.

● **Spill drill**

It's very easy to spill coffee, tea and other liquids over the keyboard but they can be cleaned off easily with a special computer cleaning fluid, as long as the drips are easily accessible.

## CLEANING YOUR MOUSE

Your mouse gets dirtier more quickly than any other part of your computer, because it constantly rolls back and forth over the mouse pad, collecting dust. It needs to be kept really clean if it is to continue working properly. It is actually the internal parts that you need to keep clean, especially the rollers. This is done by simply removing the ball and scraping the grimy rollers with the head of a match. Refer back to our guide (see Stage 1, page 91) for step-by-step tips on mouse maintenance.

## ● Screen wipes

A particular problem with the screen is the build-up of static electricity. Its most obvious effect is that it attracts dust and makes the screen dirty very quickly. Since you look at the screen whenever you're working on the computer, it is worth getting into the habit of cleaning it regularly – at least a couple of times a month.

The easiest and cheapest way to clean the screen is to use an antistatic, lint-free screen wipe. These are typically sold in packs of 100 for around $10 and are widely available in consumer-electronics stores or through mail-order office and computer supply companies.

If you don't have a special cleaning fluid on hand, then a glass-cleaning fluid and a soft cloth will do almost as good a job – but do not use any cleaner that is not specifically sold for use on glass.

A longer-term way of dealing with screen dirt is to put a protective screen filter in front of the screen. Such filters are designed mainly to reduce glare and to shield you from potentially harmful emissions, but they also reduce static electricity, so less dust is attracted to your screen. You will still have to clean your screen, but not quite as often.

## ● Where there's smoke

Computer users who smoke risk the added danger of tobacco ash and smoke being drawn into the computer through the floppy disk drive (the cooling fans operating inside the computer suck air – and smoke – through the computer). So you should do everything you can to keep cigarettes away from your computer at all times.

# Keep your machine clean

**Try to clean your computer on a regular basis – don't just wait until it's filthy. Here we show you a good cleaning routine to try.**

**1** Turn off your computer, making sure it is also unplugged. If you use a spray while the computer is still on, you not only risk getting an electric shock, but you could also damage your computer.

**2** Start on the monitor, using a special antistatic spray. Squirt a small bit on to a lint-free cloth and then immediately wipe it over the screen. This is safer than squirting the cleaner directly onto the screen, because excess liquid might drip between the screen and the monitor casing, causing damage. Avoid using too much cleaner or you'll create smears.

**3** Now start on the keyboard. You should use a mini vacuum cleaner, if you have one, to suck out all of the dust and debris. Don't press down too hard between the keys unless your cleaner has a special narrow attachment. If any of the keys are especially dirty, wipe them with a cloth or use special keyboard fluid. Do not use any liquid other than special computer cleaning fluids.

**4** Cleaning the casing of your computer is not such a delicate task: the casing can be cleaned much like any other appliance. To remove stubborn dirt from the casing, rub gently with a cloth.

## WHAT NOT TO DO

**NEVER** use a general household cleaning liquid on the screen, keyboard or connecting slots. Household cleaners could damage circuitry and encourage static electricity.
**NEVER** use an alcohol-based fluid on the screen. The screen has an invisible coating that can be damaged by these cleaners.
**NEVER** clean anything while the power is on.
**NEVER** place an ashtray or hold a cigarette just in front of your computer's floppy disk drive.

**NEVER** use a household feather duster to clean your computer as it will have gathered dirt from around the house. The static on the computer will attract dust from the duster, making the situation even worse.
**NEVER** try to push a feather duster, or anything else, into the inside of your computer.
**NEVER** get water or other liquids inside any part of your computer. Even small splashes can cause damage.

# Adding a subwoofer

*Adding a subwoofer is an easy, 5-minute job, with the reward of deeper sound for your music CDs and your games' soundtracks. If you're serious about multimedia, here's how to get more bass.*

Although your PC probably came with a pair of speakers, it's unlikely they are particularly powerful or of a high quality. They are, after all, bundled with the PC, and manufacturers give greater consideration to the small amount of desktop space they take up rather than their sound quality.

Standard PC speakers tend to be relatively quiet, tinny and have a poor frequency range. In particular, their small size limits the diameter of the speakers inside: the smaller the size, generally the poorer the bass response. Consequently, multimedia programs – and particularly games – can sound rather harsh and lifeless.

### ● Pump up the bass

One solution is to buy newer and better speakers, but although this will certainly help, the central problem remains: speakers with good bass output are too big to sit on your desktop. The best solution is to add a subwoofer. This is a specially designed amplifier and speaker, which is intended to work with your existing desktop speakers. Some are so simple to install that you have to make no further changes to your system other than finding space for it (see PC Tips, opposite).

You need only connect the subwoofer to your computer and – without the need for any extra programs (there is no software to

install when you add a subwoofer) – your PC's sound will be transformed.

### ● One is enough

You need only one subwoofer, even with stereo desktop speakers. This is because a subwoofer plays only bass notes; your ear continues to use the sound from the desktop speakers to detect the sound's stereo position.

You can alter how much the subwoofer affects the sound with simple controls – the on-off switch and, generally, a volume control knob that you turn to adjust the sound level. Don't turn it up too loud, though. Just a small amount of bass makes a lot of difference. Once you have heard this remarkable change in sound, you may never want to switch the subwoofer off.

## BUYING A SUBWOOFER

All new multimedia PCs come with speakers. Adding a subwoofer is a simple do-it-yourself matter and will cost around $20. If you don't have a pair of speakers, you can buy a combined speaker and subwoofer bundle from most computer stores (expect to pay $60 or so). Of course, you should be sure that your computer has a sound card (check in the manual).

If your computer doesn't have a sound card, it's worth getting a dealer to supply and install one, together with speakers and a subwoofer. Adding a sound card requires opening the computer system unit and is best left to the professionals. The total cost should be around $150, including installation.

# Installing a subwoofer

**Assuming that you already have a pair of speakers attached to your computer, we'll show you how to install a subwoofer. The exact process may vary with different makes of equipment, particularly the color and labeling of the cables, so if in doubt, consult the manufacturer's manual.**

**1** Before you install any new hardware you should make sure your computer is turned off and unplugged. Remember: your speakers probably have their own power supply to turn off and unplug.

**2** At the rear of your computer, locate the cable that links your sound card to your speakers. Unplug it and replace it with the cable that came with your subwoofer.

**3** Plug the other end of that cable into the input socket on the subwoofer. There may be sockets on the subwoofer for connecting it to a stereo system, but these will be a different size. You will have to plug the subwoofer, as well as your original speakers, into the electrical outlet.

**4** Now plug the cable from the subwoofer into one of the speakers. Remember that, unlike stereo speakers, computers generally have one stereo cable going into the first speaker, then out of that speaker to the other, so make sure that this cable is also in place.

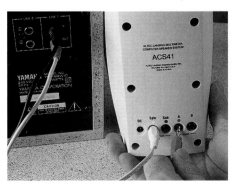

**5** Your subwoofer is best placed on the floor (see PC Tips box), under your desk. As you can see below, there isn't much room for anything else when it's on the desk! It will also need to be plugged into the electrical outlet. There is a power switch, usually on the front, which you should turn on. There is also a volume control to adjust.

## PC TIPS

The subwoofer is fairly large, so you probably won't want to put it on your desktop. Most people usually put it under the desk. The only problem with this is that the subwoofer can make an awful lot of noise and vibration, so be aware of this if there are people on the floor below who could be disturbed.

# Making music

*Connecting a simple piano-type keyboard to your computer can turn it into a sophisticated music maker.*

Nearly all modern music has been influenced by computers in some way. Musicians such as the Pet Shop Boys and Jean-Michel Jarre have long been using computers to generate almost every type of sound, but even acoustic music has benefited, as computers are used extensively during record production to mix and process music tracks.

However, the most common musical use of computers has been to link them to a piano- or synthesizer-type keyboard. The PC can then be used to store a whole series of notes and play them back later – a technique called sequencing.

*Controller keyboards, such as the RolandED PC-180A, don't have any built-in sound synthesizer of their own. Instead, you use them to input notes to your computer, which can then play music through its sound card's synthesizer chip.*

## ● A one-man band

Sequencing means that a single musician can record parts for several different instruments and play them back all at the same time so that it sounds like a whole band. It also means that a would-be musician no longer has to have the manual dexterity to play lots of different instruments. Once the basic notes have been entered, the computer can be used to edit the music (taking out any wrong notes, for example), then play it back fluently and at any speed. This has opened up enormous possibilities for home music-making. With a moderate grasp of the principles, even the inability to carry a tune need no longer be a barrier to having fun with your music-making.

## ● Computer requirements

Any computer able to run Windows 98 can run music sequencing software. You will, however, need a sound card. Fortunately, all the modern multimedia PCs have a built-in sound card, which will be fine to start with. This has a synthesizer chip, which can be 'played' by sequencing software. You don't even need a music keyboard because you can tell the computer which notes to play using the mouse,

and it sends the information to the sound card. You hear the music as if there were a tiny – and perfect – musician inside. For creating music, however, this approach is not really practical. A music keyboard lets you input notes more naturally. The computer can also record the key you've hit, how hard you've hit it and for how long. You can then replay this information using any sound available on your sound card, such as a guitar, trumpet or even a barking dog.

Once it's on the computer, you can edit it, perhaps changing the tempo or moving the melody up an octave. The key to all this is a system called **MIDI**, which is what makes music on a computer so flexible and efficient. The important thing to

---

### WHAT IT MEANS

**MIDI**

*Standing for Music Instrument Digital Interface, MIDI is really two things: a standard way of connecting one MIDI instrument to another, and a type of computer file that stores the notes of a piece of music.*

*A MIDI file stores details of which note is being played and its sound characteristics – such as how strongly it is being played. You could think of it, if you wish, as the electronic equivalent of a musical score.*

*Your computer sound card is a MIDI instrument in its own right. With the correct cable, you can connect it to any other MIDI-compatible instrument.*

This top-quality Roland keyboard costs over $1,200,
but it is a professional model with many advanced features.

HOW BIG ARE
MIDI FILES?

Because they record instructions rather than sounds, MIDI files take up very little space. A MIDI file for an entire CD's worth of an orchestral composition can actually be stored on a floppy disk.

remember when you play a MIDI file, is that the sound quality depends on the caliber of the synthesizer. If you are unhappy with the sound quality of your MIDI synthesizer you can get your PC to send the MIDI information down a cable to a MIDI music keyboard for a better sound.

### ● Keyboard types

You can choose from a wide range of keyboards to suit all budgets and aspirations.

Cheapest of the options is the controller keyboard, which doesn't actually make a sound itself – it is the computer that makes the sound. The controller keyboard plugs directly into your computer and allows you to play the notes on the keyboard and

then edit them on the computer screen. When you have finished, you can play the notes through the sound card's synthesizer chip and out of your computer's audio speakers.

A controller keyboard is basically all you need to get started, although you can buy several extra

This mid-priced Yamaha keyboard is programmed with sounds suited to a wide range of music, from classical to pop.

components to increase the sounds available. The next step up is a music keyboard that has synthesized sounds and effects built in. This type is very popular for home use. However, many low-cost models don't work with MIDI. For computer use, it's essential to have a MIDI keyboard.

You will find a wide variety of MIDI keyboards available from music and computer stores. When buying, remember to tell the sales assistant that you need a cable to connect it to your computer. Some music keyboards designed for home use plug straight into the sound card's joystick port and come with a suitable cable, but many don't come with a cable.

### ● Built-in sounds

MIDI keyboards differ widely in price, depending on the quality of the sound inside. The cheapest have a limited range of sounds – more akin to the home organ – and might not sound much better than the synthesizer chip on your sound card.

At the top of the range are professional and semiprofessional keyboards. These often have almost unlimited sound possibilities, because you can tweak the built-in settings in many different ways.

You can also buy add-on hardware called MIDI expanders. These devices connect to the PC in just the same way, but they don't have a keyboard of their own. They are mostly used when you simply want to increase the number, or quality, of sounds that you can hear.

## MUSIC SOFTWARE

The most important piece of software for the computer musician is a MIDI sequencer. This program is used to record the notes you play on the music keyboard, edit them to correct any mistakes, and then to save the MIDI file on your hard drive. If you're not comfortable with the idea of playing a piano keyboard, most sequencers also let you create music by placing notes on a musical stave on screen.

You also use the MIDI sequencer to play the MIDI files you create, getting it to direct the notes through your sound card's synthesizer chip or out through a MIDI cable to a music keyboard.

You can move and/or copy the notes around at any time, so if you write a song, you need only write the chorus once and then copy and paste it as many times as you need.

The best aspect of a MIDI sequencer is that you can record different parts to build up a piece of music one instrument at a time. For example, you can record a bass part first, and then replay it through the synthesizer, while recording a string section at the same time. What's more, the MIDI sequencer will always play back the music perfectly.

A sequencer screen can look confusing at first. All the on-screen tools act just like the equipment available in a real-life recording studio.

*Once you have bought a MIDI keyboard, it takes only a matter of minutes to connect it to your computer. You can then install the software and be ready to make beautiful music.*

# Connecting a MIDI keyboard

On the previous pages, we have shown how adding a MIDI music keyboard to your computer can open up a new world of sound. However, the MIDI keyboard and computer must be connected before you start exploring the joys of creating music on your PC, using music composer programs and sequencing software.

### ● Types of connection

Some MIDI keyboards are connected to your computer via a cable that is permanently wired into the back of the keyboard itself. More commonly, a special cable (called a MIDI cable) is used. This has a pair of round 5-pin plugs on one end that fit into the music keyboard's MIDI sockets.

The cable from the keyboard plugs into your PC's joystick socket, which is internally connected to the sound card. Once connected to each other, MIDI music information – including which notes you play, how long you hold the keys down and how hard you hit them – is able to pass along the MIDI cable between the sound card and the keyboard.

## THE SOFTWARE

The software you choose will play an important part in making sure that your computer and the music keyboard work properly together.

You will need to tell the software – usually a sequencer – that you have a MIDI music keyboard attached. You will almost certainly need some of the information from the music keyboard's manual to set up the software so that it knows how to get the most from your music keyboard.

Connecting the keyboard to your PC is a relatively simple plug-in process, as shown in the step-by-step guide opposite. You then need to install the music software that you intend to use – either a program that came with the keyboard or a separately purchased MIDI sequencer.

### ● Software setup

All multimedia computers have a sound card that is suitable for use with a MIDI keyboard. If the sound card has been properly set up under Windows, and is working with other applications, it is ready to work with your music keyboard. However, you will need to set up the computer using the software and instructions supplied with the keyboard.

Once your new keyboard is set up, and with a sequencing program to organize the notes you enter, you'll soon be composing your own music, laying it down instrument by instrument, and then combining it all together using the power of your PC. The only limit is your imagination.

# Making the keyboard connections

**Thanks to MIDI connectors being standardized, plugging in a music keyboard is simple and takes just moments.**

YOUR FIRST step should be to read the instruction manuals that came with the keyboard and sound card (or that part of your computer's manual that covers the sound card). The physical connections (shown below) are quite simple to make – and even easier for those keyboards that have a cable permanently attached, because you can skip Steps 2 and 3 in the connection sequence.

You will also need to read the instructions for your choice of music sequencing software, making sure it knows from where the data is input. Again, music keyboards specifically made for connection to a computer often come bundled with music software and have more detailed instructions about getting started once the connections are made.

**1** Turn everything off before you start. Always adopt a 'safety first' attitude when you add anything to your PC. Make sure everything is properly closed down and switched off before trying to connect any cables. Unplug the computer to avoid the risk of damage, not only to yourself but also to your PC.

**2** Most MIDI keyboards use a cable that's specifically made to connect the keyboards to PCs (you may have to buy one as it usually isn't included with MIDI keyboards – expect to pay around $30). It has a chunky PC-type plug at one end and a pair of smaller, round plugs on the other.

**3** Locate the MIDI sockets on the back of your music keyboard. There will be two or three close together, marked MIDI IN, MIDI OUT and – if there's a third – MIDI THRU. MIDI THRU is used only for connecting extra MIDI devices. IN and OUT refer to signals passing into and out of the keyboard (see box below).

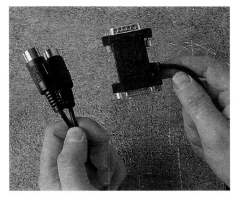

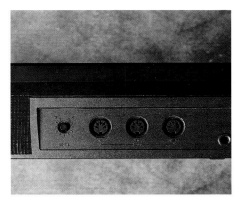

**4** Fit the plug marked MIDI IN into the socket marked MIDI OUT, and the MIDI OUT plug into the MIDI IN socket. This might seem confusing, but there's a way of understanding it to make it seem quite simple, see MIDI IN to MIDI OUT box (right).

**5** Look at the back of your computer and locate the joystick socket. It will be close to where the speakers connect. The chunky end of the cable plugs into this socket.

If you already have a joystick connected to your computer, remove it. Some MIDI cables have a pass-through socket that allows you to plug the joystick into it. If not, you'll have to swap between the two plugs manually.

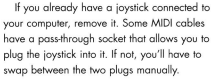

## MIDI IN TO MIDI OUT

At first glance, the way MIDI cables and sockets connect may seem a little confusing. You connect the MIDI IN plug from the computer's sound card to the MIDI OUT socket on the music keyboard, and vice versa.

It will help to think of the MIDI connections as a flow of musical notes: the notes you play on the music keyboard flow out of its MIDI OUT socket into the MIDI IN plug of the sound card cable and then into the computer. Likewise, when using the computer to 'play' the keyboard with a musical composition program, notes flow from the computer, along the sound card cable and out of its MIDI OUT plug into the keyboard's MIDI IN socket.

# Home Learning & Leisure

# Fun with math

**Kids want to play games; parents want kids to learn from their PCs. With CD-ROM software that combines the two aims, you can lay the groundwork for formal school work by teaching premath skills to children as young as three.**

Getting a head start in any school subject is useful, but with math being central to so many other subjects in later school life, any grounding you can give your young children is bound to pay dividends later. Many parents are aware of math programs for juniors and seniors, but even preschoolers have their own CD-ROM software.

### ● Math with a mutt

*Blue's 123 Time Activities* – produced by collaboration between Humongous Entertainment and the Nickelodeon TV channel – aims to give preschoolers fundamental know-how that they can build upon later in the classroom. In this CD software, Blue – the endearingly blue dog – is your child's companion on a tour around the Backyard Fair.

*In Blue's 123 Time Activities, the aim is to solve math puzzles so that you can win enough Blue Dollars to buy blue canine companion prizes.*

After a friendly welcome from Steve Burns, the zany Nickelodeon TV presenter, you're introduced to Blue and given a Blue Dollar to get your visit off to a good start (you collect more as rewards for completing the math puzzles that follow). Then you sign in and enter the Fair, a collection of half a dozen stalls, each manned with different cartoon characters. As your child travels from one stall to

*In the Mother May I game, basic counting and addition skills are involved in guiding Blue along the number line according to numbers called out by the Pail cartoon character.*

*Modern PC-based programs are far removed from the traditional methods of teaching mathematics. Some of them are so much fun that the essential key to success with numbers – practice – isn't a problem.*

another, there's a different problem to solve, each one designed to encourage math-oriented thinking.

### ● Math skills

The most basic math skill covered is counting, which plays a part in several of the puzzles. For example, at the *Mother May I* game stall, you guide Blue along a number line, depending on the number called out by the Pail cartoon. You must add each new number to your current position on the line to move correctly. Get to the other end of the line before the Shovel cartoon to win extra Blue Dollars.

It's not just the more obvious counting and addition premath skills that are taught – other math concepts are included, such as sets and subsets, and color, shape and number matching. For example, in *Baby Bear's Card Game*, you can match either shapes or numbers to get rid of all your cards. The puzzles get subtly more advanced as the game – and your child's skill level – progresses.

Blue collects the Blue Dollars in her backpack. Once the riches have mounted up, you can visit the Prize Tent and use them to earn prizes for Blue. Even here, math is needed: you must count money out of Blue's backpack to pay for different components for the prize. If you don't have enough, you can return to the Backyard Fair to earn more.

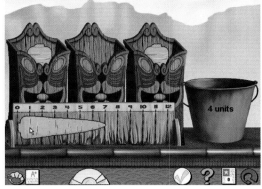
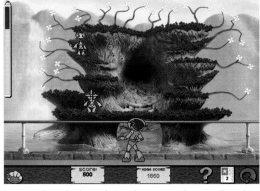

*It's time to feed the Woozerp's but before you can play the game – where you throw food into their wide-open mouths – you'll need to carefully measure it first.*

### ● Friendly encouragement

The software developers have taken care not to discourage younger children who may have difficulty with the puzzles. The cartoon characters always give friendly support and encouragement to try again following any wrong answers, and a smaller number of Blue Dollars are awarded when you lose a game - the aim being to provide a reward for trying hard.

The manual also includes suggestions for real-world parent and child activities based upon each of the puzzles in the game. Few need anything more elaborate than some straws or a wire clothes hanger.

### ● For older children

*Knowledge Adventure's Math Blaster* is aimed at slightly older children, with a succession of three programs covering ages 6-7, 7-8, and 8-9. They

*Aimed at older children, Math Blaster has a slick graphics interface and a combination of math puzzles with more sophisticated arcade-style gaming.*

share the same approach with *Blue's 123 Time Activities* – using game play as the incentive for getting young kids interested in math.

In keeping with the demands of an older age group, the graphics – characters and scenes – are more smoothly shaded than the chunkier but easier to see graphics in *Blue's 123 Time Activities*. The soundtrack is also less childish and uses modern music to good effect. These extra-cool factors should help it appeal to kids who are growing up quickly.

In *Mission 1: Comic Critter Challenge*, the scenario is an intergalactic zoo, where the animals have become too lazy. There are five games, each designed with specific skills in mind. For instance, in the Gnat Zapper race simple addition and subtraction questions are posed, and by giving the right answer, your child's character races faster across the screen.

### ● Better game play

*Math Blaster* is designed with the idea that older kids are attracted to arcade games, and that they have the motor skills needed to play such games successfully. The math lessons are combined with arcade-style gameplay. In many of the games, the first step is to solve the math puzzles. Only then can your child go on to play the game.

For example, the principles of measuring length, weight, and temperature are covered at the Woozerp enclosure. Once your child has successfully measured out the Woozerp's food, he'll need to pay for it, counting out the right number of nickels and dimes. Only when that's done, is it time to play the game,

throwing food to the hungry Woozerps clambering on their island. The game itself is trickier than the math puzzles – so you can be sure your child will come back to the puzzles in order to have another chance at the game.

Throughout *Math Blaster*, Activity Cards are awarded for good math performance. Once you have enough Activity Cards you can try the *Tickle Tag* – a PacMan-like game that includes the animals you have met in the zoo.

Like *Blue's 123 Time Activities*, *Math Blaster* keeps track of which puzzles have been tackled, and the math puzzles get harder over time. There's a report card that shows scores and progress through the difficulty levels. Beyond the ready-made puzzles and games, *Math Blaster* also includes a number of extras. For example, there are math question sheets that you can print out for your child to do away from the computer.

### CONTACT POINTS

**Blue's 123 Time Activities**
Humongous Entertainment
Tel: 1 800 499 8386
Price: $19.99
www.humongous.com

**Math Blaster Mission 1: Comic Critter Challenge**
Knowledge Adventure
Tel: 1 800 545 7677
Price: $19.99
www.knowledgeadventure.com

$(1-a)(1+a)=?$

# Successful math exams

*It's often difficult for parents to help children with schoolwork, but your computer can run programs that guide them successfully through their exams.*

Almost as soon as children start school these days, they seem to be required to take tests of one kind or another. Of course, these do not all involve sitting formally in a structured setting, but the results are nevertheless taken seriously by the majority of schools.

But it is when students are about to apply for college and when they need to take an aptitude test – the SAT – that a good performance is vital. Success in this is usually essential for entry, as acceptance is not based solely on grades obtained at school.

The SAT (Scholastic Assessment Test) is a 3-hour standardized college entrance exam administered seven times each year. It contains two portions, one covering math and the other covering verbal skills. In general, the key to passing the test is not the number of questions answered but the percentage answered correctly. This is why practice is so important. Questions are presented in ascending order of difficulty.

● **Getting ready**
The Educational Software Institute offers several CD-ROMs that can be helpful in preparation for the SAT. The *SAT Math Engine* CD-ROM for grades 9-12, for instance, aims to give students test-taking confidence and experience, while helping them boost their SAT math scores. Students are presented with complete tests to that areas needing improvement can be recognized. Each of the 25 tutorials covers a different area of math and includes a quiz to test skills. Solutions can be reviewed.

A further CD-ROM from the ESI, for grades 9-12, and adults, entitled *SAT I - Math*, offers practice in fractions, ratios, equations, algebra, geometry, quantitative analysis, rates, and consecutive integers.

● **Revising online**
But you do not necessarily have to buy a CD-ROM to get practice in math. You can revise online. Majon's Test Prep Center provides numerous examples of the math section of the SAT, and gives clear explanations of how to calculate these.

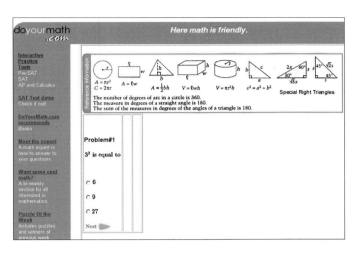

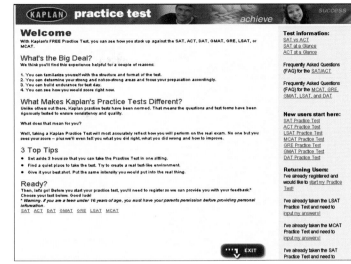

*The Interactive Practice Test at the www.doyourmath.com site include basic pre-SAT questions that younger pupils should be able to answer.*

You can also consult Doyourmath online. Here you will find everything about math, from SAT math tests to amazing math puzzles. There are pre-SAT tests (PSATs) in algebra, for example, providing 20 questions to be answered in 25 minutes. Details about the next national testing date are also given.

But that is not all. There is an online facility, too, provided by Doyourmath entitled Meet the Expert. You simply give your name and your email address, and then submit your question. We have experimented with this, and an acknowledgment of the inquiry came back right away. You should not expect an immediate answer to the question, however. It is obviously impossible to assess how many such inquiries are being received at any one time, so be sure to allow some days.

*You must first register at www.kaplanpracticetest.com before you can take the SAT practice tests so that you can receive feedback on your results by email.*

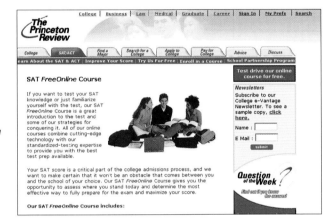

*The Princeton Review site includes a free section with a full-length test and interactive online lessons. A coach is also on hand to help with students' questions.*

The *Princeton Review* also provides online SAT courses with interactive, multimedia lessons and a 'coach' available at any time of the day or night to answer your questions.

Kaplan Testprep, meanwhile, offers the free opportunity to try some SAT math test questions online, but you need to become a registered member of KAPTEST.com first. You can do

this online. A student is advised to set aside 3 hours to take the sample test so that he or she will have the same amount of time as in the math SAT for real.

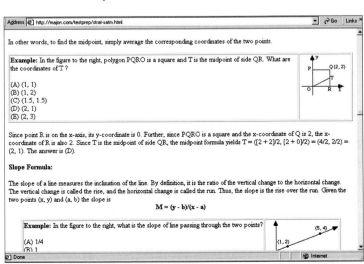

*At the www.majon.com Web site, there are many examples of SAT-level questions to help prepare students for the test. In addition to the answers, the reasons are fully explained.*

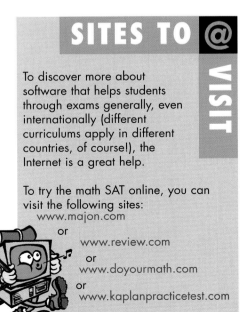

**SITES TO @ VISIT**

To discover more about software that helps students through exams generally, even internationally (different curriculums apply in different countries, of course!), the Internet is a great help.

To try the math SAT online, you can visit the following sites:

www.majon.com

or

www.review.com

or

www.doyourmath.com

or

www.kaplanpracticetest.com

# Designing your home

*If you've grown tired of the way your home looks, why not give your rooms a face-lift by changing their layouts? Your computer, as always, can help.*

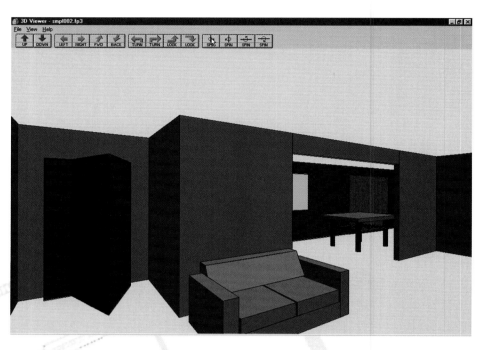

Once you've got the structure and layout right in Floor Plan 3D, you can furnish your home and take a virtual walk through to check that it provides you with the effect you want.

Have you ever spent a day moving all your furniture around to see if the shelf unit looks better in that alcove or against the wall? Everything probably ended up back where it started and all you had to show for your efforts were a strained back and aching muscles.

A far better way of rearranging a room is not to move the furniture at all, but to draw a scale plan of the room and position scale drawings of the furniture on it. This way you can try out all the possible arrangements to find the one you like the best.

### ● No drawing skills required

While it might seem like a great idea, for most of us, drawing a scale plan is about as easy as performing brain surgery. This is where your PC can help. There are computer programs that allow you to create scale room plans, letting you see what a room

would look like with your furniture in different places. The software will also add different color schemes. Some programs will even produce a three-dimensional design you can 'walk' through.

### ● Drawing floor plans

A good CD to start with is *Floor Plan 3D* in the Essentials series from IMSI. This gives you many of the tools used in professional design, but in a simplified form. You can draw floor plans using the set of easy tools provided or you could take one of the sample plans and modify it to your own taste.

The floor plan shows the outer walls, doors, windows, and the internal dividing walls. To add features, you simply select from a drop-down menu, view the options and then drag and drop the desired

element – such as a window or fireplace – into position. For complicated features such as staircases you might have to select dimensions from a dialog box. To see what your dream home looks like in three

### DON'T FORGET THE KITCHEN

It has to be said that most people don't give too much thought to designing the rooms in their house. Furniture tends to go where it fits and that's that. But there is one room that almost everybody 'designs' – the kitchen.

Now you can draw your own floorplan, see it in 3-D, 'walk' through it and experiment with the colors and textures of walls, surfaces and units by using a 3-D kitchen design program. Some packages include a specialized 3-D kitchen designer. Using this could prove more useful in the kitchen than in any other room, since the cost of the units prohibits real-life trial and error.

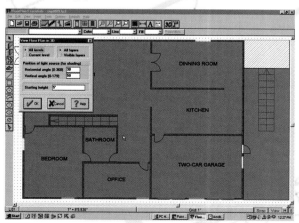

**Floor Plan 3D** *lets you take a preexisting design and modify it – and you can choose to view it in 3-D, too.*

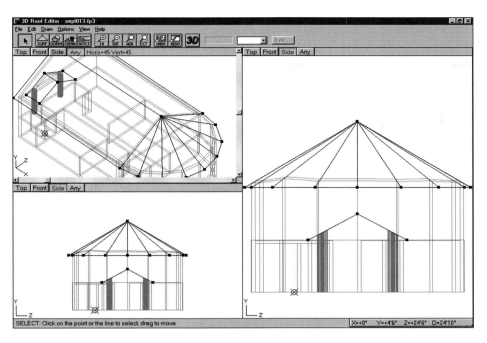

Bob Vila's Home Design *has handy wizards to help you through the trickier parts, such as this 3-D Roof Editor, which helps you design a roof for the building you are planning.*

dimensions, *Floor Plan 3D* gives you a three-dimensional view that can be modified from a simple dialog box, allowing you to select which layers of the building will be displayed, where the light source comes from, and so on. You can also take a three-dimensional tour through the

*There's no shortage of furniture choices in* Complete Home Designer.

interior, viewing the rooms with their furniture in position. *Floor Plan 3D* is a great way to judge the effects, for example, of demolishing an internal wall. There's no mess or expense and you can rebuild, instantly.

● **Complete Home Designer**
*Complete Home Designer*, from Data Becker, is a larger and more fully-featured program, offering higher levels of control and precision. It comes with a correspondingly hefty manual, which you will need to spend some time with to get the most out of the software, but the effort is repaid in the richness of the designs and views you can create. As with *Floor Plan 3D*, you can choose to start from scratch or to use a sample design. Begin with a blank sheet and

then play around with the samples. The program supplies a handy wizard to get you through the first few steps. You can view your construction as a plan, but in 3-D you can see it both in perspective (solid) or in wireframe.

Once you've got a structure and room layout, you need to furnish it. *Complete Home Designer* scores well on this point; there's a huge range of furnishings to put in the rooms.

● **Do-it-yourself home design**
*Bob Vila's Home Design* from Mattel Interactive supplies much the same mix of architecture and design as *Floor Plan 3D* and *Complete Home Designer*, but it aims to provide a friendlier approach, in the shape of Bob Vila – the popular do-it-yourself television host. A separate module of the CD gives video sequences of Bob's tips on designing and building.

The design software is similar in operation and features to *Floor Plan 3D*. This means it's pretty easy and intuitive to use. It also contains a range of 1001 sample homes. When it comes to dealing with intricate, but essential, elements (such as a roof) the software is helpful, giving you three separate views on screen.

All three of these programs require quite a bit of effort if they are to be genuinely useful. But that is only to be expected from design software that gives you desktop tools that only a few years ago were, for price reasons alone, available only to professional architects and builders.

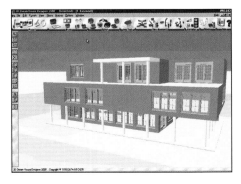

Complete Home Designer 2000 *allows you to view the house as a solid 3-D image...*

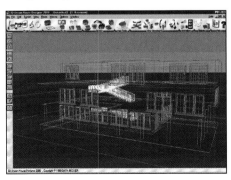

*...or as a wireframe, so you can see internal structures, such as staircases.*

## CONTACT POINTS

***Floor Plan 3D***
IMSI
Tel: 1 800 833 4674
Price: $29.95

***Complete Home Designer***
Data Becker
Tel: 1 781 453 2340
Price: $29.95

***Bob Vila's Home Design***
Mattel Interactive, distributed by The Learning Company
Tel: 1 800 395 0277
Price: $14.95

# High school biology

**Books can only do so much when it comes to teaching biology, but some software developers are so confident that their biology CD-ROMs can boost grades that they give a money-back guarantee.**

Away from the classroom, there's little opportunity to reinforce academic learning in biology. Natural science TV shows are great for boosting interest in the natural world, but they rarely provide the depth of knowledge needed for proper study of biology as a science. At the other extreme, books can provide this depth, but many children struggle to maintain motivation for reading large chunks of text. Biology CD-ROMs can combine the benefits of both. There's enough storage space on the CDs for both in-depth text information and images to illustrate complex processes. Of course, the PC adds the unique element of being interactive, allowing your kids to work at their own pace, and assessing progress through quizzes and puzzles.

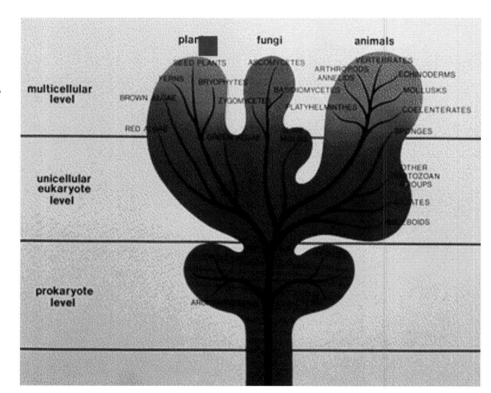

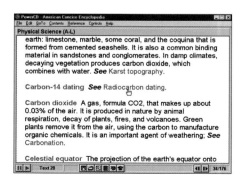

*Each of the CDs in the **High School Biology** package includes the **American Concise Encyclopedia**, allowing you to quickly look up words and phrases that you don't know.*

### ● Education guaranteed

Fogware Publishing, the developer of *High School Biology*, is so confident of its combination of multimedia entertainment and solid knowledge that it gives a money-back guarantee that it will boost your child's grades over a semester. Make sure to keep your receipt, although you're unlikely to need it to claim a refund.

*High School Biology* is a package of five CDs: *The Five Kingdoms of Life*, *Genetics*, *Heredity*, *Ecosystems*, and *Plant Anatomy*. Each is arranged as a series of self-running multimedia presentations–over 6 hours in all. These are narrated screens of information, with images and text. At any time, you can pause the presentation to use the built-in glossary for more details about an unusual word, or to zoom in on an image, for example. The software makes it a snap to print any of the 2,600 images for use in homework projects.

*High School Biology's **first CD**, The Five Kingdoms of Life, goes into great depth about the way biologists have divided the living world into species, phyla and classes.*

### ● Testing times

Each of the CDs contains a set of multiple-choice questions that you can use in a quiz. You set the number of questions and time limit, and the program poses the questions one after the other. At the end, there's a score and you can see how you did on each

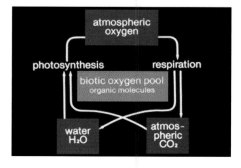

*As the presentations in **High School Biology** progress, students are asked to test their understanding of the topics just covered.*

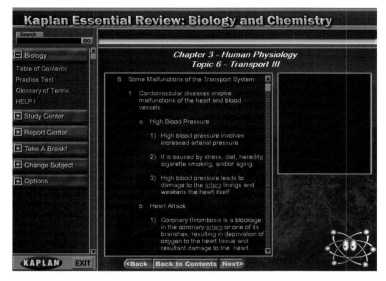

*Kaplan Essential Review: Biology and Chemistry focuses on presenting solid information in the guise of text, with very few images.*

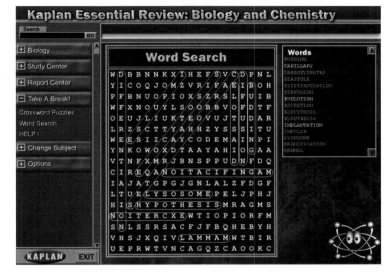

*To help make scientific terms more familiar, Kaplan Essential Review: Biology and Chemistry uses word searches and crosswords.*

on the CD to chapters in several standard biology textbooks, such as *McGraw Hill's Biology: Living Systems*.

● **Help with homework**

As a tool dedicated to serious study and – ultimately – exam success, *Biology and Chemistry* also provides help when it comes to producing assignments. The Study Center section includes an idea creator. This lets you brainstorm the structure of a paper onscreen, adding bibliography and supporting clip-art images.

A section of Tips and Strategies contains advice on managing preexam stress and also gives vital guidance for taking multiple-choice tests – such as watching out for 'pick all that apply' questions that can trip up students in tests where normally only one choice is required. You can take practice tests at any time.

Commendably, *Biology and Chemistry* exploits some novel ways to help students learn the biology vocabulary. The problem is that many of the scientific words are unusual and rarely used outside of class; however, by using word-search puzzles, which include tricky words such as 'exocyotosis' and 'diastole', the program can reinforce the familiarity of the terms.

The crossword puzzles are even more useful. The words aren't listed as they are in the word-search puzzle, so you must answer questions where the only clue is the number of letters in the answer, and the letters already in place from other answers. There's no multiple-choice element, so the questions are actually a better test of understanding than the practice tests.

question: click on the questions you got wrong to retake them–this time with an explanation of why your choice is right or wrong.

Fogware Publishing also deserves a special merit for understanding that CD-ROM software can clutter up your hard drive. The *High School Biology* CD-ROMs run directly and instantly from the CD-ROM drive, adding no extra folders to your hard drive.

Taking a rather different tack is the single CD program, *Kaplan Essential Review: Biology and Chemistry*. Once you have chosen the subject (Biology or Chemistry) the program encourages you to start by assessing your knowledge level instead of just jumping into the subject topics. You take the Diagnostic Test, and then the program analyzes the results to create a study program to tackle areas

where it can see that your knowledge is lacking – really useful.

You don't have to take the test, however. Click the No option and you can work through the program's main areas yourself. The program is arranged much like a book, with chapters and topics within chapters. The first topic of the first chapter discusses the concept of life, and subsequent chapters go on to cover human physiology, evolution, and ecology. Lab skills are also covered. *Kaplan Essential Review: Biology and Chemistry* is heavily text based; there are illustrations and clip art, but these are definitely a sideshow to the main act – even the 'musak' soundtrack is created not to distract you. As a study aid, the software aims to cover the same ground as biology textbooks. There's a Textbook Correlator to help you match material

**CONTACT POINTS**

*Kaplan Essential Review: Biology and Chemistry*
Encore Software
Tel: 1 310 719 2890
Price: $9.99
www.encoresoftware.com/

*High School Biology*
Fogware Publishing
Price: $29.99
www.fog-ware.com/

# Driver education

**Auto accident statistics speak for themselves: thousands of young drivers' lives are wasted every year. Education CD-ROMs can teach teens about safety in addition to teaching everyday driving skills.**

Excited and enthusiastic about gaining automotive freedom, teenagers are understandably eager to take to the road. Getting a license and starting out on the road is a significant achievement, guaranteed to improve a teen's social life as well as being an early sign of adult responsibility.

However, in spite of – or perhaps because of – this enthusiasm, this group of young drivers is greatly over-represented in the auto accident statistics. According to the AAA Foundation for Traffic Safety, 16-year olds have 20 times the number of crashes per mile than average drivers. Decreasing this figure is a key target of medics, teachers, politicians, moms, and dads alike.

CD-ROMs in the form of driver education software can help. Some programs focus on teaching the basics – the meaning of road signs, right of way at intersections, and so

You need to stay alert to potential hazards in driver-ZED's Drive mode or there will be a noisy crash.

on. Others use highway simulations to get practical lessons across.

## ● Learning how to drive
*Right of Way*, from Guidance Associates, focuses on basic driver education but does include some sensible road-safety advice. Using a multimedia soundtrack and onscreen slide show, the program presents information in a clear, if basic, way.

The first lessons cover Traffic Controls – the easy aspects of road-sign shape and color. In the fast flow of today's traffic there are many visual cues for drivers to act upon, and being able to quickly pick out the right type of sign, while ignoring the others is a vital skill. This section – and the test that follows it – makes sure the principles of sign shape and color are learned.

The lessons move on to cover other areas of driving such as Passing, Parking, Special Situations, and Sharing the Road. Each is subdivided into smaller sections, and each of these has its own multiple-choice test. Only when all the questions have

been answered correctly can the student move onto the next section.

## ● Safety advice
There are two sections that deal with safety concerns: Defensive Driving and Alcohol/Drugs. The first gives plenty of commonsense advice on being proactive to avoid accidents – looking out for other drivers' mistakes and describing the two-

**Right of Way *starts with the very basics – making sure the student driver has a sound knowledge of road signs and their meanings.***

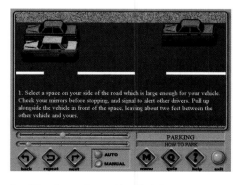

**Parallel parking – *the stumbling block for many a would-be driver – is explained in simple step-by-step form in* Right of Way.**

## STATE DIFFERENCES

Bear in mind that some states have different driving codes, and make sure to check your driver education software against your state's driving code.

*Right of Way*, for example, is based on the New York State Driver Education Curriculum – one of the country's stricter driving codes. Some aspects – speed limits and maximum permitted alcohol levels, for instance – vary from state to state.

*In driver-ZED's Spot mode, the video action freezes and you need to point out all of the hazards you must consider.*

second rule, for example. It also covers life-saving basics, such as the facts and figures supporting the need for seat belts.

Within the Alcohol/Drugs section, the vastly increased risks of accidents due to intoxication are explained, and the 'designated driver' principle explained. In addition, reasons are given why even cold remedies and over-the-counter allergy medications need to be checked out before driving while taking them.

### ● By teens, for teens

The first thing you notice with *driver-ZED* is that it's an altogether more polished and modern affair than *Right of Way*. Four teens introduce this innovative educational game, which has been produced by the AAA Foundation for Traffic Safety itself. The result is a program that is both more appealing to more of the target audience, and more informative through use of more multimedia content.

**Driver-ZED** *is a more modern program, offering an interactive and fun learning experience hosted by a lively group of four teen presenters.*

Whereas *Right of Way* is primarily an overall driver education program, *driver-ZED* is aimed squarely at reducing accidents. ZED stands for zero errors driving, and the software uses real movie clips to help teen drivers spot potential hazards in everyday traffic scenarios.

### ● Realism

*Driver-ZED*'s unique feature is its combination of movie clips and risk assessment. For example, you see the driver's eye view as a real car travels real streets. More important, the emphasis isn't on controlling the car – so there's no chance that your kids will treat it as a driving game. Instead the job is to spot problems before they happen.

Hazards that must be identified range from the drumming sound of a flat tire while driving on the freeway, to inattentive or aggressive road users pulling out into your automobile's path when you least expect it. There are four modes. In Scan you see a short driving clip and then have to answer questions afterward. Spot mode is similar, but instead the movie clip freezes and you must use the mouse to point out the hazards.

Act mode takes a similar approach, but when the action freezes at a particular point, you must work out and select the best course of action. In Drive mode, you decide when to take action, and which action to take. Get it wrong and there'll be an accident. Throughout *driver-ZED*'s 83 driving sequences, you get points so you can monitor progress.

One of the commendable benefits of the *driver-ZED* approach is that all aspects of observation are tested. This helps novice drivers understand that in addition to the more obvious risks from other vehicles on the road, there are many other risks – such as cars leaving driveways and pedestrians. It's good to see that attention to the car's mirrors is also required.

Overall, *driver-ZED* is a very useful aid together with regular driver-education. Despite the inclusion of accident simulations when hazards are missed, these events don't undermine the object of the software.

### CONTACT POINTS

**driver-ZED**
Electronic Learning Facilitators
Tel: 1 800 305 SAFE
Price: $27.50
www.driverzed.org

**Right of Way**
Guidance Associates
Tel: 1 800 431 1242
Price: $39.95
www.guidanceassociates.com

# Family health encyclopedias

*Help yourself and your family to better health by using your computer and its multimedia capabilities.*

Modern-day pressures and emotional stresses conspire with the pollution of our air and water to make us work a bit harder to stay healthy. And eating fast-food on the run, not to mention what we drink, can be doing little good for us. But, with a little application and help, you can learn how to stay healthy and get fit by understanding how your body works and knowing what you can do to keep it working properly, or what to do if you become sick.

### ● Fully booked

There are many medical reference books available, but these are often full of difficult medical terms and provide little practical, day-to-day information. A better alternative is to use the multimedia power of your computer in the form of an electronic medical encyclopedia. As with books, these CD-ROMs are not a substitute for expert advice – if in doubt, always contact your doctor.

A CD-ROM medical reference will enable you to quickly find the information you want and instantly and efficiently cross-reference all the

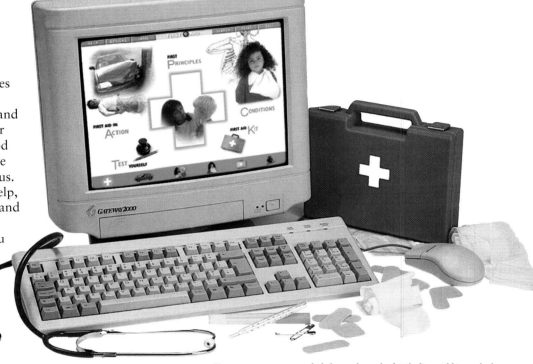

*Your computer can not only help you keep the family first-aid kit stocked, but it also shows you what to do in the event of an emergency.*

*You don't have to wait until you're ill before you use your computer health advisor. There's also lots of comprehensive information about medicines, fitness and family care.*

information relevant to the subject. Video demonstrations, animation and illustrations are used to show how to exercise correctly or perform life-saving first aid. On some of the discs, animation demonstrates how parts of your body work. The choice of which program to go for is up to you.

### ● A wealth of choice

One of the programs available is *BodyWorks*, a 3-D tour around the human body. It might sound gruesome, but it's actually fascinating to see beneath the skin, view the bones of your skeleton and journey through all the internal organs to discover how they work.

## A LITTLE REASSURANCE

If you're the type of person who prefers not to know what your medical treatment might involve, you are probably not the ideal candidate for a medical encyclopedia program. However, the clear and concise explanations, narration and video footage of simple surgical procedures could reassure a worried patient that this is now a relatively minor and commonplace procedure that offers a chance for a return to good health.

### ● Consult the ACP

One of the most innovative guides to family health and medicine for a general audience, the American College of Physicians *Complete Home Medical Guide* comes with an interactive CD-ROM covering human anatomy. *The Family Medical Reference Library* CD-ROM, meanwhile, presents step-by-step flowcharts that take you from symptoms to diagnosis; definitions of more than 650 diseases and disorders; and practical health tips as well as a glossary of more than 700 over-the-counter and prescription drugs.

The package comes with two other CD-ROMs: *The Ultimate Human Body* and *The Ultimate 3D Skeleton*. Both of these are more multimedia-orientated than the main CD and combine fun with education instead of offering medical guidance. For example, you can take a Body Quiz with *The Ultimate Human Body*, or look up amazing facts about the body's bones in *The Ultimate 3D Skeleton*.

*The Merck Manual of Medical Information* CD-ROM is derived from their best selling book. It explains over 1,200 conditions in easy-to-read everyday language, clarifying complex medical concepts and terms, and provides links to many health-related Internet sites.

The program's content is stored in

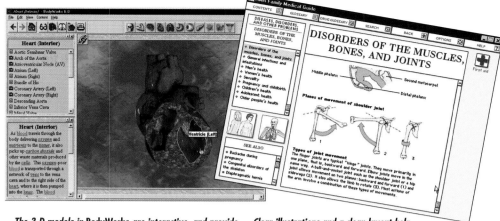

*The 3-D models in BodyWorks are interactive, and provide a helpful insight into the way the human body works.*

*Clear illustrations and a clean layout help to make the Family Medical Reference Library a quick and easy to find your way around.*

website form on the CD-ROM, and once it is installed, you use your Web browser to access the information. It's not as slick, nor as attractive, an interface as the *Family Medical Reference Library* CDs but the content is very impressive in breadth and depth. There are 3-D animations and video clips, but they are secondary to the text information.

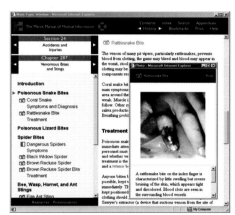

*Hopefully, you'll never need to know what a rattlesnake bite looks like, but Merck's CD-ROM has information on this and other insect and animal bites.*

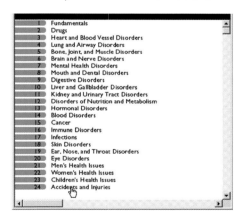

*Merck Manual of Medical Information may lack the slick interface of other health CD-ROM's, but its range and depth are impressive.*

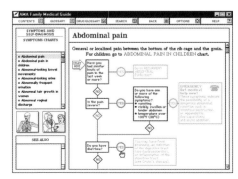

*The Family Medical Reference Library has dozens of flowcharts that can help to diagnose illnesses from your symptoms with a few clicks of the mouse.*

---

## FIRST AID

The American Institute of Preventive Medicine has contributed to an Internet site (www.healthy.net/clinic/firstaid), providing information about emergency care in situations ranging from breathing problems, chest pain, cuts, and electric shock to fainting, frostbite, burns, and animal bites. However, clearly, in an emergency there should be no delay in calling an ambulance or rushing a patient who can be moved to the emergency room of a hospital.

St. John Ambulance, Canada, meanwhile, has recognized the need to complement existing instructions with computer-based training in a CD-ROM entitled *First Aid*. It gives advice on the prevention of injuries and suggests how to avoid complications if accidents do happen.

---

## CONTACT POINTS

**ACP Complete Home Medical Guide (with interactive CD-ROM of Human Anatomy)**
Price: $40
***Family Medical Reference Library***
Dorling Kindersley
Tel: 1 212 123 4800
Price: $30
www.dk.com

**BodyWorks**
The Learning Company
Tel: 1 800 227 5609
Price: $12
www.learningco.com

**Merck Manual of Medical Information**
McGraw-Hill
Tel: 1 800 352 3566
Price: $40
www.bookstore.mcgraw-hill.com

# The Internet

# Buying books and CDs from websites

*Are you having trouble finding that out-of-print book or unstocked CD in your local stores? Broaden your horizons – and chances of success – by shopping on the Internet.*

The Amazon.com website claims to be the world's biggest bookstore – and with over 2.5 million titles in stock, it's difficult to argue with that. It would be a problem to find any store locally that is as well stocked. Buying books and other items, such as music and software CDs, via the Internet is really the only way to gain access to almost limitless choices. Because Internet stores have lower overhead than chain stores, they are often able to offer their goods at competitive prices.

### ● Shop until you drop

Buying items from websites is very much like buying from a catalogue. Besides the increased range of items offered, the sites also allow you to use the power of your Web browser and its own search engines to look for specific books or CDs (or any other item you are after). These site-specific search engines allow you to look for books by a particular author, search for books when you know only a portion of the title, just look for those that cover a specific subject or those published during a certain period.

Most sites organize their wares into useful categories, such as fiction and biographies for books, or jazz and

hip-hop for music. Some of the larger sites go even farther and offer reviews of their products (often written by members of the public who have bought the items), buyer's guides, author/band biographies, links to related fan sites and much more.

Now that e-commerce has really taken off, the breadth and depth of what's offered has increased. So you won't just find the best-selling books and the top 10 CDs. Instead, you can explore just about any interest you have, from audio books to 16th-century music.

Over the next few pages we describe some of the most popular sites around. But if your own particular interest isn't listed, don't despair. Simply use the powers of

your favorite search engine (see Stage 2, pages 136-137) to seek it out; the chances are that there will be a choice of sites out there that can deliver the goods.

## LANGUAGE BARRIER

Thanks to the Internet, getting hold of foreign books or CDs has never been easier. You'll pay more in postage to have a book sent from France, of course, but the online stores offer such a wealth of stock that you probably won't mind the extra cost. It's easy to find the sites as well. Books On Line (www.bol.com), for example, has a menu giving access to their sites in Europe. Amazon also has sites worldwide.

# Books and CDs on the Web

**Here's a selection of Internet sites from all over the world, where you can browse through millions of books, videos and CDs.**

BOOKS AND CDS were the goods that kicked off the Web as a way of doing your shopping. Now these sites offer not just a massive range of stock and discounted prices, but, in many cases, extremely sophisticated designs packed with information about the goods for sale. All the sites mentioned here use secure online ordering, and most of them allow you to use an ordinary debit card as well as a credit card. If you can bear to wait for a few days to get your hands on what you want, these sites are a great way to buy both your music and your reading matter.

# Online bookselling giants

**Amazon – the 'first mover' of online bookselling – has been in business for years. It has been joined by other excellent sites, developed both by other media giants and innovative specialist organizations.**

## Amazon

www.amazon.com

Amazon is an online behemoth, with a presence on the Web you can't escape; it advertises on just about every site you visit. It's one of the biggest e-businesses and worth an absolute fortune. It's not hard to see why investors are excited; Amazon was the first to launch online bookselling, did it very well, and keeps getting better. It has a massive stock of books – around 1.4 million titles – and offers substantial discounts on popular ones, with smaller savings on other books. It also supplies plenty of content, from features and reviews to readers' comments about their purchases. The site now covers a variety of other areas, including music.

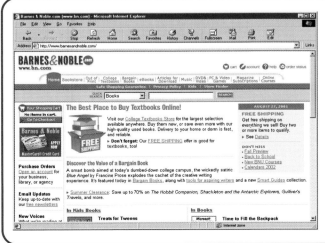

## Barnes & Noble

www.bn.com

Although Amazon had a head start in online bookselling, it doesn't have things all its own way. The renowned Barnes and Noble bookstore chain has extended its enterprise to include its own online site. This well-stocked site offers a database of 1.5 million books, plus it is an invaluable source when searching for those hard-to-find college textbooks (both new and used), out-of-print titles or rare classics. There are plenty of other features, including a useful newsletter with email updates and recommendations from your own profile of tastes. In addition, it's all attractively presented in a lively and easy-to-use format.

## Audiobookclub

www.audiobookclub.com

In the modern era you don't have even to read a book to enjoy it: you can listen to it instead, in the shape of an audio book on cassette or audio CD. There's a surprisingly wide range of these, and this site gives you access to thousands of titles, covering everything from current best-sellers to unabridged readings of enormous classic novels, which will keep you occupied for a number of days, to say the least. The Audiobookclub's special features include reviews, author interviews and chats, and you can preview clips before you buy to make sure that you'll like what you purchase.

## Suncoast

www.suncoast.com

Suncoast is a giant of cybershopping, with books and music as two of its specialities. In terms of music, the Suncoast site offers one of the better shopping experiences. It has a comprehensive range of titles, with prices that work out very competitively. Whatever your taste in music – from the latest releases to essentials for your collection – you are sure to find them on this site. What's more, it has a neat and attractive layout, while a search for an artist or title brings up not only the thing itself, but also plenty of background information. Ordering is quick and easy, and they even send you emails to let you know your order is logged and then on its way to you.

## Rand McNally

www.randmcnally.com

If you love to go a-wandering, you'll probably need a map or two to help you find your way. For an unusual or particularly detailed map, the choices at most stores tend to be limited and large-scale or rare maps tend to be stocked only by a few specialty bookstores. Because of this, it's extremely handy to have an online store like this one, which keeps a massive stock of maps and guidebooks. You can even get a map of the polar regions and a guide book on the Arctic or Antarctic. Closer to home, you can join the Road Explorers and personalize your trip plans along with getting email updates relating to your road trips. Once you start using this site, you'll return to it again and again.

## Half.com

www.half.com

This is the one-stop site for everything you're likely to need in the modern world: movies, DVDs, games, sporting goods, computers, music – there's even a category called 'Everything Else New!' There is a huge amount of choice, as you would expect from an eBay company, and many products are heavily discounted. Buying online is simple and pain-free. What is more, if you have something to sell, you can do that here, too. There is an easy route to becoming a member to make your trading simpler still. And the many regular announcements, special offers and What's Hot alerts make checking out the site frequently well worth your while.

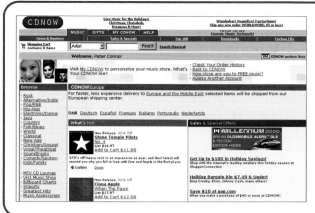

## CDNOW

www.cdnow.com

This is a giant American music store, with European distribution centers, that offers to ship any order worldwide. Add this to what seem to be extremely competitive prices on the CDs themselves, and you need to check this site out before buying elsewhere. In addition, the site is full of useful information, and contains excellent 'beginner's guides' to various genres, such as jazz and classical music. If you can assemble its recommended basic collections, you'll not only be enjoying the music, but also, within a short while, be chatting on equal terms with the experts.

## The Book Pl@ce

www.bookplace.co.uk

This British online bookstore has the same range of stock as the multinational giants, but has a number of extras. For instance, they offer two different magazine-style areas, Bookends (www.bookends.co.uk) and The Book Monster (www.thebookmonster.co.uk), aimed at adults and children respectively. These give more detail on what's happening in the book world and are worth looking at, even if you're not actually thinking of buying a particular book. The delivery of books is available worldwide, and you can expect to receive your purchase in 7-10 days by airmail.

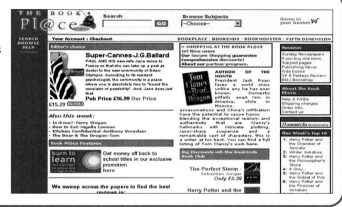

## Fatbrain

www.fatbrain.com

This large distributor of computer books and training materials has a functional and easy-to-use site. It has an easily searchable database, and it will keep you up to date with new books by email if you want. Fatbrain is just the place to look if you want heavyweight computer manuals, tutorials, training resources and related do-it-yourself material. You can also use this site to leap off into other sectors such as engineering and science, business or medical. And if you've lost your car manual – or maybe never had one – you can get it here.

## Coda

www.codamusic.co.uk

This Scottish online retailer specializes in folk, world and blues music. The site has a pretty large stock, easily searchable by artist or title, and offers to find what you want if it's not in stock. Shipping and handling is included in the quoted prices 'wherever you are in the world', so you don't get any nasty surprises at the virtual checkout. There is no doubt that this is a good resource if the music genres it offers are what turn you on. In addition to CDs and cassettes, the site sells music, song books and even traditional musical instruments, such as bodhrans (Celtic drums) and penny whistles. The site lives up to the statement on its home page: 'Traditional by name, traditional by nature'.

# Planning a vacation

**One time when you're sure to need plenty of information is when you are planning a trip. So why not use the Internet to discover the wealth of up-to-the-minute travel data and vacation bargains online?**

Travel and vacation sites were one of the first categories to make it big on the Internet, for obvious reasons: anyone choosing a holiday – whether a package or a do-it-yourself trip – wants as much information as possible prior to arranging it.

However, in the early days of the Internet, finding this information was something of a hit-and-miss affair, throwing up personal experiences from individuals, as well as thoroughly researched and credible sites. There was also little in the way of solid information or online reservations systems from major travel companies or airlines. But now you can do just about everything on the Internet that used to be done over the telephone or sitting in the travel agent's office.

### ● No-frills flights

The major worldwide airlines have been on the Web for quite some time, offering flight information and online reservations. However, these premium carriers charged premium prices; there hadn't been much going cheaply. But a significant development in the late 1990s was the boom in bargain-basement airlines offering no-frills flights at low-cost prices.

Now all major airlines offer bargain fares on their websites. Some have banded together to create sites such as www.hotwire.com that offer only low-cost restricted fares to national and international destinations.

Online reservations is an integral part of the strategy of all airline companies. It's much cheaper than using phone operators. And it can be easier for the consumer, although as these services become more popular, you sometimes find the sites are slow because they are busy.

*The Internet has a vast array of vacation information and travel destination choices just waiting for your browser to open. Reserving tickets, checking flights and viewing hotels before you arrive are just a few Web facilities.*

### ● Package tours

Another important development is that while the major package travel companies were fairly late to get on the Internet bandwagon, they are now out there in force. Many of them have bold and attractive websites, although the quality and depth of the information available varies widely from site to site.

There's a good range of sites, from economy to deluxe – and many sites offer the chance to take advantage of tempting last-minute bargains. In spite of all the information on the sites, you may still want to pick up the printed brochures and spend a few hours browsing through them.

### ● Do-it-yourself travel

Many people prefer to organize their own vacations and the Internet caters to them. It can be especially helpful when trying to find somewhere to stay in just about any country. Generally, typing in a search of the town and country you want to visit, together with the word 'accommodation' or 'hotel' presents you with a wide list of possible choices. The sites listed on page 137 contain literally thousands of hotels worldwide, in a range of categories and often with the facilities detailed in an easy-to follow format. An increasing number of hotels now also offer online reservations.

# Reserving a flight online

**The Internet shopping revolution now means that you can research and arrange all kinds of travel – including air travel – online.**

HERE WE'LL FIND out how to reserve a ticket from Dallas–Fort Worth to Minneapolis–St. Paul with American Airlines. The procedure shown is similar to reserving a

ticket on other airlines that offer online reservations, such as Northwest Airlines (www.nwa.com), Delta Air Lines (www.delta.com), and most others.

**1** Type American Airlines address (www.aa.com) into your Web browser's Address box and press [Enter]. When the American Airlines home page has loaded, you will see that you can immediately begin to fill in your trip details. However, if you lose track of this page when you are using the site, just click on BOOK FLIGHT to get back to your information.

**2** Use the online sales area to specify what you're after. Simply fill in the spaces with the relevant information, either by typing or by selecting from the pull-down menus. When you've completed all areas of the screen, click the 'choose by price' button (see inset) or 'choose by schedule'.

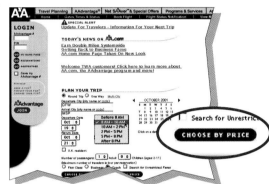

**3** Now you're shown the flight information for your chosen location. Check that the details are correct at the top, then look at the options you have been given – these will indicate different times and flights. Click on the radio button next to the flight you want to book (inset) and then click the Next button.

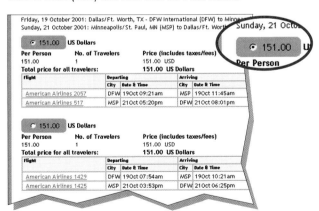

**4** The next screen displays the flight you have selected and the price of the ticket. If you are happy with your selection, check the details carefully and reveiw the Detailed Fare Rules to make sure you are aware of any restrictions to the ticket you are purchasing. You don't have a ticketing clerk to alert you to these. If you still wish to proceed, click on the Purchase now button.

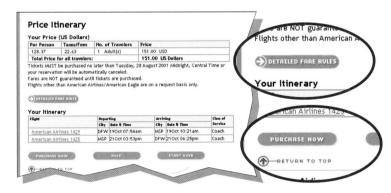

**5** On the next screen, all you have to do is fill in the details of the passenger, including your name and address, so that a seat in the correct name can be booked. Scroll down the page to fill in the final details including your payment information.

**6** You can also select seats if the airline allows early assignments. Click on Continue to complete your purchase. Unless you select an e-ticket, your tickets will be mailed to you at the address specified, or you can pick them up at the airport.

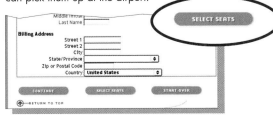

# Finding out about... Amsterdam

**The Internet provides easy access to lots of information about any travel destination. So now you've made the flight reservations, here's how you can discover where to go and what to do while you're in Amsterdam.**

**1** A good place to start is a search engine, such as Yahoo!, that categorizes content. Go to www.yahoo.com, and start by clicking on the Countries link in the Regional section. Click the Netherlands link when you see a list of countries of the world. Click Travel when the list of subcategories appears.

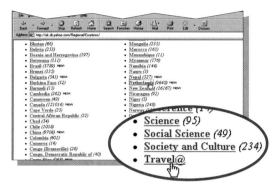

**2** Finding a place to stay is a priority, so click on the Accommodation link and then the Hotels link. This page leads to a substantial list of hotels and other places to stay. Read the brief descriptions to see if they're your kind of place. The Hotel Barbacan seems interesting and has a website, so click on the link. It offers plenty of information, so you could come back and make a reservation, once you've checked out the other places.

**3** To get a few ideas on what to do while you're in Amsterdam, search Yahoo! for 'Amsterdam', then click on the Local Guides link. TimeOut Amsterdam offers a guide to what's on and where to go. Use your browser's Bookmark or Favorites command and it will note the page; you can return later by selecting this Bookmark or Favorites again. Now return to Yahoo! to follow some other links.

**4** The Internet Guide to Amsterdam is packed with useful information, including annual weather graphs and downloadable maps. The Guide also has a small, but select, section of links to other Amsterdam sites.

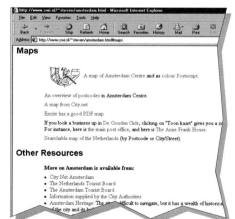

**5** One of the reasons we're visiting is to see the museums dedicated to Holland's great artists, Rembrandt and Van Gogh. To find out about these, go back to Yahoo! where there are links to sites such as The Rembrandt House Museum (below) and the restored Van Gogh Museum. Both sites give a good view of the respective artists and their work, information on where the museums are and opening times.

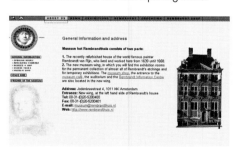

**6** It might be nice to do a little shopping – particularly for antiques. Yahoo! has lots of sites under its Business and Shopping links. The Antiques and Collectibles category contains a link to the Aronson Gallery, which gives us a good idea of what's on sale.

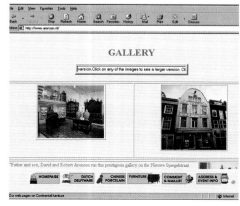

**7** Finally, to check current weather conditions before you go, click the Weather link on the Yahoo! home page, then choose Europe and then type in Amsterdam. You will get a two- to four-day forecast – giving you a good idea of what to pack for your trip. Remember that temperatures are given in Centigrade!

# Top travel sites

There are plenty of travel-related sites on the Internet, but a few stand out from the crowd for the breadth and depth of what they offer.

## Orbitz

www.orbitz.com

You certainly feel that you are in touch with the travel business when you visit this comprehensive site. Choose the type of trip you want and every page comes up with a thorough search facility and links taking you deeper and deeper into details on the vacation you are looking for. In general it is more of a catalogue than an information center, but you do have a huge number of deals and packages to choose from.

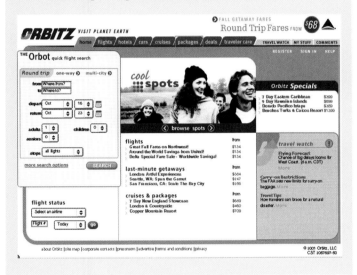

## Caribbeans.com

www.caribbeans.com

If you are planning to visit these beautiful islands, this could be the site for you. Caribbeans.com doesn't only provide the 'standard' offerings of hotel booking and car rental, but also provides you with the opportunity to select a romantic escape for a wedding or anniversary, and for the more energetic, you can opt for a 'tropical adventure' of scuba diving or chartering a yacht. There are also air travel special deals and maps of the islands to help you orient yourself, making this a useful and informative site.

## Expedia

www.expedia.com

This is Microsoft's gigantic Expedia travel site. It's huge, so its tentacles reach just about everywhere that a travel site could go; the chances are that you can find information here that might only otherwise be found on half a dozen individual sites. Weather, late bookings, flights, maps, hotel directories, car rental, health advice, city guides and generous travel discounts – you name it, Expedia's got it. And it does it so very well.

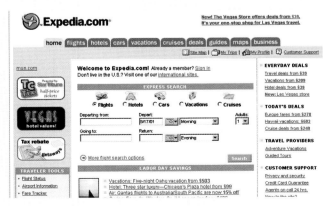

## Lonely Planet

www.lonelyplanet.com

Lonely Planet is the big daddy of printed guides for the 'independent traveler'. The website offers plenty of good stuff but what makes it vital to anyone thinking of an exotic trip is the Upgrades section, where you find the very latest information on border crossings, visas, safety and so on, that did not make it into the guidebook.

# Internet fan clubs

O ne thing that the Internet is justly famous for is providing a forum for fans of just about anything. Whether you spend your spare time mulling over the various theories on the TV series *The Prisoner*, or the exact wording of the *Monty Python* parrot sketch, the Internet can guide you toward like-minded people.

For no matter how alone you might feel in your own particular interest, you can guarantee that someone else on the Web feels the same way.

**Whether you're a fan of Daphne in Frasier or Joey in Friends, you're sure to find a website to suit. We take a look at Internet fan clubs, from the hugely popular to the downright obscure.**

## UNOFFICIAL SITES

You might be wondering how it is that unofficial sites get away with using copyrighted words and pictures. The fact is that often they don't. While copyright holders are often happy to ignore infringements and reap the free publicity, their lawyers sometimes like to flex their muscles and try, usually successfully, to ban various sites.

This happens most frequently with valuable brand names, such as *Star Trek* and *The X Files*, and usually results in torrents of abuse from fans, and a retraction by the copyright holder.

To attract these lost souls, many fans create websites for their chosen subject and often start up fan clubs around them.

### ● Official and unofficial clubs

The term 'fan club' can mean anything from a small group of enthusiasts who keep in contact via email, to an extensive organization (either official or unofficial) with its own magazines (print or email-based) and annual conventions.

Many unofficial fan clubs are free to join, but some charge a nominal fee. Most, though, are nonprofit. However, the same cannot be said of the various official fan clubs you might find.

Although they usually have the more extravagant websites, the amount of information and content on official sites can sometimes be less than that offered by more obsessive fans. Of course, this all varies according to the subject of the club and the company behind it.

In the next few pages we look at some of the more reputable official clubs and the more enthusiastic fan sites. As always, be careful about handing over your hard-earned cash when joining any club. A brief chat with an existing member should soon fill you in on what's what...and, of course, this is incredibly easy thanks to the exhaustive email links that many sites contain.

# A selection of official and unofficial sites

As you can imagine, there is an almost infinite number of fan sites for just about everything you could possibly think of. Many don't actually advertise themselves as fan clubs, but are still just as effective at bringing mutual admirers together.

## The Prisoner Appreciation Society: Six of One

www.theprisonerappreciationsociety.com

*The Prisoner* is the granddaddy of all cult TV shows. The program, starring the American-born British actor Patrick McGoohan, was unique at the time and, even now, is regarded by many as unsurpassed in terms of ambition and execution.

The series told the story of Number Six (played by McGoohan), a top British secret agent who resigns his job, but is kidnapped and sent to The Village – a surreal town that serves as a prison, and from which he is determined to escape.

This website is the focal point for fans around the world to talk about the show and discuss exactly what they think was going on in it.

The surreal nature of most of the episodes has created enough controversy to keep the series alive for decades. Although surfing around the website is free, The Prisoner Appreciation Society does encourage you to join the Six of One club. For a fee of $45 you receive a quarterly newsletter and the chance to join the annual anniversary of the show, which usually takes place in the Welsh village of Portmeirion – where the series was filmed.

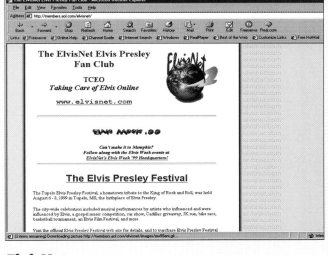

## ElvisNet

http://members.aol.com/elvisnet

On the Internet, the King is certainly not dead – with a few of the sites even claiming to have been created by the man himself. This is one of the saner sites and tries to concentrate on the facts of his life and music.

## Harry Potter Fan Site!

www.angelfire.com/wi/harrypotter

The publishers of J. K. Rowling's best-selling children's books have done Harry proud, creating a fan site that overflows with content – even if it's not the most attractive. News

## FRIENDS

http://friends.warnerbros.com/cmp

This is the official site for the hugely popular TV series featuring the young, beautiful but not always very happy (or smart) New Yorkers. It's very well presented and has just about anything a fan could want, including cast biographies, story updates and peeks behind the scenes. There are also well-presented and heavily used message boards and chat areas.

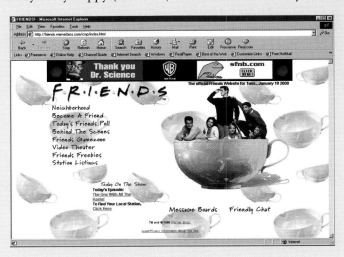

includes details of forthcoming books in the series, together with information about the first Harry Potter film. There's a chat area, an online Quidditch game (a sort of trivia affair), and readers are encouraged to contribute their very own Hogwarts stories, which could be displayed on the site.

*The Beatle death clues debate still rages among fans on the Internet.*

## Sgt. Pepper's Lonely Hearts Club Online

http://members.aol.com/AMBeatle/club.html

When you are dealing with a worldwide phenomenon such as The Beatles, it's often difficult to know where to start in terms of finding online resources and fans. Sgt. Pepper's Lonely Hearts Club Online, or SPLHCO, as it is also known, professes to be the world's largest online Beatles fan club.

On first visiting this site, this fact isn't particularly believable as the main page is rather amateurish and very slow to download. However, if you dig just below the surface, you'll find a wealth of interesting content. For starters, the club boasts free membership, via email, and over 1,200 worldwide members. On the site itself you can find interviews, news, memorabilia, pages created by other fans, the music itself in various file formats, and much, much more.

Finding out about the legend that was The Beatles and making new friends in the process has never been so easy, especially as the fan club organizes regular conventions all around the world.

## The BarryNet

www.barrynet.com

Whatever your musical tastes, you'll find them catered to somewhere. The devotion of Barry Manilow's fans is legendary, and they can boast a website that is far more professional and attractive than most of its peers. You get a comprehensive biography and discography, complete with pictures and sound clips.

There's a lot of emphasis on making pen (or email) pals, as well as taking part in the traditional conventions and, of course, concerts. Tickets can be bought at a reduced rate if you're a member, and there are also various deals on albums and other Barrymania items. If you're one of his fans, you need never feel alone; after all, this site has had over 1,000,000 visitors.

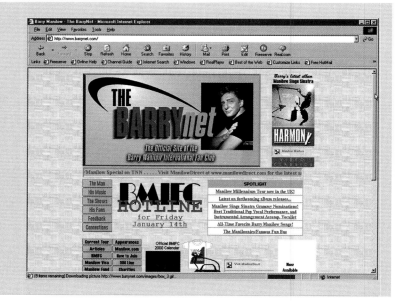

## Indiana Jones

www.indianajones.com

This site is great fun for all those follows of the intrepid hero – both in his guise in the blockbuster movies and in the earlier series. There are storylines from all the features and lots of pictures in the scrapbook section, with a close-up look at the exciting artifacts that Indy encounters. Of course, you can buy the videos here, and other paraphernalia such as PC games, so all in all, it's a fun, amusingly written site that is very entertaining.

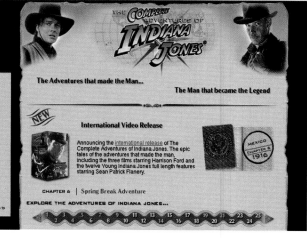

## The Rocky Horror Picture Show

www.rockyhorror.com

The film and stage show that has the most online fan clubs is *The Rocky Horror Show*. This is just one of the many sites all over the world. Unlike some fan sites, this one actually goes out of its way to make visitors feel welcome, rather than frightening them away with obscure lingo and references. In fact, if you haven't been to a live

show before, there's a page of Rocky etiquette that covers everything from the clothes you wear to what you're allowed to throw on stage and when. You can also purchase memorabilia online, including custom-made costumes. Remember, the average *Rocky Horror* fan favors fishnet stockings – regardless of gender. Despite the potential for lewdness, the whole site is very much tongue-in-cheek, so there's little danger of anyone being corrupted by Riff-Raff's devilish ways.

## Ricky Martin

www.rickymartin.com

Ricky Martin appeared from nowhere in 1999 to become a world megastar, hence this official site dedicated to the crooner of *Livin' La Vida Loca* and other Latin-flavored tunes. It's a curiously understated site but there is some

solid content – a generous stack of Real Audio sound bites from the music and a similar amount of videos. There's also an online store where you can buy your Ricky products.

## MAILING LISTS

One of the most refreshing aspects of fan sites is the genuine, heartfelt input from the fans themselves – an input you can have delivered to your own email address, courtesy of a mailing list. Here's how it works. You send an email to the mailing list address asking to subscribe. Any subsequent mail sent to the list – in much the same way as a message is posted on a newsgroup – will be sent on to you. Similarly, any email you send to the list will be sent on to all the other subscribers. The amount of traffic varies from list to list, but it's not unusual to find yourself getting dozens of emails every day for each list you've subscribed to. The level of policing varies from strict to none, but it generally reflects the subject matter; anyone sending offensive mail could be taken off the list.

## Babes and Hunks

www.babesandhunks.com

Forget Hollywood. The film world's new power center is none other than Bombay – hence the name Bollywood. Films from the Indian subcontinent are becoming increasingly popular with all types of audience worldwide, and so, too, are their stars. This site, the work of one dedicated fan, is a slick and content-rich guide to dozens of major Bollywood stars. At the core of the site are the pages dedicated to the stars. Here you get good photos, plus a page or so of text, which gives a brief biography of the stars and their latest activities. There are also message boards and chat rooms, free screen savers and wallpaper to download, and all the latest news from the industry. There are also dozens of film clips to view – but you'll need Real Video to view them properly.

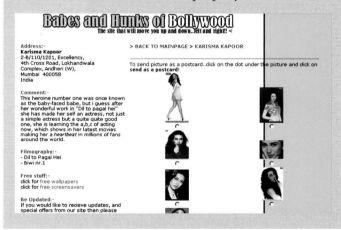

## PythOnline

www.pythonline.com

One site that is most definitely not sane – and would be a great disappointment if it were – is this official *Monty Python* page. With input from the stars, this is an extremely impressive site for all fans of the surreal and amusing Pythons.

# Royalty-free graphics

**If you want jazz up a poster or create a striking website, use the Net to find suppliers offering the graphics you need on a 'royalty-free' basis.**

We have already looked at the advantages of using ready-made clip-art images in your documents (see Stage 2, pages 78-81) and explored the useful range of professionally drawn images supplied free with CorelDRAW, Windows and other programs. However, there are, of course, some occasions when none of these is quite suitable.

No matter how specialized your illustration requirements, you are likely to be able to find and buy a suitable picture in the format you want on the Internet. Basic, ready-made clip art is usually supplied as professionally drawn bitmap or vector images, although you might also find the odd photo. Among the many options available are professional-quality **stock photography**, Web buttons and animations, fonts and 3-D pictures.

### ● Paying for graphics

A photographic image is often costly to produce, so it's rarely given away or sold in the usual way. It is much more likely to be supplied as a 'royalty-free' graphic. This doesn't usually mean that the graphics don't cost anything – although a few may actually be free. Instead, it refers to the basis on which copyright pictures are often sold for professional use, where the user must pay a sum of money (a royalty) every time the image is used.

This isn't the case with royalty-free graphics, where a single up-front payment allows the image to be used

Ian Lauder 1997

*No matter whether you are looking for a tranquil image of Canadian sealife or a photograph of a shipwreck, a host of professional-quality photographs, graphics and 3-D imagery is available via the Internet.*

again and again (subject to a few restrictions), making it much more practical for home computer use.

The restrictions exist to protect suppliers from misuse of their work and to ensure that they get a fair payment for images which might have been expensive to produce. The controls imposed vary, but some common ones are listed in the Royalty-free restrictions box (see opposite page).

Most of these are concerned with people who will be using the images in a commercial environment and selling products based on them. For a home user who just wants to make a better website or create a few professional-looking posters, this is rarely going to be a problem; it will be, though, if you intend to run off vast quantities of your poster or reproduce the shot in thousands of magazines.

[San Juan Islands]

[Wrecks]

### WHAT IT MEANS

**STOCK PHOTOGRAPHY**

*Stock photography describes images that are kept in stock by picture libraries, which charge a fee for finding you the image and another if you want to use it. Fees can range from the modest to the expensive, depending on the rarity of the image. The price also depends on how the picture is used; if it is for a poster publicizing an event, it should cost less than for a large-circulation newspaper.*

### ● Picture planning

Royalty-free images are provided in familiar graphics formats and most can be used just as easily as any other piece of clip art. One exception is 3-D imagery, which you might find is supplied in the form of 3-D **models**. But, unlike free or shareware clip art, such graphics are seldom purchased on the spur of the moment or for general use – usually, you will want a particular image for a specific job.

Most companies providing royalty-free graphics realize this and organize them into themes. Some of these are downloadable from the Internet, but even where they are supplied on CD-ROM, you can often use the company's Web site to search for them. You can then buy a CD that is full of landscape photography, 3-D models of the human body or people at work, for example. Many companies specialize in a particular area, such as wildlife, sports or aerial photography.

### ● Where to find what you need

On the following pages we look at the various formats and types of royalty-free graphics, as well as the companies that supply them and the costs involved. Although some collections can cost hundreds of dollars, because they are primarily aimed at designers and companies, you'll find that many cost much less than that and are a reasonable purchase for any home user. Check the agreement details to ensure that you can accept the conditions and you'll find royalty-free graphics provide almost effortless results.

| WHAT IT MEANS |
| --- |

**3-D MODELS**

*Each object or shape in a 3-D picture or 'world' is referred to as a model. This is because the 3-D imagery is created by manipulating simple wireframe objects in a program such as CorelDREAM 3-D. These objects are just templates, or models, for the shapes in the finished picture, which does not appear in its final form until the PC displays the 3-D image on your screen.*

# *Royalty-free restrictions*

WHEN YOU BUY royalty-free graphics, you will be asked to sign an agreement to use them in accordance with certain restrictions. The following is a rough outline of some typical examples, but you should always check exactly what conditions you are accepting.
● You must agree that the copyright of the graphics remains with the publisher. You can't copyright any pictures that you create using a royalty-free image, or claim it as your own.
● You can't use the graphics to create postcards, calendars, prints or anything else that you intend to sell in quantities over 100,000. Usually you can buy a resale license to do this, but that will cost you much more.
● You must not use the graphics to create any offensive or libelous material.
● You must agree to free the supplier of any legal actions arising from the use or misuse of the graphics. This is the company's way of saying: 'If you get into trouble through use of the images, you are solely responsible.'
● There will also be clauses similar to those imposed on any other software purchases, stating that the data is delivered 'as is' and that as far as the company is aware, the images are not infringing on anyone else's copyright.

## Photodisc

www.photodisc.com

This site offers over 33,000 images on a collection of CD-ROMs. As with many stock photography libraries, it's cheaper to buy lots of images at the same time. The site organizes photos into CD-ROMs that cover a vast range of subjects, from abstract backgrounds to family life. For example, a CD-ROM covering Retro People, 'sophisticated charm and squeaky-clean, wide-eyed innocence' has 120 images for only $219.

You can use a Lightbox page to preview the images on the CDs, and if you find an image you like, you can download a small version to use for layout purposes until the CD-ROM with the main photo arrives.

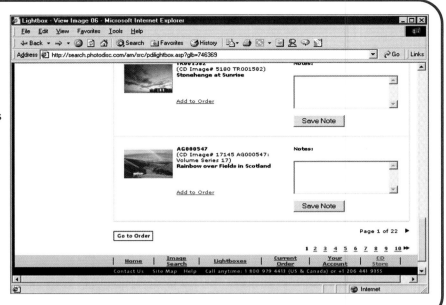

## ImageBuy.com

www.imagebuy.com

If you are looking for a comprehensive range of high-quality royalty-free graphics, ImageBuy.com brings you the MIXA and HFS range of CD-ROMs. Subjects are as diverse as desert islands, clay models of family groups, and fruit and vegetables. The prices vary, depending on the resolution, dpi, and number of images that you want. While the very high-resolution images are primarily used by professional designers (and have the price tag to match), you can buy a general CD-ROM with 4,000 images for just $69.95, providing plenty of material for the enthusiast. Look out for deals on free shipping, which are also available.

## Dynamic Graphics, Inc.

www.dgusa.com

There's a wide range of stock photography and other graphics on this site, covering topics such as babies, people at work, travel and so on. Much of the content is probably of more interest to the professional designer than the amateur – especially because a CD with 90 nature photos will cost from $329.

However, of slightly more interest is the range of stylish maps – often hard to find in the royalty-free world – which costs only $49 for a 250-image CD. There are links to other sites, which give access to royalty-free illustrations or even footage, for example, if you are looking for a different type of image.

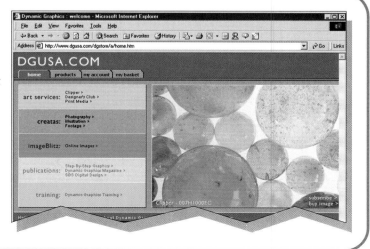

## ArtToday

www.arttoday.com

The ArtToday site is unusual in the way it prices its products. Instead of paying for what you use, you pay a yearly subscription of $29.95 to gain unrestricted access to the entire ArtToday archive, with absolutely no extra fees or royalties. This is a good deal, as most of the images are of a high quality and are sorted into numerous types, including clip art, Web icons, photos, line drawings and fonts. The fonts are particularly useful as they are all royalty-free and are also of good quality. The images can be downloaded by simply entering your subscription password and clicking the download button. This really is one of the best art sites around and well worth the modest investment, particularly if you are often in need of new images and fonts.

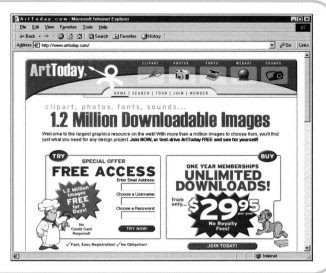

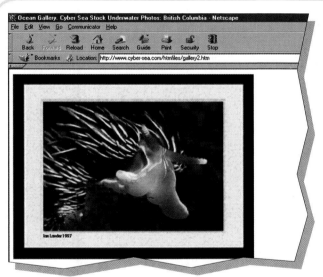

## Cyber Sea

www.cyber-sea.com

All the previously mentioned sites have specialized in particular formats or types of royalty-free graphic. This site takes the opposite tack, offering a range of image types, but all based on the theme of underwater scenes from around the coast of the United States.

Cyber Sea has massive amounts of sample art and many different CD-ROM collections for sale, in addition to such peripheral items as screen savers, postcards, wallpaper and editorial articles. Despite their specialized nature, prices for the CDs are reasonable, with even the most high-resolution collection costing as little as $29 for personal use and $99 for commercial use.

You might be surprised at how many specialty sites like this exist. If you look long enough, you can find everything, even sites dedicated to images of clouds.

## 3DSite

www.3dsite.com/3dsite/

Creating your own 3-D images and models is becoming increasingly easy. 3DSite is dedicated to making the process of producing your own complex 3-D images even easier with a range of tutorials, discussion forums and features. It also has well-researched articles on new hardware and software, and interviews with prominent artists and professionals.

The site also has an exhaustive section of links to companies that provide royalty-free 3-D models, and a wide variety of associated products. On top of this there is also a very handy section of totally free 3-D models and textures provided by various companies and individuals. Many of these illustrations are quite complex and have clearly taken a long time to put together. So now there's no excuse to let yourself be restricted to plain 2-D clip art: you can try out the third dimension as well.

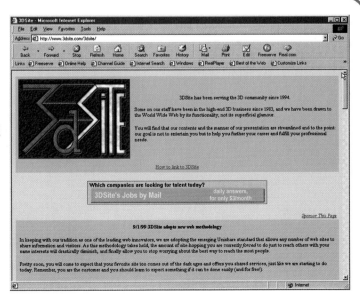

# All creatures great and small

*If you or anyone in your family has an interest in natural history, let the Internet bring that interest to life. It's a rich source of knowledge about everything in the natural world.*

N atural history is a huge topic, covering the origins, evolution and ecology of the Earth and the plants and creatures living on it. As such, it cuts across many more specific areas, making it somewhat difficult to find all the information you require in a single book or encyclopedia.

However, the Web offers a vast range of natural-history sites, so PC users of all ages can explore their interests in many exciting ways.

### ● Going batty

For example, if you've just watched a wildlife program about bats on television and want to know more, you can instantly find information from a 'bats' site on the Internet. School assignments will be enriched by Internet research, with many of the best natural-history sites on the Web, including the outstanding American Museum of Natural History in New York City (www.amnh.org), a world-famous educational resource.

Quite often there will be a list of FAQs (frequently asked questions) on a given topic and they may well provide just the information you're looking for. You can download text to add quotes to an essay or project or even save pictures from a website

to use in your work. Of course, the interest in natural-history sites is not limited purely to those doing schoolwork. The living world fascinates and astonishes all of us, and the Web is the ideal place to follow up even an idle interest in something you've seen on TV or read about in the newspaper.

### ● Practical pet help

There's even a practical value too, at the level of caring for pets and other animals. This is particularly true of

the rarer or more unusual domestic pets. If your taste runs to snakes, for example, you'll find dozens of richly informative sites on reptiles, offering expert advice on buying, rearing and breeding serpents.

It's a fascinating world and such a large one that we can only scrape the surface here to point out some of the best sites around. You can be sure that whatever your interest, from fish or fowl to ferocious beasts, you will find not just a couple, but many sites to inform and entertain you.

# It's a jungle out there

**As the Internet embraces the latest computer technology, the amount of information available about the natural world may prove surprising.**

THE SITES we've selected over the next few pages offer a broad example of the range of what can be found on the Web, from the great institutions of the world to small groups of enthusiasts. What they all have in common is that you'll be entertained as well as informed if you visit them.

The major museums featured all have an 'online gallery' of one kind or another – whether it's a guided virtual tour of the permanent collection or a special exhibition on a specific topic. Some of these museum sites also have

excellent interactive and collaborative learning sections, where schools and individuals can contribute to ongoing projects with help from the museum's experts.

We've also looked for sites that will have a special attraction to smaller children – ones that introduce an element of play into learning.

Naturally, we've picked out a number of sites that deal especially well with dinosaurs – an eternally popular subject with both children and adults.

---

## Florida Museum of Natural History
www.flmnh.ufl.edu

This site is notable mainly for its Fossil Horse virtual museum, which lets you learn about paleontology and evolution by exploring the fossil record of horses. Clicking on the horse skulls tells you about the creatures, while clicking on the different geological eras tells you about the ecology of the period.

*This virtual museum allows you to uncover the fascinating history of the horse in fossils.*

## The Giant Squid
http://seawifs.gsfc.nasa.gov

A minority interest, perhaps, but the giant squid is the world's largest invertebrate – and a pretty elusive creature to boot. This online version of a special exhibition at the Smithsonian Institution National Museum of Natural History succeeds in its aim of displaying the mystery, beauty and complexity of these mysterious, sea creatures.

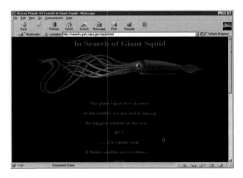

*Discover the mysterious squid – how has such a seemingly fragile creature survived so well?*

## The Natural History Museum, London
www.nhm.ac.uk

This is a site that does justice to a fine collection. There's a great 3-D-surround video tour of the Earth and Life galleries, allowing you to take a 360-degree look at the giant dinosaur skeletons. There are even virtual-reality fossils, such as this trilobite (below) to look at. To get the best out of this site, you may need to download plug-ins (see Stage 2,

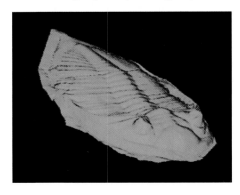

pages 146-147). There's also a Science Casebook section where you can post questions or initiate discussions relating to the areas covered. You might find a discussion of whether dinosaurs really could be recreated from DNA, or even a discussion on whether or not the legendary Beast of Bodmin Moor actually exists.

## Seaworld
www.seaworld.org

This is the site of the aquatic theme parks of the same name, with outposts in both Florida and California.

*At the Seaworld site, you can journey to Florida and visit the wonderful aquarium.*

It's bright, breezy and commercial, but nevertheless contains lots of educational resources. Choose the aquatic safari option and you'll be able to discover a wealth of information about fish. And, by viewing the animal enclosures with the Webcam, you can check out what's happening as it happens.

*Chicago is home to a fine aquarium. The Shedd Aquarium houses fish, reptiles, birds and mammals.*

## Shedd Aquarium

www.sheddnet.org

This Chicago aquarium is one of the biggest and best-stocked in the world. The colorful site contains lots of entertaining information about the aquarium itself and is also packed with fascinating information about the creatures of the deep. Fact sheets give you an informative picture of the exhibits and provide you with statistics – all of which make a visit to this site rewarding.

## Smithsonian Institution National Museum of Natural History

www.mnh.si.edu

This leading natural-history institution has an excellent presence on the Web. You can find out all you need to know about the museum and examine a number of well-presented and informative online exhibits. The virtual tour of the museum is easy and you won't find it hard to get to the dinosaurs. There's a section on global warming and an innovative exhibit called the Hologlobe, which shows the world from an astronaut's viewpoint to demonstrate various ecological and climatic points.

*See Earth as the Galileo spacecraft saw it – looking back on its journey to Jupiter. The Smithsonian's Hologlobe (left) lets you do this.*

*The Smithsonian Institution also has a section called Portraits of Smithsonian Science (right), which discusses some of the personalities who usually remain behind the scenes.*

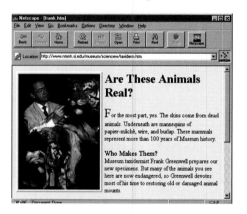

# Sites for children

There are special sites to encourage younger children to learn about animals over the Internet.

## Bats4Kids

http://members.aol.com/bats4kids

This is a site that aims to take the terror out of bats! Designed clearly for children, this site removes the mystery of these nocturnal creatures by presenting true and fascinating facts about them. For example: Where do bats live? Why aren't they birds? What are the myths about bats? All the answers are here in a colorful and clear site. You can play a game of bat concentration (a simple memory game) or you can enter the bat quiz – or even visit a bat cave. Children will love this site, but adults may also learn much of interest.

*Bats may be frightening for some children, but this site quickly explodes the myths, revealing much about these fascinating creatures.*

*The bat cave provides a bat puzzle, bat crossword and a bat word search game to test young visitors on how much they can remember.*

## Walking with Dinosaurs

www.bbc.co.uk/dinosaurs

Even if they've never seen the popular British TV series it is based on, your dino-loving youngsters will enjoy this lavish site, rich in resources. Here you'll find information on the creatures and their habitats.

## St. Louis Science Center
www.slsc.org
This site contains an Ecology and Environment Past online gallery, which is subdivided into several sections, including Geological Timeline, Fossils and Do or Die. The Geological Timeline is of most interest, giving a guided tour of living beings since the dawn of time. Dinosaurs are an obvious feature, with colorful dioramas, but there are also plenty of other creatures, down to the tiny shrew of 200 million years ago. Besides the natural-history content, the site contains a rich vein of other interesting scientific material to peruse.

*At the St. Louis Science Center site there are 300 pages of photographs, video footage, drawings and informative text – and that's just in the Ecology and Environment Past section.*

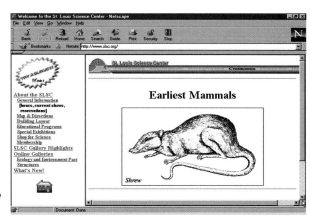

# When dinosaurs ruled the earth

**Dinosaurs provide endless fascination for both young and old alike, so step back in time several million years and search for them on the Web.**

## The Field Museum of Natural History
www.fmnh.org
This great Chicago museum has a marvelous collection of just about everything, and good virtual tours. You can take several dinosaur tours, each one of which is informative, richly illustrated (below) and easily accessible to children of all ages. There are games and quizzes, and you can even download a running triceratops. The Field is worth visiting regularly, and it's recently bought Sue – the largest and best-preserved *Tyrannosaurus rex* remains in existence – so you can follow the preservation process through the months.

## UCMP Web
www.ucmp.berkeley.edu
A Geological Time Machine is the highlight of this site from the University of California at Berkeley. It takes you through millions of years of history, discussing the ecology and the creatures that lived in various eras – including the dinosaurs. The site is rich in links to related information and is well illustrated.

*The UCMP website is a vast source of knowledge about fossils, such as this trilobite.*

## National Geographic
www.nationalgeographic.com/dinoeggs
This 'online egg hunt' is developed from a National Geographic-sponsored expedition and the subsequent magazine article. Researchers 'hatch' fossilized dinosaur embryos, and you can then follow their progress. Although this is not an extensive or in-depth site on dinosaurs, what it does, it does well. And there are good links to other dinosaur sites. Of course, anyone interested in natural history is likely to be interested in much of the content of National Geographic.

*The National Geographic site is of the same high quality as the respected magazine. Discover the dinosaur egg hunt (right) that was featured in a 1996 issue of the magazine and get a behind-the-scenes view, unique to the Internet user.*

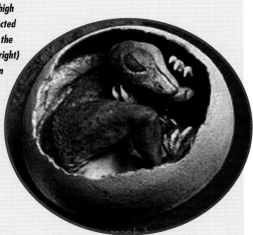

# Internet chat

*Internet chat systems offer the opportunity to communicate live online with other computer users all around the world.*

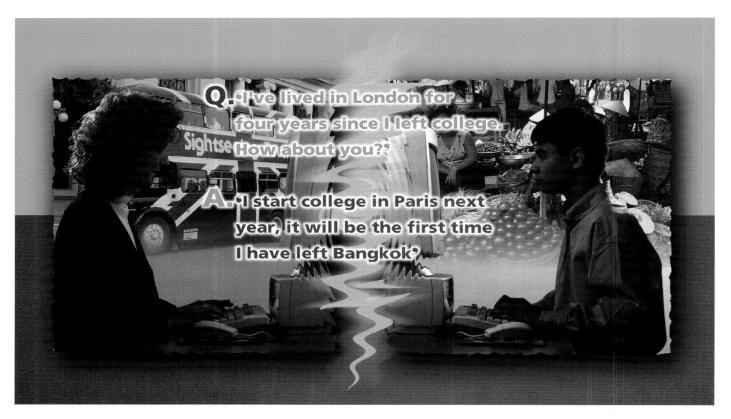

Q. 'I've lived in London for four years since I left college. How about you?'

A. 'I start college in Paris next year, it will be the first time I have left Bangkok'

Sending messages to people all over the world via email has long been, and is still, the main reason people use the Internet. But email does not happen in 'real time': it's more like sending a letter than making a phone call. But it's actually very easy to talk, or 'chat', to other people on the Internet in real time, and not just to a single person, but to a host of participants all over the world. In fact, Internet chat is so easy that it has become one of the fastest growing areas of use.

In the earlier days of the Internet, real-time chat was an extremely complicated business; you had to download substantial programs that could be confusing to use. And finding the 'chat rooms' where people gather was no easy business. Nowadays, the whole thing has become much simpler, largely because the software that powers the chat-room system downloads in a matter of seconds. That, together with the massive and growing number of people online, means that Internet chat has never been easier. Just log on to the home page of any major ISP (Internet Service Provider) and you'll find a link taking you directly to chat areas. We show how, and what is available, over the next three pages.

● **People and topics**
Chat rooms cover every conceivable interest. There are rooms dedicated to dealing on the stock market, to soaps, to football and to pop music, to name but a few. There are also many rooms created specifically for certain age groups, such as teens, 40-somethings and so on. And, of course, there are many rooms – with names such as Love Shack, Singles Bar and the like – where the chat often takes the form of more flirtatious conversation.

Whatever the room or the ISP, the format is very similar and easy to use. The screen generally presents a main window showing the participants' contributions. A narrow window at the bottom is where you type your own, before clicking on Send or hitting [Enter] to send it to the chat room. On the right you will nearly always find a list of the users currently active: in many services you can click on these to get personal details (if supplied) and to send email to or chat one-to-one with other users, away from the main chat room.

## A WORD OF WARNING

Although some chat rooms – such as those on AOL – are monitored, the general rule is that they are a free forum. People can, and do, say just about anything, sometimes in very suggestive language. So you need to exercise caution about which chat rooms you, and especially your children, enter. Fortunately, potentially unsuitable ones are nearly always easily identifiable by their names.

# Using Yahoo! Chat

Yahoo! is one of the Internet's most popular sites. It offers a range of services, including numerous chat rooms which are easy to access and use.

**1** Go to the Yahoo! site (www.yahoo.com) and click on the Chat link under Connect near the top of the page.

**2** As a first-time visitor, you'll have to register in order to get a user ID and a password. Remember that you don't need to use your real name – and it's probably advisable to use a pseudonym if you value your anonymity. Just type in your chosen ID and password in the boxes at the top of the page. You'll also be asked to provide some personal details so that Yahoo! can help out should you forget your password.

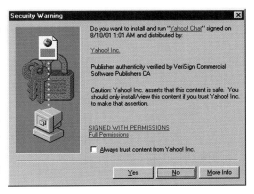

**3** Once that's done, you are taken to the home page of the Chat area where you'll see links to some featured rooms organized by topic, such as music and surfing the Web, as well as a listing of the main Chat categories. Simply click on the one you want to go to.

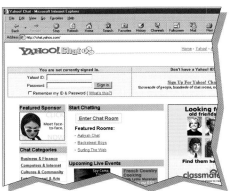

**4** Before you can actually enter the Chat room, you may have to install the Yahoo! Chat software. This is a Java program that downloads almost instantly; all you need to do is click the Yes button.

**5** Now you're ready to chat. The main screen window shows who is entering and who is leaving the room, and the sender and text of any messages. To join in, all you do is type your contribution in the narrow Chat: box near the bottom of the screen and click the Send button. On the right is the Chatters window showing a list of those in the Chat room.

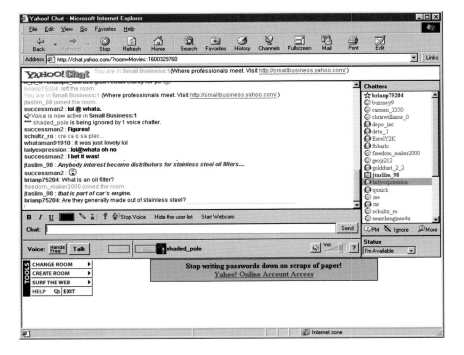

## CHAT TOPICS

The front page of the Yahoo! Chat area offers a number of featured rooms that you can jump right into. If you're new to Chat then it's probably a good idea to check these out first. But these are far from being your only choices. Yahoo! Chat offers hundreds of chat rooms, covering just about everything from business and computing to romance and religion. And there are dozens of rooms dedicated to local chatting, so you can check out folks from your very own area.

The vast majority of these rooms are safe and welcoming places, where people go to interact with others and benefit from their advice and experience. The one category you should be wary of, particularly if children or teenagers are going to be online, is romance. There is a wide variety of chat rooms within this category, and generally they are pretty safe. But rogue chatters can and do make appearances, sometimes with pretty offensive material. Enter these rooms at your own risk, and monitor them carefully if your children are going to use them.

# Chatting on AOL

**If you are a member of AOL (see Stage 1, pages 146-149), you'll probably find a topic to talk about in one of its chat rooms.**

**1** Getting into the Chat areas on AOL is relatively simple. Once you've logged on, just click the Chat channel icon (inset) on the left of the AOL Welcome screen.

**2** The AOL Chat page appears. From here you have a variety of options. Click on the Find a Chat button (inset) to go to a list of what's available.

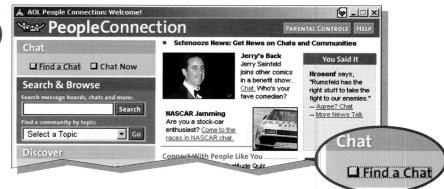

**3** You can now scroll through a list of categories covering a wide range of topics, from the practical to the frivolous. Click on the View Chats button to see the Chat rooms in that category to the right of the screen. Highlight a Chat and then click on Go Chat to enter the room.

**4** Here, we've entered the Love Lounge room. This is a lighthearted romance Chat room, which is generally very busy and usually has fairly innocuous content. The list of members in the room is displayed to the right of the screen. To join in, just type in your message in the box at the bottom and click Send or hit the [Enter] key.

**5** Because AOL is a worldwide service, Chat rooms are not limited to the US. From the Find a Chat page (see Step 2), just click on the area that interests you – UK, Canada, Japan, Brazil – and you could be chattering away in a foreign language in no time.

**6** AOL also gives you the opportunity to participate in live celebrity chat sessions. At the bottom of the AOL People Connection page (see Step 2), click on the Meet Celebrities link, which will take you to the AOL Live channel. Here you can see what's happening in any given week and then log in at the relevant time.

## CHAT-ROOM SHORTHAND

New chatters will find plenty of shorthand is used in Chat rooms on the Web. One of the most frequently used abbreviations is 'lol', which is a little bemusing at first. It means 'laugh out loud' and is added to the end of your comment if you mean it as a joke, as in: 'Yes, my other car is a Ferrari lol'. Another popular one is 'ROTFL' – rolling on the floor laughing – used only when you find the comment extremely unfunny.

# Internet Relay Chat

**There is more than one way to chat on the Internet and here we show you how to use the Internet Relay Interface.**

INTERNET RELAY CHAT, or IRC, has been around since 1988 and has evolved alongside the early Internet standards. Like most chat systems, IRC offers channels or rooms that people can use to converse, exchange files, or participate in chat games and other activities. Because IRC developed from an open standard, there are many different networks of servers to choose from, but among the largest and most popular are EFNet, Undernet, and Dalnet.

Using one of many freely available IRC clients, anyone can connect to an IRC network and visit one of hundreds or even thousands of channels. Alternatively, IRC users can start their own channels devoted to whatever topic they like. Some networks, such as Dalnet, support the registering of nicknames and channels, giving the channel owner rights to restrict or moderate access to the chosen few. As with most chats, IRC users can also send private messages to an individual user.

**1** The first step in using IRC is choosing the IRC client software you wish to use. You can download it from shareware and freeware sites such as http://download.cnet.com, which also offers many different clients which you can view by popularity (the easiest way to find them is to search for 'IRC'). Among the most widely used is mIRC, a shareware IRC client, but the basic features are the same in all clients.

**2** When you first start mIRC, you will be prompted to enter some information to identify which network to login to and how you wish to be identified. You will need to complete the mIRC options for the type of network (often subdivided by geographical region for speedier access), your full name, email address, and both a nickname and an alternative nickname in case the first is being used. You are not required to divulge your full name and email address – just enter something in these fields so the server can distinguish you from other users.

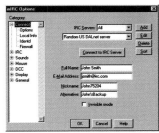

**3** Upon connecting with an IRC server, you will see a quickly scrolling series of messages in your main text window. These usually consist of introductory messages and administrative notes, and can be a helpful place to start to learn the ins and outs of a particular network or server. Then a mIRC dialog box pops up showing a list of default channels to join.

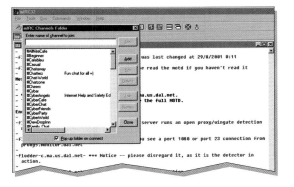

**4** You can search through a list of existing channel names using the List Channels button on the toolbar (inset), this will find any channel with specific text in its name or description. From there you can browse through the channels until you find one that interests you. To join a group, highlight it and click on Join in the top right of the dialog box.

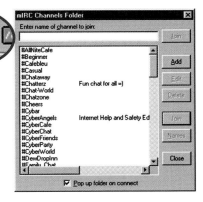

**5** When you join a channel, a new text window will open. It's wise to observe the style of the chat for a few moments before joining in. There's almost always a help channel (often just called 'help' or 'IRChelp') for people new to IRC. As you become more experienced, however, you may well be able to keep conversations going in multiple channels at the same time.

## NEW USERS

One place you can go to learn more about IRC is 'IRC for newbies' (at http://desperado .port5.com/irc/newbie.html). This page will give you an overview of some of the basic terminology and the types of things you can do in IRC. Another web page with useful information is 'IRC FAQ' (at http://www.rt66.com/support/faqs/irc/ircf aq.html). There is also mIRC's official site (www.mirc.com), which offers both instructions on how to get the most out of mIRC and some good tutorials on general IRC use (such as which network to choose).

I f you have an account with one of the well-established ISPs, then you almost certainly have some free Web space as part of your package deal. By taking advantage of this space, you have the ability to create your own website for other Internet users to see.

You could use this space to set up a site for your hobbies, to advertise your business if you're self-employed or even a site that simply says 'Hello world' and shares details about you and your life.

Most ISPs provide at least 5MB of space free of charge. Additional space is available at extra cost, but 5MB should give you plenty of scope to make an interesting site.

### ● It's just another document

Just like the documents you create in Word or Excel, the pages you make for a website take up disk space. Similarly, when you create the pages, you store them on your computer's hard drive. The difference is that to make the Web pages visible to all Internet users, you copy (or upload) them to your ISP.

Your ISP has powerful computers, called Web servers, which are dedicated to storing hundreds or even thousands of Web pages for its customers. Anytime someone types in your website address, your Web pages are retrieved from the server.

### ● An address for your site

Once your Web pages are copied to your ISP's computer, Internet users can then see them by typing the address of the pages into their Web browsers. This address will usually be based on the ISP's own address. For example, AOL users store their websites in

# Creating your own website

**One of the great pleasures of the Internet comes from creating your very own site and having people access it. To actually produce your own website is nowhere near as difficult as you might imagine – and we'll show you how.**

hometown.aol.com. Similarly, CompuServe users' sites are at ourworld.compuserve.com. If you use a different ISP, check your sign-up documents for information on free Web space and addresses. If you visit one of the CompuServe sites, you'll be

*The Internet is great at giving us the opportunity to find people all over the world with similar interests. With a website of your own you can announce your own interests – and people will be able to find you!*

able to see huge categorized lists of people's websites and their contents (some are shown opposite). Although the space given to each site might be similar, the contents are as diverse and unique as the people who made them.

Subjects can range from *Star Trek* trivia to how to look after unusual pets; from needlework to the fuel consumption of a 1940s roadster; or from technical PC information to Elvis' inseam measurement.

## ● HTML – the Web language

The one thing that deters many people from creating a website is that it uses a programming language called HTML (HyperText Mark-up Language). But don't worry – HTML is one of the simplest languages in the computing world and the basics are no more complicated than typing normal text sprinkled with a few special commands.

There's no denying the fact that a page of HTML code can look complicated, but as soon as you start learning what a few of the commands mean, you'll see that everything is quite logical.

## ● Breaking the code

You might find yourself wondering what this odd looking code has to do with the pictures and text you see when you type an address into your Web browser. After all, you don't see a single piece of HTML code.

What happens is that your browser strips out the HTML commands, which it uses to work out how to display the real content. The browser reads the code to determine where to place the images, words and links and displays them for the user, who need never see the underlying code that makes it possible.

The following exercises will show you how to create some simple HTML pages. When you've worked

### HTML COMMANDS

Many of the most commonly used HTML commands are used in pairs. For example, you can add bold to some text by adding a <B> command in front of the text and a </B> command at the end. Here, the second command stops the function of the first command. Similarly, to center some text on the page, you use <CENTER> and </CENTER>. If you accidentally omit the second </CENTER> command, you will find that the rest of the text on the page will become centered. However, no harm has been done, and to correct the problem all you need do is insert the </CENTER> command correctly.

through both of these exercises, you'll be able to put centered text on the screen, as well as pictures and even links – which are all you need to produce a perfectly usable page. In fact, many slow-loading pages are usually caused by their creator trying to use too many fancy commands.

### ● Begin with the basics

Learning to take full advantage of the basic HTML commands is important, not only from a technical standpoint, but also from a design one. However, once you've learned how basic HTML works, save time and trouble by using a Web editing program, such as FrontPage Express (included with Windows 98) or Adobe PageMill. These easy-to-use programs create all the HTML code for you.

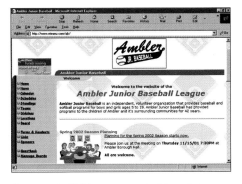

*A page on the Web is a great way to let people know what's going on in a society or club, as with this page detailing the activities of a little league baseball team.*

*You don't even have to finish the site completely before you display it to the world; a simple Under Construction graphic will let people know you're working on it.*

### UPLOADING PAGES TO YOUR ISP

When you have finished creating your own personal website on your computer's hard drive, you just upload or copy it to your ISP's server (which is just another computer).

This process varies from ISP to ISP; for detailed information, look through any instructions that you received when you first signed up with your ISP. You might find that the software your ISP supplied included a special program to make the copying easy. If you can't find any instructions, check the ISP's website or call the ISP's technical support number.

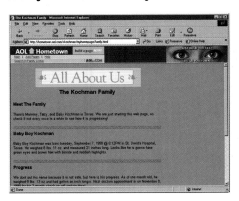

*It can be fun for a family just to introduce themselves to the world and tell other people what they are interested in. It's by no means necessary to have a complex site.*

*Some personal sites can have a stylish, smart appearance that differs little from the results achieved on a professional or commercial site.*

# Making your own Web page

**It's easy to make your presence known to the world. Here, we show you how to make a start at constructing your own website.**

**1** The first thing to do with any Web page is to type the simple commands (we're using Notepad) that identify it as an HTML document. Type <HTML> on the first line and then </HTML> on the next line. The second command will let the browser know the Web page is finished. The rest of our page will be typed between these commands.

**2** Now we'll create a heading for the page. Between our two lines, type another: <H1>My First Web Page!</H1>. The <H1> and </H1> commands tell the browser that the text between them is going to be the heading; it will use a bigger and bolder typeface when it displays the page.

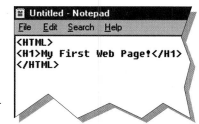

**3** Finally, type <CENTER> in front of the <H1> command and </CENTER> after </H1>. Now your text will be centered when it appears in your browser window.

**4** You can now type in the main text for your Web page. Start by typing a few sentences. Begin on a new line under the heading and type as if you were typing on a word processor. However, when you get to the edge of the Notepad window press the [Enter] key to move on to a new line. Since these words come after the </H1> and </CENTER> they won't be centered or bold.

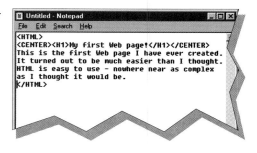

**5** To finish off this simple text page, we'd like a simple line across the bottom of the page. We could add lots of underline characters, by pressing [Shift]+[-]. But there are better and more powerful options built into the HTML language. Create a new line just before the </HTML> line which finishes the page. On this new line type <HR>. This is one of the few HTML commands that doesn't need a </HR> command to switch it off.

**6** Now we'll save the Web page. Select Save As from the File menu, and locate a suitable folder in the Save in drop-down list. Type a simple name into the File name text box, and use an .htm extension. This file extension identifies it as an HTML file. Make sure you don't forget the period beforehand. Then press the Save button.

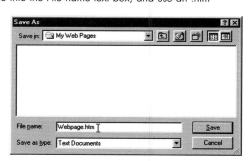

**7** Now we want to see the page as it would appear on the Worldwide Web. The easiest way to load the page into your Web browser is to double-click on the My Computer icon and locate the folder on your hard drive. Find your file and double-click on it. After a few seconds your page will load into your browser and you'll see it on screen (far right). Depending on the way your browser is set up, a dialog box might appear before the page loads, asking if you want to logo onto your ISP – just click the Cancel button.

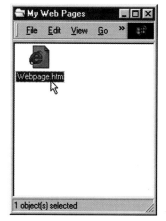

# Adding a picture that's a link

**Besides telling people all over the world about yourself, you can also show them what you look like. All you need is a picture – the rest is easy!**

**1** To liven up our Web page we're going to add a picture between the title and the main text. The first thing to do is find a picture. However, as Web pages use two types of picture, GIF and JPG, you might need to convert it first (see Pictures for websites, below). Copy the picture into the same folder you used for your Web page.

**2** Now start Notepad so that you can edit the HTML file you created on the previous page. Click on the File menu and select Open. Use the Look in section of the Open dialog box to locate the relevant folder. You won't see the .htm file at first; this is because Notepad normally looks for files that end in .txt. Click on the Files of type drop-down list and select All Files (*.*). You will see your file appear, along with any others in the folder. Select the file and press the Open button.

**3** Now you can edit the file. First we'll add our picture. Insert a new line under the heading and type <IMG SRC="family.jpg">, with the name of your picture in quotes.

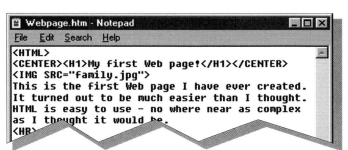

**4** As it is, this picture will appear at the left of the page, directly before the paragraph text. To tidy things up, place a <CENTER> command before it and </CENTER> after it. After that, create a new line and add a <BR>. This will place a space between the picture and the text.

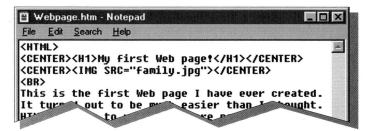

**5** We can also make the picture a clickable link. This means that when the mouse pointer of the person viewing the page moves over the picture, it will turn into a hand informing the person they can click on the picture to go to a new page. First, though, we need a second page to switch to. That's easy: we'll just edit this page and save it under a new name. Change the page to read as shown here. When you save the file in the same folder, name it link.htm.

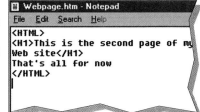

**6** Now repeat Step 2 to open the first page of your website again. To create the link for the picture, type <A HREF="link.htm"> before the picture command (it doesn't matter if it is before or after <CENTER>) and then type </A> after the picture. Select Save from the File menu to save these changes.

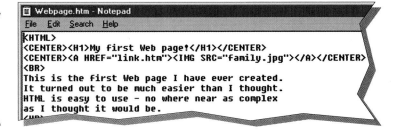

**7** View your Web page by double clicking on the first Web page you created (Step 7, previous page). Your page will load with the picture in place. Click once on the picture and you'll see the second page appear. This is the principle on which the whole Web works. While there are some Web design techniques that are hard to work out, perhaps 90 percent of all websites are created with commands as simple as these.

## PICTURES FOR WEBSITES

Most pictures on websites are in GIF or JPG format. These are special formats that are suitable for use over the Internet, since they are compact and are quick to download. Other types of pictures, such as the Windows format, BMP, will need to be converted before use in your Web pages. Do this with a graphics program, such as Corel PHOTO-PAINT (see pages 74-77).

### ● About the index

Text in italics is used for cross-references within the index (as in *see also...* ). Page numbers in bold type denote the main entries for a topic.

● **Acknowledgments**
Abbreviations: t = top; b = bottom;
r = right; l = left; c = center;
bkg = background. All cartoons
are by Chris Bramley

8      Lyndon Parker/De Agostini
9tl    Lyndon Parker/De Agostini
12     Stockmarket
13t    De Agostini
15tl   Stockmarket
16     Lyndon Parker/De Agostini
18     Lyndon Parker/De Agostini
22all  Steve Bartholomew/De Agostini
23tr   Steve Bartholomew/De Agostini
26     Steve Bartholomew/De Agostini
28     Jennie Child/De Agostini
30     Lyndon Parker/De Agostini
34     Lyndon Parker/De Agostini
38     Lyndon Parker/De Agostini
40     Lyndon Parker/De Agostini
42tall Lyndon Parker/De Agostini
45tr   Lyndon Parker/De Agostini
46     Lyndon Parker/De Agostini
50t    Lyndon Parker/De Agostini
50b    De Agostini
53t    De Agostini
54     De Agostini
56     Lyndon Parker/De Agostini
58     Getty One Stone
60     De Agostini

62     De Agostini
64     De Agostini
66     Performing Arts Library
68     De Agostini
70     De Agostini
73     De Agostini
78     De Agostini
80     De Agostini
82     De Agostini
83all  De Agostini
85     De Agostini
86     De Agostini
87all  De Agostini
88all  De Agostini
89all  De Agostini
90     De Agostini
94     De Agostini
95all  Lyndon Parker/De Agostini
96     (elephant) Getty One Stone
96     De Agostini
97tr   (elephant) Getty One Stone
97cl,cr,bl De Agostini
98all  Lyndon Parker/De Agostini
99all  Lyndon Parker/De Agostini
100tr  Courtesy Ricoh
100bl  Courtesy Agfa
101t   Lyndon Parker/De Agostini
102t   Lyndon Parker/De Agostini
102b   Ray Dunthorn/De Agostini
103all Lyndon Parker/De Agostini
104t   (family) Imagebank

104t   (computer) Lyndon Parker/De Agostini
104c,b Warrender Grant/De Agostini
105tl  Courtesy Hewlett Parkard
106    Lyndon Parker/De Agostini
107    Lyndon Parker/De Agostini
108    (dancers) Stockmarket
108    (speakers) Lyndon Parker/De Agostini
109all Lyndon Parker/De Agostini
110t   Courtesy Roland
110b   Lyndon Parker/De Agostini
111t   Lyndon Parker/De Agostini
111c   Courtesy Yamaha
112    Lyndon Parker/De Agostini
113all Lyndon Parker/De Agostini
116    Steve Bartholomew/De Agostini
126    Steve Bartholomew/De Agostini
130    Lyndon Parker/De Agostini
131t   Lyndon Parker/De Agostini
134    Lyndon Parker/De Agostini
138all De Agostini
143    Lyndon Parker/De Agostini
146    (tiger) Getty One Stone
146    (boy) Lyndon Parker/De Agostini
147t   (tiger) Getty One Stone
147t   (boy) Lyndon Parker/De Agostini
150    Lyndon Parker/De Agostini
154all De Agostini
157tr  Steve Bartholomew/De Agostini